HELLENIC STUDIES 18

Poetic and Performative Memory in Ancient Greece

Heroic Reference and Ritual Gestures in Time and Space

Other Titles in the Hellenic Studies Series

Plato's Rhapsody and Homer's Music
The Poetics of the Panathenaic Festival in Classical Athens

Labored in Papyrus Leaves
Perspectives on an Epigram Collection Attributed to Posidippus
(P.Mil.Vogl. VIII 309)

Helots and Their Masters in Laconia and Messenia
Histories, Ideologies, Structures

Archilochos Heros
The Cult of Poets in the Greek Polis

Master of the Game
Competition and Performance in Greek Poetry

Greek Ritual Poetics

Black Doves Speak
Herodotus and the Languages of Barbarians

Pointing at the Past
From Formula to Performance in Homeric Poetics

Homeric Conversation

The Life and Miracles of Thekla

Victim of the Muses
Poet as Scapegoat, Warrior and Hero
in Greco-Roman and Indo-European Myth and History

Amphoterōglossia
A Poetics of the Twelfth Century Medieval Greek Novel

Priene (second edition)

Plato's Symposium
Issues in Interpretation and Reception

http://chs.harvard.edu/chs/publications

Poetic and Performative Memory in Ancient Greece

Claude Calame

Translated from the French by Harlan Patton

CENTER FOR HELLENIC STUDIES
Trustees for Harvard University
Washington, D.C.
Distributed by Harvard University Press
Cambridge, Massachusetts, and London, England
2009

Poetic and Performative Memory in Ancient Greece: Heroic Reference and Ritual Gestures in Time and Space
   by Claude Calame
Translated by Harlan Patton
Copyright © 2009 Center for Hellenic Studies, Trustees for Harvard University
All Rights Reserved.
The Center for Hellenic Studies and the author wish to express their gratitude to the Fondation Chuard Schmid at the Université de Lausanne for their generous support of the creation of this translation.
Published by Center for Hellenic Studies, Trustees for Harvard University, Washington, D.C.
Distributed by Harvard University Press, Cambridge, Massachusetts and London, England
Production: Kristin Murphy Romano and Ivy Livingston
Cover design and illustration: Joni Godlove
Printed in Ann Arbor, MI by Edwards Brothers, Inc.

LIBRARY OF CONGRESS CATALOGING-IN-PUBLICATION DATA:
Calame, Claude.
   [Pratiques poétiques de la mémoire. English]
   Poetic and performative memory in ancient Greece : heroic reference and ritual gestures in time and space / by Claude Calame ; translated from the French by Harlan Patton.
      p. cm. — (Hellenic Studies Series; 18)
   Includes bibliographical references and index.
   ISBN 978-0-674-02124-2
   1. Greek poetry--History and criticism. 2. Space and time in literature. I. Title. II. Series.
   PA3095.C35313 2009
   881'.0109--dc22

                                                                                    2008014630

Foreword

I T IS DIFFICULT TO FIND WORDS to describe the intellectual challenge offered by the invitation from the Classics Department of Harvard University in Fall 2000 to present the four Carl Newell Jackson lectures to an audience which managed to combine critical attention with a welcoming acceptance for the non-traditional positions I have always defended. The suggestions made at these opportunities for learned exchange, punctuationed by convivial gatherings organized by my hosts, were so numerous that it would be impossible to name all who made them. Arguing as I do for collective and practical concepts of time and space, I would like to lend to my expression of sincere gratitude that same character of community by combining my thanks and those of my family to colleagues and the learned community. I would also like to express my thanks to the students of the Ecole de Hautes Etudes en Science Sociales graduate seminar, who listened with attentive engagement to these same reflections in French.

The idea of concentrating not only on poetic and practical concepts of space but also on the spatial component of these specifically Greek temporalities came from a lively interdisciplinary post-graduate seminar with Jean-Michel Adam and Mondher Kilani at the University of Lausanne in 1994/95, centered on the topic "Time, memory, discourse: Local temporalities, learned temporalities." The discussion continued during the academic years 1998/99 and 1999/2000, focusing on "Discursive representations of time." It was marked in June 1999 by the international colloquium organized with our anthropologist colleagues from Pavie, Turin, Milan, Lausanne, and Paris (the "Patomipala" group), the theme of which was "Discursive representations of time: Historiography and Anthropology." All this is to say that the thoughts expressed in the five chapters which follow owe a great deal to that other collective and interdisciplinary enterprise. Anyone who does not much appreciate (French) theory is invited to skip the first chapter.

Claude Calame
Lausanne—Paris, April 2003

Forward to the English Version

DURING THE TRANSLATION OF THIS WORK INTO ENGLISH, I had the intellectual pleasure of being in regular contact with my colleague, the fine translator Harlan Patton. To him and to the Fondation Irène Nada Andrée Chuard-Schmid (University of Lausanne), which supported the translation, go my heartfelt thanks, as well as to Gregory Nagy, generous friend and Editor-in-Chief of the Hellenic Studies Series, and to Lenny Muellner, Emily Collinson, and other members of the editorial staff of the Center for Hellenic Studies.

Claude Calame
Paris—Reckingen, February 2008

Translator's Preface

THIS TRANSLATION, undertaken with the support of the Fondation Chuard Schmid at the Université de Lausanne and the Center for Hellenic Studies, is intended in part to address our ambivalence about translation. Translation nearly always represents compromise in our various fields of study. Academics, especially those specialized in some specific language area, naturally prefer the original of any work, in its original language. Everyone accepts compromise in this as in many things, as there would be little time left for much else if we attempted to master all the languages required for the study of Western thought, particularly at the high level required to discuss and debate proposed interpretations of those texts. We all find ourselves obliged to rely on translations from time to time, sometimes even translations of major works and primary sources in languages where our skills are limited, but we don't really like it any more than we like our students reading the Cliff Notes rather than Dickens in the original.

On the other hand, translation of scholarly works is not very different from part of what many of us do. In our teaching, we read others' works, we attempt to become expert enough to speak with some authority on them, and we try to make them accessible and understandable to others. For the scholar as for the translator, the first problem is to become sufficiently competent in the matter to speak with some authority, to represent accurately the content of the original document. Sometimes we do this through dispassionate traditional research and impartial comment, sometimes (as Calame stresses) we interpret those texts (critically, rather than linguistically) by applying our own contemporary biases, to see how well the texts suit our academic viewpoints, rather than the other way around, though there is less danger of that in translation, where any academic biases should be limited to those of the original work.

Like translators, students of the humanities are already well-accustomed to becoming at least moderately knowledgeable in numerous fields of study. Simonides' image of the unpredictable flight of a fly (cited in Calame's concluding chapter) could as easily apply to many questions in the Humanities as it does to the time of human happiness. There is no telling when an art history question may branch off into chemistry, textiles, history, anthropology, or optics, or when verification of a Greek text may depend on accurate carbon dating, advanced computer-imaging techniques, or centuries-old notes from an archaeological dig. Translation nearly always involves similar complications: alongside literary matters, it has for me meant becoming reasonably familiar, at various times and among other things, with French patent and contract law, geotextiles, marketing, industrial uses of asbestos, the standard terminology of a private investigator's report, and auto mechanics, all finite and limited domains, far less complex and demanding than Claude Calame's study. But there is a very different dialectic in this more traditional translation in the Humanities, and considerably more help available: some of those who will be obliged to trust this English translation are the same scholars I have trusted to translate and interpret for me the Greek texts being studied here. Translation is something we do for one another.

There have been irritations in this translation, as in most others. Some are language based: I can find, for example, nothing better than the conventional but inelegant putting-into-discourse to translate *mise en discours*, which recurs in Calame's semantic analysis in the text. Occasional problems stemmed from my own lack of familiarity with the details of a culture geographically and temporally distant from our own: the use of astragales (meaning both 'knucklebones' and 'bitter vetch' in English), among items placed in a basket during Dionysian initiation rites (along with a rhombus, a top, and a mirror), could as easily have been the one as the other to me, until various scholarly sources clarified the ritualistic representation of toys the Titans used to tempt the young Dionysus within their grasp.

Given my relative inexperience in this subject matter, I've been grateful for help given by a number of people. This project required reading and studying a number of primary and secondary texts unfamiliar to me. I'd read Hesiod only in survey courses many years ago, and had never come across Bacchylides' dithyrambs or the texts of the gold lamellae before accepting this translation project, and I am grateful to several Hellenists whose works clarify and interpret those texts. I thank a number of my colleagues at Furman University for their kind assistance: Chris Blackwell in the Classics Department for proposing, facilitating, and organizing this entire project at its inception, and for occasional Greek help along the way; Tom Kazee, our Academic Dean, for his enthusiastic support for release time for the translation; David Morgan in my own department for his quick answers to Greek spelling and language questions; Bill Allen in the French section of the department for working out how to replace me for one entire semester; Chantal for not being too upset at finding the dining room full of books, papers, and computers. I thank Gregory Nagy and his colleagues at the Center for Hellenic Studies for proposing the project, and Lenny Muellner for guidance and answers along the way. Steve Clark's careful editing has made this translation vastly more readable and precise. Thanks also to the Fondation Chuard Schmid of Lausanne, which helped in funding this project along with the Center for Hellenic Studies. And of course my thanks to Professor Calame himself, with whom I corresponded while in France last fall. He will have many readers far more qualified than I to appreciate his work fully, though I have done my best here to insure that he will never have a more careful or attentive reader.

Harlan Patton
Professor of French, Furman University

TABLE OF CONTENTS

I

SPATIO-TEMPORAL POETICS OF THE PAST IN ANCIENT GREECE

"Memory is the present of the past."

Saint Augustine, *Confessions* 11.20, 26

THE TRANSITION FROM THE TWENTIETH TO THE TWENTY-FIRST CENTURY has helped history to experience a real renewal, both as a determining influence on our social life and as an academic discipline. Historians can no longer consider it enough merely to denigrate the collective actors of social history as being too Marxist compared to the mainstream perspective fashionable at the end of the twentieth century, one marked by selfish individualism and imposed by the economic practices of global neo-liberalism (fashionable at the end of the twentieth century). Nor is there any question of seeking an erudite refuge in the local specifics of a micro-history that tries to shelter itself from comparative generalizations and from overblown theories. Historians can no longer avoid facing a "social question" that will yield center stage to textual refractions or relativistic diversions rendering illusory any grasp on reality and any practical engagement. It will not suffice to reconstruct great characters as history's actors and actresses in the frenzy of an essentially economic competition, nor will it suffice to hand over indigenous peculiarities to some epistemologically agnostic specialist, nor will simple textual objects suffice if they call only for the intellectual practices of writing as a game.

This renewal of history has been forced on us by our need to re-think our shared knowledge of the recent past and thus how we represent our fathers and our grandfathers as they participated in the worldwide conflict that created a political and moral point of no return for Europeans in the middle of the 20th century. We needed to reformulate a recent past that we had generally rejected or idealized. We are witnessing the (re)birth of a history that is documentary, certainly disenchanted and conscious of its ideological presuppositions, but a real "history" nevertheless: a history based on the etymology of its name—an inquiry consequently determined to investigate from the present, if not to act upon the present; a history whose anthropological dimension could be much more developed, as we shall try to show; a history neither national nor European, but widened to include territories opened by the process of globalization to what were originally economic interests; a history sensitive to events, which are primarily made up of representations and accounts with symbolic overtones; consequently a social history of moments that have marked the development of a cultural community; and so a history of manifestations and representations of communities that identify themselves within a culture, however composite that culture may be. But this is a history which—far from ignoring its narrative and poetic foundations—is written under an imperative which must not be underestimated, in that historians from now on will be asked to sketch and formulate responses to present questions and needs. And so a history searching for itself, and which, by its sensitivity to anthropological methods as well as those of the science of discourse, may question itself openly about different practical concepts of space and time in different cultures which care about their memory.

1. Prelude: History, memory, and the present

For the Swiss citizen attempting to address both a French and an American readership, this critical movement is inscribed between two poles; we can illustrate these poles schematically by means of two recent ideological events. On the one hand, we might evoke the mandate given by the Swiss government to a group of respected professional historians, to furnish the public with new insights on the attitudes and policies of federal authorities regarding Nazi power during the Second World War. The attention of these professional archivists and scholars was to be focused on official relations with Hitler's Germany, on economic links between big businesses and banks and their German counterparts, and on the restriction of the rights of asylum applied especially to refugees of Jewish origin.[1] This attempt at a collective rewriting of official history based on a rereading of archived documents

---

[1] This five-year work of historiographic inquiry has been completed and published as *La Suisse, le national-socialisme et la Seconde Guerre mondiale. Rapport final de la Commission indépendante d'experts Suisse-Seconde Guerre mondiale, ou rapport Bergier*, Zürich (Pendo) 2002; on this *Rapport Bergier*, see Boschetti 2004.

coincided with a fundamental revision of the shared image of a traditionally neutral and humanitarian Switzerland. It brought about a debate which could have been healthy, had it had a practical effect on the current attitude of Swiss authorities toward those requesting asylum from regions in a state of civil war. Whatever may happen with what once was a right of asylum and is now a policy of dissuasion and return, the various reactions to this report on how Swiss economic interests accommodated the Nazi regime—reactions to news of the report's preparation and reactions upon its publication—show that the (re)writing of history is not without pragmatic impact.

The work of historiography does indeed depend upon a putting-into-discourse (*mise en discours*) as well as on large distribution through the media, both of which involve its authors as well as its intended readers, whether they be ideologues of neutrality or defenders of secret banking practices. In creating an account intended to be public, this work cannot help but have a practical effect, even if that effect is relatively limited. Community memory is not cut from history, but rather—as I will try to point out—is maintained and reoriented by the work of historians.[2]

But at the moment when this controversial investigation's first results were being published, President Bill Clinton was singing Gorgianic praises to America's eternal youth on the other side of the Atlantic.[3] In addressing his best wishes to the world (a world dominated by the United States) at the beginning of a new millennium, he extolled the eternally renewed dynamism of an entire people: an implicit defense of historicity reduced to the current actions of the new generation, the generation which from an economic, ideological, and even military viewpoint (depending on circumstances) imposes on the world its concept of history and civilization, using powerful resources of finance and the media developed in the move to new technologies.

Certainly we can consider the successive wars in the Middle East, wars conducted by those who hold world economic and military power, as new efforts to annul time and space by repeated assertions against a "terrorism" that is seen as a global menace to the immutable and universal values of liberal and capitalist democracy. Yet I have no intention of reviving the worn

[2] Regarding the remarkable work by Y. H. Yershlami, *Zakhor: Histoire juive et mémoire juive*, Paris: (La Découverte) 1984, Vidal-Naquet 1994:54 concludes an urgent call to integrate memory with history in the following words: "Of course, this does not mean that we must separate the true from the false; it simply means that man does not identify himself with the moment when he is alive, and that he must from now on integrate himself into historical discourse as a temporal being with the gift of memory. *Zakhor*, 'remember,' must be the watchword of today."

[3] See his address to the American people published in the *New York Times* 2 Jan. 2000.

and erroneous opposition between a young United States, without depth or historical consciousness, and an old Europe, with not only its secular cultural traditions but also the weight of its unenviable colonial past.

We must realize that such tension—between an economic projection into a very near future and a political concern about the depth of history—does not coincide exactly with the apparent geographic division that the Atlantic Ocean would seem to form. This is more and more true at a moment when several European Community countries are lining up behind the United States of George Bush, in a military-ideological crusade against an allegedly extremist Islam, in order to defend their oil interests rather than their civilization. This tension between looking back toward a past which questions us and forward to a future animated by the fastest possible profits and consumption is inherent in any political community observing the great principles of neo-liberal modernity.

There is tension on the one hand to reread one's own past in order to reformulate it critically, knowing that it largely determines our actions, and on the other hand to focus on the present instant, oriented toward the immediate future, with the incitement to consume ever new goods and services, thanks to accelerated techniques of advertising and to the media, for instantaneous profit. Consequently, this is a tension between two "regimes of historicity," between two ways of representing oneself, of managing and practicing individual and community relations with the passing of cosmic time.[4] Finally, it is a tension between two different feelings for history, one for the person who sees his own actions on his environment as oriented and constrained as much by his own experience of time and space as by his own knowledge and representations of the past of his social and cultural community, and on the other for the person who, as a citizen voluntarily subject to the global market economy and its logic of quick profit, intends to live in a state of youth constantly sought and renewed, a youth seemingly offered by an economic system based on consumption and on immediate gratification.

This is no doubt an exaggerated dichotomy, especially in that it inscribes itself in a sequence of binary oppositions, oppositions of contraries which are sometime forced upon us by a reductive version of structuralism. Do we want to draw a very artificial division between on the one hand the hedonistic

---

[4] The notion of "regimes of historicity" is taken up by Hartog 2003:26–30, and will be discussed and defined in §5.3 below. In analyzing the parameters of the temporality of modernity, Chesneaux 1996:7 and 84–85 (see also 27–41) speaks of "time crushed into the immediate," and of "presentist regression." See also Hartog 2003:127–133 especially, on "the rise of presentism."

image and practice of fluent capitalist time, and on the other a more-or-less thoughtful image and practice of social time with historical depth? The former would come through immersion in a present time from which, by adopting the all-consuming values of exchange, we extract what material advantages we can. The latter we would retain from social and symbolic temporality by our efforts at a critical revision of conventional values relative to the past. Such a division would have to be, in any case, nuanced to the extent that the practice of a present constantly lying in wait for the immediate future is animated by an obsessive desire to anticipate the future constantly. Brought to life by the media, this burning desire coincides with an anguish not to be *dé-passé* "outdated or overtaken." This is most certainly our fear of being bypassed, in a logic based on competition among individuals; but, less obviously, there is also the muted fear of being dispossessed of one's past and space, which gives life to numerous nationalisms, despite globalized modernity. And so, in one of those word games which postmodernism likes so well, the incitement to constant projection into the immediate future invites us not to break basic attachments with a recent past, even if it has a bad reputation, attached as it is for Europe either to the largest organized massacres that humanity has ever known (thanks to Western technological progress) or to a series of social gains which have been widely denigrated for the past three decades. In a logic of symbolic memory, it is the acceleration of a breathless immediate which requires a return to history.

For that is one of the essentials in the four case studies presented here: to give food for thought about the paradigms of time and space we depend on, by choosing practical concepts of time and space in that different culture, both geographically and historically, which is the one constantly recreated by the ancient Greeks. And since the learned journey proposed here is that of discourse analysis inspired by the approaches of cultural and social anthropology, the four configurations and practical concepts of time and space taken up here invite us to reflect briefly on four of the paradigms which have marked the development of human sciences since the 1960's: in order of their presentation, structuralism, gender studies, philosophical idealism *redivivus*, and neo-mysticism.

2. Pragmatics of spatio-temporal representations

Schematic though it may be, the division between two contemporary manners of practicing social time which was briefly sketched as a prelude should at least call our attention to other ways of seeing and of living one's relation with one's own past and with one's own individual future, quite apart from the one held by the social and cultural community one belongs to, and which extends itself in space. The general point of view adopted here will nonetheless be that of a present in tension not only between the individual and the collective, but especially between a past with a certain depth, inscribed in space and attached to different forms of memory, and a near future, fashioned by ways of organizing time and space in the present. And so the well-known philosophical concept of time sketched by Saint Augustine may come to make sense to those who consider themselves concerned with practical concepts of temporality as they appear in an anthropological perspective: "Indeed, what is time (*quid est enim tempus*)? How do these two times, the past and the future, exist when the past is no longer and the future is not yet? As for the present, if it were always present and if it did not change into the past, it would not be time, but eternity." Even philosophically, the present cannot be conceived of except in tension between the past and the future! To give consistency to the present, and thus to time, one must see it in a tensive way, both as remembrance and as anticipation.[5]

It is important to state from the outset that the present moment also implies spatial location and consistency. While physicists have been pondering for nearly a century the question of the curvature of a time inseparable from space, historical spatio-temporality imposed by the anthropological and discursive dimension of history is defended in these pages. That poses the question of the ontological status of this dynamic of temporal flux whose axis runs through present time and present space. To make of the passage of time a movement of the *animus*, as Saint Augustine proposes, in a dialectic between *intentio* and *distentio*, is finally to see time in a psychological dimension. But this dodges the question of how interior temporality is articulated with social time or cosmic time, and it erases the spatial parameters of all temporality. This first chapter is intended to show that, on the contrary, spatiality is consubstantial with any form of temporality.

In this regard, texts from the cultural and symbolic manifestations of ancient Greece offer especially significant representations of time integrated into space. They are all the more interesting in that, conveyed by poetic texts with a practical function, they are always created and conditioned, as are ours,

---

[5] Saint Augustine, *Confessions* 11.14.17; see also 11.20.26, 27, 36, and 28, 38. Ricœur 1983:19–53, and 1985:1936, bases his own concept of narrative time on the reflections of Saint Augustine, whose theological implications and practical inadequacies he shows; on this, see Gilbert 1996:42–52.

by a preoccupation with the *hic et nunc* in relation to the past. Generally oriented toward a ritualistic action done in a precise place, these spatio-temporal manifestations also maintain a pragmatic relationship with the immediate future. They are thus sensations, but also representations, and finally, because of the putting-into-discourse whose object these representations are, they are configurations of temporality and spatiality. In their practical aspect, they are strongly distinguished from the philosophical concepts of time which have been too easily attributed to the representatives of Greek culture in general; some have tried to make metaphysicians of simple poets who define themselves as having a certain savoir-faire (*sophoí*). Representation, configuration, and putting-into-discourse are three notions we shall soon return to, but their relevance we can try to illustrate immediately with an example.

A poem by Bacchylides is given over to ritual praise of a young man from Metapontum in Magna Graecia, a winner of the Pythian games at the dawn of the Classical Age. Most of the praise is accomplished through narration, in the story of the flight of the daughters of King Proïtos of Argos. In a reading sensitive both to the development of the narrative and to the marks of enunciation presented by this ritual poem, I have tried to show the practical effects of combining several temporal threads and several sites in a complex poetic configuration: the line of the account of the legendary flight of the Proitides, abandoning Tiryns which was founded by their father, then the cultural and etiological honors that the girls pay to Artemis in Lousoï in Arcadia; the thread of the story narrated whose chronology goes back to the founding of the "Mycenaean" city of Tiryns by Proïtos, with its causes; the thread of enunciation (uttered in the poem) to celebrate the present victor in his native city in Magna Graecia (in a *hic et nunc* of a discursive and enunciative order). These three temporal and spatial lines (narration, story told, enunciation) intertwine in the poetic discourse as sung (on an "intra-discursive" level) to converge finally toward the ("extra-discursive") moment of the poem's "performance," with its cultural and social implications, in the colonial city of Metapontum, in the first half of the fifth century BC.[6] The discursive and narrative operation of this melic poem is all the more significant in that it poetically reconfigures,

---

[6] Bacchylides 11, with the commentary formulated in the study of 2000c: 399–412; also specifics on the temporal levels of a discursive order are mentioned there. See also Borutti 1996:250–252. Without taking into consideration the extra-discursive time of the situation of enunciation, Griffith 1993 presents an analysis of the temporality of Pindar's *Epinikia* which distinguishes the levels of story (approximately equivalent to *erzählte Zeit*), account (equivalent to *Erzählzeit*), and text or narrative (which seems to relate to the *énonciation énoncée* "uttered enunciation").

both on the discursive level and in the fictional mode, a form of social time; this "regime of historicity" is shared between the memory of the founding of the colonial city to which the young victor of the Pythian games belongs and the ritual cyclical celebration of the goddess Artemis, who proves to be both the goddess honored in Arcadia by the girls in the legend and the goddess of the city in southern Italy where the athlete's pan-Hellenic victory is ritually celebrated. This work of poetic representation and temporal and spatial configuration is accomplished in a subtle interplay of anticipations and returns along the chronological timeline and in the space recounted; these spatio-temporal movements combine with the rhetorical structures of an (intra-discursive) ring structure which evoke the cyclical character of the (extra-discursive) ritual celebration. In addition, a final enunciative and narrative passage through the heroic past of the Trojan War leads at the end of the poem to the realization in the near future, by the community of citizens of the colonial city of Metapontum, of the spirit of justice throughout the exemplary great acts of the Achaean heroes. Through the intermediary of the "instance of enunciation," the sung ritual performance thus ensures the pragmatic transition of the different (intra-discursive) spatio-temporal threads woven into the poem toward the (extra-discursive) time and space of the ritual act of enunciation.

2.1. Philosophical temporalities

So we have too often overlooked that Greek concepts of time and space are situated at the intersection of several temporal lines which appear as constituents of our being in a social space. As an operating statement, and thus schematically, we must remember that one can distinguish several lines of realization in our thoughts and in our expressions of a temporality (and a spatiality) which are essentially existential. I shall readily and naïvely take up here the distinction that is traditionally made between cosmic time and lived time. The former corresponds to physical time (and space), and it is this universal time/space which draws the world into an apparently inexorable dynamic of material and organic changes, most probably from a principle of entropy which assures its irreversibility; the second, often viewed as psychic time or ordinary time, coincides with the perception that every human has of physical time, and with the experience that he has of it in his own body and intellect. Concomitantly, this allows a complementary distinction, equally operational, between "natural" or organic space and perceived space.

It is precisely in these practices of history that the philosopher Paul Ricœur proposes to find the points which will permit us to overcome the aporia of a temporality divided between the "objective" time of the world and "phenomenological" time. Or, to use the terms of a Heideggerian phenomenology which has once again become fashionable, it is in the domain of history that one must seek the bridges between an exterior, measurable time, and interior time, the time of the *Dasein*. In a highly meaningful paradox, the former would have to be rejected, in the name of the latter's ontological status, as "vulgar" time, time designated as such because it would be awash in a succession of anecdotal and contingent events. Consequently, the time of the *Dasein*, based essentially in man, would be marked by a tension toward the future. Despite its ontological status, such a tension could be stimulating were it not animated by an unhealthy existential and metaphysical concern and if it did not end up coinciding in a decidedly morbid mode with "being toward death" (*Sein zum Tode*).[7] Using artifices of language which were denounced by Pierre Bourdieu and Henri Meschonnic, and formulated in such a way that the usual etymologizing redundancies are underlined by the typographic ingenuities of an absurdly mimetic translation, Martin Heidegger can affirm, for example:

> Thrown and entangled, *Da-sein* is initially and for the most part lost in what it takes care of. But in this lostness, the flight of *Da-sein* from its authentic existence that we characterized as anticipatory resoluteness makes itself known, and this is a flight that covers over. In such heedful fleeing lies the flight from death, that is, a looking away *from* the end of being-in-the-world. This looking away from ... is in itself a mode of the ecstatic, *futural* being *toward* the end. Looking away from finitude, the inauthentic temporality of entangled everyday *Dasein* must fail to recognize authentic futurality and temporality in general.[8]

Indeed, if there is a "being toward death" for each individual—we'll see that Hesiod himself would not have disagreed—the *Dasein* depends entirely on lived time, on "exterior" time which is itself founded on the physical and cosmic flux of space/time. And so it is a complete reversal of perspective that we hope to achieve here.

---

[7] Ricœur 1985:147–182, attempting to resolve the aporia with which Heidegger 1996 (1927):373–398 (§407–437) finds himself confronted in his scornful rejection of everyday time; concerning these troubling pages, see also Ricœur 1983:125–129, and 1985:90–144.

[8] Heidegger 1996 (1927): 389 (§424) (trans. Stambaugh); cf. also n31 below. Bourdieu 1982:167–205, showed and denounced the misleading inconsistency of such sophistic formulations. See also, in the same sense, the excellent critical remarks by Meschonnic 1990: 258–345.

This makes obvious the aporia which an ontological and philosophical time oriented toward death leads to, disregarding the potential for realization and construction of social and practical time. Faced with this philosophical impasse, one might willingly re-examine Ricœur's twofold attempt, to return to history its function of "rewriting lived time on cosmic time" and to base man's historic condition with its hermeneutics in the dialectic of memory and forgetfulness. We must remember that his first effort was based on a model representation of the construction of historic time in three phases, in a processing sequence whose cognitive status is not specified: "prefiguration" operations, understanding both the practical and symbolic natures of human action and its temporality (*mimesis* I); a process of "configuration" by narrative and discursive *mise en intrigue* "emplotment" of man's actions organized in a temporal sequence (*mimesis* II); and "refiguration" of configured time by narrative means, when this time is in some way given back to human experience (*mimesis* III). Because of the attention given to semio-narrative analysis which developed in the 1970s, the arrangement is part of the definition of a hermeneutics which claims for its own the tripartite structure and the procedures implied by a communication schema applied to literary production. "Hermeneutics, on the other hand, is careful to reconstruct the entire range of operations by which practical experience gives itself works, authors, and readers. (...) The issue therefore is the concrete process by which textual configuration mediates between the prefiguration of the practical field and its refiguration by the work's reception. (...) Aristotle, as we have seen, ignored the temporal aspects of emplotment. I propose to disentangle those aspects from the act of textual configuration, and show the mediating role of this time of emplotment between the temporal aspects prefigured in the practical field and the refiguration of our temporal experience by this constructed time. *We follow destiny from a prefigured time to a refigured time, through the mediation of a configured time.*"[9]

On the other hand, in the most recent stage of his lengthy itinerary, Ricœur has noticed that by defining the works of historians as discursive and more especially narrative configurations of different prefigurations of time, he was confronted with the thorny problem of linguistic reference. It is obvious that if one conceives the general problem of articulation between phenomeno-logical time and cosmic time in terms of emplotment (*mise en intrigue*) or even of (historic) putting-into-discourse (*mise en discours*), an immediate question

---

[9] Ricœur 1983:86–87 (1985:147). The three moments of *mimēsis* which are the basis of hermeneu-tics are described by Ricœur 1983:87–100, 101–109, and 109–129, respectively.

arises: from what mediations are events, the spatio-temporal "reality" of the past, events, constituted in history? Beyond the role of prefiguration played by the indispensable individual memory, beyond the materialization of archived singular and collective memories, simple narrative emplotment proves insufficient to account for intellectual operations relative to the configuration in the movement of *mimesis* II. These operations would be grouped into three categories implying an order of succession: after archiving operations would come explanation/comprehension procedures, which would lead to representations grasped as interpretations in "representance." "The problem of referentiality appropriate to history seems to me to stand out clearly, in that a tendency to closure, inherent in the act of emplotment, becomes an obstacle to the extra-linguistic, extratextual, even referential impulse by which representation becomes representance."[10] We shall see that we must go much farther critically, concerning the privilege granted emplotment (*mise en intrigue*) in procedures relative to the act of configuration and representation, independent of the question of reference.

Defined in the first part of Ricœur's first investigation on the time of history, the process of three mimetic moments proves to be essential when, in the third part of Ricœur's work published in the 1980's, there appears the question of "third time" (*tiers temps*) capable of ensuring mediation between lived time and cosmic time, to find some way out of the impasses of the (Heideggerian) phenomenology of time: "a third option, opened up by pondering the aporias of the phenomenology of time, is to reflect on *the place of historic time between phenomenological time and that other time which phenomenology does not succeed in constituting, whether it is called world time, objective time, or vulgar time.*" We understand that the "third time" he seeks coincides with history, which truly does the work of poetic ordering, using "instruments of thought" such as the calendar, the succession of generations, or recourse to archives and documents.[11] Lacking the reversal of perspective proposed here, and given the ontological status conferred on the temporality of the *Dasein*, it is not surprising to see Ricœur placing the work of the historian among procedures of the refiguration phase. Indeed, in returning to the philosophical question of time, Ricœur assimilates the fabrication of history to a process of reading and rereading temporal configurations already constituted in the *mimesis* II moment. The "third time" which is supposed to serve as mediator between lived phenomenological time on the one hand and physical, organic,

---

[10] Ricœur 2000:302–307, and 307–320, (for the quotation, 319).
[11] Ricœur 1985:147 and 153.

even cosmic time on the other, would consequently be found in the interpretive procedures of reconfiguration in *mimesis* III!

Due to the reversal of perspective proposed here, the concept of "third time" must be replaced by the concept of "spatio-temporal mediations" (plural): mediation on the one hand in the prefigurations of lived time and space (anchored in physical time and space) with the individual and collective memory which corresponds to them; mediation also in the different operations of history which rework these configurations in order to base them not in philosophical or even metaphysical time, but rather in a community memory of a discursive and practical sort; mediations finally by the fact that operations of the historical memory, well known by everyone in the community through different oral and written genres, are in turn inscribed in a historicity and spatiality which is both individual and collective, and find a practical effectiveness in refigurations. To that extent, whether entrusted to poets specializing in the memory of the community or to university professors using erudite academic methods, history as a re-creation practice using different ways of emplotment is not refiguration, but configuration. It is poietic—as we shall see in 4.5—in the etymological sense of the term; as at the time of the Greek *aoidoi*, it remains the daughter of Mnemosyne.

But as a social practice, this discursive recreation also has an impact on the spatial and temporal flux of what we live collectively and individually. From the perspective of hermeneutics, the realization of this pragmatic dimension essential to any operation of emplotment and historian configuration no doubt belongs among refiguration operations. It is by refiguration that history-configuration can reorient the spatio-temporal flux which makes up our historicity in physical space/time. Far from being accidental and "vulgar," this flux is the referent for the memorial operations of history as a poietic genre and as an academic discipline, operations which should help us manage it!

So we willingly recognize that the practical effects of the putting-into-discourse (*mise en discours*) implied by any narrative configuration in the work of *mimesis* II is based on interpretive refigurations; its social effects consequently belong to *mimesis* III. The same is true, really, of the practical consequences of any manifestation of the symbolic process seen in its pragmatic dimension. To this extent, and looking at all imaginable operations to account for symbolic and fictional production in general, the historian's activity and production surely belong to the procedures of configuration and emplotment of *mimesis* II.[12] But we shall see that the perspective of "configurational"

---

[12] An historian of historiography, Prost 1996:247–252, sees the "founding act" of plot construction

emplotment must be enlarged to include all the procedures of schematization and modelization which relate to putting-into-discourse. Although we shall return to define and delimit it later in this study (2.3), it would be best to state immediately that the notion of configuration, through putting-into-discourse and well beyond simple emplotment, includes a whole series of procedures of placing into discursive form; along with placing into sequence, these procedures combine description, schematization, different varieties of metaphor, and logic of an argumentative sort, if not an explicative sort; configuration tends toward a modelization designed to make things intelligible.[13]

In this way, the notion of configuration goes back to the most inclusive concept of representation, which subsumes the different ways we grasp a state of things in a figurative and symbolic form, which is to say in a po(i)etic form in the Greek and etymological sense of this term to which we shall return later. Developed at the end of the final stage of Ricœur's investigation, the concept of "representance" could not be substituted for representation. Designating as it does "anticipation (*attente*) linked to historical knowledge of constructions constituting reconstructions of the past course of events," and founded as it is on "historian intentionality" (*l'intentionnalité historienne*), "representance" once again draws us wrongly toward *mimesis* III.[14]

On the other hand, we would do well to remember that, conceived as *enárgeia* by the rhetoricians of antiquity, the faculty of "placing before the eyes" is central in the operation of restitution of a spatio-temporal referent. But this visual faculty of discourse takes place in the operation of configuration before deploying its pragmatic effects in the moment of refiguration, which may be marked by a "pact between writer and reader." If it is convincing to the public through the force of literary writing,[15] this means that it is impossible to make a clear distinction between historian operation (*opération historienne*) and a work of fiction. Both are definitively founded on fictional effects, on the "as

---

as a work of configuration. In 1996b:15–68, I tried to show the practical and social impact inherent in any symbolic putting-into-discourse.

[13] On several of these operations of historiographic configuration, see the recent contribution of Revel 2001:62–74. Ricœur 2000:320–328 recognizes the existence of "rhetorical resources of verbal attestation," most notably in movements of attestation and protestation given in the narratives of the Shoah.

[14] Ricœur 2000: 302–307 and 359–369. The reference in the lengthy note 77 (367–369) to the concept of "Vertretung" developed by H.-G. Gadamer in *Wahrheit und Methode* reveals a philosophical hermeneutics which, ignoring the linguistic turn, is incapable of grasping the effects of the poietics distinctive to the verbal putting-into-discourse; cf. Calame 2002b:67–77.

[15] Cf. especially Chartier 1998:91–99; for evidence in ancient historiography, see Hartog 2005: 61–74.

if" of the putting-into-discourse and the work of poietic writing, from spatio-temporal referents provided by a natural and social environment, inscribed in the flux of physical and cosmic time.

Ricœur thus seems to be the victim not only of his dependence on the narratological paradigm of the 1970s, but also of his fascination with Heidegger's metaphysical phenomenology. By making of the emplotment of historical discourse a "third time" operation, and by situating this "third time" not in a sequence of movements of configuration beginning with our way of living physical space/time, but rather in discursive refiguration, as well as by erasing the spatial points of reference of every temporal and historical configuration, the hermeneutic philosopher sustains a fundamental misunderstanding in his effort to resolve the unmistakable aporia of the phenomenology of time by defining an intermediary situation between history and fiction. This ambiguity stems largely from silence about the fictional effects of any use of language and any putting-into-discourse; these effects of fiction themselves also contribute to relativizing strongly the ontological status accorded to the philosophical temporality of the *Dasein*. This misunderstanding has as corollaries no fewer than four other misunderstandings which we must now dispel in order to change them into instruments of analysis.

2.2. The double articulation of calendar time

Stemming from the singular and ambiguous position assigned by Ricœur to "third time," the second misunderstanding which must be pointed out in Ricœur's quest for a bridge between lived time and cosmic time is maintained by the notion of "calendar time" as borrowed from Emile Benveniste. According to the propositions formulated by the eminent linguist, calendar time would indeed be characterized by the linear organization traced by a computation originating from an axial point of origin. From a point generally corresponding to a founding event, a homogenous and dynamic scansion would thus orient a "chronic" time; this time is presented by Ricœur as the very example of a "third time" allowing psychic time to articulate with cosmic time.[16]

Now I would like to point out that in every cultural community, the temporality of the calendar is in fact founded on a combination of conven-

---

[16] Ricœur 1985:154–160, from Benveniste 1974:67–78 (a chapter which corresponds to a study entitled "Language and Human Experience," and originally published in *Diogène* 51, 1965, pp. 3–13.)

tions which rest not only on a regular measure which allows one to move in a linear manner in the past, but also on a series of recurrences of a more or less cyclical sort. Certainly, by virtue of the reference point concerning a founding moment taken as axial point, calendar time in its linear dimension depends on the representation which every society creates of its own community past; to this extent, in its practical effects, the temporality of the calendar corresponds to a way of living collectively, intellectually, and symbolically, the inexorable progress and flight of cosmic time. On the other hand, in its cyclical dimension, calendar time depends on points of reference furnished by the "natural" world, with astronomical phases or meteorological repetitions such as the cycle of the seasons or the rhythm of monsoons, but also with the recurrent biological successions attached to the mortality of the human being. Through the rhythm which it imposes on social behavior, calendar time also creates a communal way of living the cyclical aspect of organic time by symbolic and cultural practice. And because of its twofold dimension, both linear and circular, calendar time does indeed furnish, well before historiographic operations, a privileged mediation between physical, biological, and cosmic time on the one hand, and psychic and social time on the other. Before the intervention of the writing of history with its fictional effects, the temporal mediation being sought takes place in this complex symbolic organization and scansion, starting from a specific spatio-temporal environment and from collective representations of the past.

While organizing a social space, calendar time thus offers a composite and rhythmical temporality. It is in its realization that the conjunction between all the cultural representations of the past which we class in the vague category of "myth," and all the regulated and recurrent symbolic practices which we place under the no less vague name of "rite," take place. The former is not opposed to the latter, as Ricœur and some others think. But the socially shared narrative representation of the past with its spatial points of reference combines with the somatic and anthropopoietic practice of the community inscribed in calendar recurrence attached to precise places. This combining confers an additional symbolic and practical depth on a time which is far from ordinary, which could be scorned only by a metaphysical philosopher.[17]

Inscribed in calendar time, "myth" and "rite" contribute by different symbolic means to transform, socially and spatially, the linear and cyclical

---

[17] Ricœur 1985:154–156. Relative and operative anthropological concepts, often naturalized and changed to the universals which myth and rite have become, have been the object of several critiques to which I returned in 1996a:12–25 and 1996b:15–19.

components of physical and biological time, in its flow and in its rhythmical recurrences. Thus in the Bacchylides poem cited at the beginning of this discussion, the different lines of heroic time and space recounted, through the spatio-temporal reference points of the discursive enunciation and by the annular rhythmic and rhetorical structures that the song presents, lead to the ritual celebration, *hic et nunc*, in the cult of the city deity, for the Delphic victory of a renowned citizen: from heroic Argos and Troy we move in time through the choral ritual instituted in Arcadia toward Delphi to end up (with the actual poetic and ritual performance) in the colonial city of Metapontum, under the aegis of Artemis. In so doing, the different symbolic manifestations that modern anthropology labels myth and rite transform individual apprehensions, prefigured by the time and space of the world, into a shared knowledge and practical collective memory, performed as cultic songs; these apprehensions, felt as psychic time and space based on the development of organic time and the deployment of physical space, are transformed in mythico-ritual configurations and realized as ritualized collective memory. This is far from the "vulgar" time rejected by Heidegger in favor of "historiality," a constitutive element of the projection of *Dasein* into death.

2.3. The question of putting-into-discourse

From this perspective, there is no choice but to observe that, based on the prefigurations of temporality represented by our individual feelings of physical and cosmic time, biological and psychic but also socialized, the configuration of social time and space through calendar time immediately calls for a putting-into-discourse. The temporal (and spatial) operations of *mimesis* II call immediately for representations of a discursive sort. In this regard, the polysemy of the term *histoire* in French, of *storia* in Italian, and even of *Geschichte* in German is no doubt significant: history as constituted and shared academic knowledge of the past by selection and putting-into-form of the events retained in "memory"; history as a narrative practice and as story sharing with history as knowledge the narrative and more generally poetic (but also pragmatic) narrative aspects inherent to any putting-into-discourse; but also history as (individual and collective) apprehension of and relationship to the past through a sequence of events, thus history as memory.[18] Certainly, these three modalities of history can be found in a dialectical relationship of reciprocity and interaction which ensures that one of them, history as

---

[18] On history as discourse and practice, see de Certeau 1975:27–30.

knowledge, feeds from the other two, history as narrative and history as perception and representation of the past. One could thus imagine that history as shared knowledge is founded largely on our perceptions and our practical ways of living history as past, but that this knowledge is also constantly reshaped by historians using essentially discursive means.

If narrative structures do indeed seem by their logic to transform every history into narrative, the moment of spatial and temporal configuration represented by the historian's elaboration must be expanded—as we have already indicated—to all procedures of putting-into-discourse. Since it coincides with a putting-into-discourse, historiographic configuration thus covers a whole series of procedures of discursive putting-into-form, which are not limited to emplotment; as we indicated, along with the placing into narrative sequence are combined procedures of description and schematization, elaborations of prototypes and stereotypes, different varieties of metaphor, rhetorical forms and figures proper to the discipline, and an argumentative logic, if not an explanatory one.[19] By these various means, the configuration tends toward modeling, toward the "as if" which characterizes discourse in human sciences in general. By integrating the moment of historic configuration with the various procedures basic to any putting-into-discourse, we come back to the classical Greek concept of poetics as fabrication, of the poetic as "poietic": *poieîn* based on the operations of the fictional *mimēsis* as Aristotle saw it, which Ricœur for his part takes up in the first part of his investigation of time, but in order to focus on emplotment and limit it essentially to narrative procedures.[20]

In this wider po(i)etic perspective to which I have said I shall return (section 4.5), the historian's work can be imagined as a historiopoiesis which erases the distinctions which one might be tempted to make between history and historiography, between history as doing and erudite history (configuration on the one hand, refiguration on the other?); the poietic work of the historian thus seen as construction and fashioning of temporalities and

---

[19] The role of rhetorical devices in historiographic putting-into-discourse was finally recognized by Ricœur 2000: 320–328 (cf. n8 above); see Chartier 1998:108–125. He tells not only of its argumentative functions, but also of its figurative power, producing images (2000:249–258).

[20] On the effects of modelization brought about by any putting-into-discourse, cf. Borutti 1999:136–147, and on history see Revel 2001:68–74. I have tried to clarify this fundamental trait of Greek poietics, whose fabrication function one can try to render by using the term "fictional," in 2000b:38–51; the work of several Greek historiopoietai is sketched in the work of 1996b:30–46; cf. also 2000b:145–161, with the details given below in section 4.5 and n50. On the "as if" procedures in human sciences in general, see the references I gave in 2002:67–77.

spatialities prefigured in our individual and collective apprehensions of time and space. In this respect, the historiographic operation is in fact situated in *mimesis* II as well as in *mimesis* III. Having become a *historiopoietes*, the historiographer can indeed be called on to reread a past discursive configuration in which he himself or others have already actively participated in the *mimesis* II phase; he would thus intervene, as a "hermeneuticist," in the reconfiguration operations of *mimesis* III. But these hermeneutics are a dynamic process, destined not to reveal the meaning of a fixed canonic text like the Old or New Testament, but rather to produce a new discourse, with its concrete efficacy. In their discursive dimension, spatio-temporal configurations and refigurations are thus based on procedures of selection and schematization, on description and modelization, through intermediary prototypes and stereotypes, on argumentative placing into sequence, on logical concatenation, which as we have just seen are characteristic, along with narrative structures, of any putting-into-discourse.

It is in this measure that, in the final phase of Ricœur's reflections on time metamorphosed into history, the schematizations which constitute mentalities, variations of scale, and the representations themselves can be included in the intermediate phase of explanation/comprehension. Already at the beginning of the 1970s, Reinhart Koselleck had grasped fully that it is the role of shared concepts, more than simple narrative forms, to ensure the intelligibility of history and thus of past time: "Concepts which include facts, complex relationships, and past processes become, for the historian who uses them in his cognitive approach, formal categories which may be posited as conditions of possibility of histories. It is only with concepts capable of covering a certain duration (...) that the way opens which permits one to know how a once 'real' history can appear to us today as possible and thus representable."[21] It is as discursive, configuring, and refiguring *poíēseis* that the practices of historians contribute to the cognitive stabilization of the collective temporalities known by every political and cultural community; that in an "as if" which ensures both the relationship of reference to events localized in the past with its space and their comprehension in the present, *nunc et hic*.

---

[21] Ricœur 2000:231–238 and 241–277; Koselleck 1990:141, in a contribution entitled "Darstellung, Ereignis und Struktur," published by R. Koselleck and W. D. Stempel (eds.), *Geschichte, Ereignis und Erzählung* (Poetik und Hermeneutik V), Munich (Fink) 1973:560–577. Borutti 1999:136–137, shows that in human sciences in general we work less under the system of the "object-class" than under that of the "object-example," which tends to show its own rule of construction, and thus of possibility.

2.4. The enunciative dimension

Since the constitution of time (and space) in history in the wider sense of the term falls within the different procedures of putting-into-discourse, a fourth ambiguity may spring from not taking into account the enunciative dimension proper to any act of discourse: and this once again caused by defining calendar time too restrictively. Concerning selection, succession, and logical and argumented sequencing, Benveniste says: "In all forms of human culture and in every era, we see in one way or another an effort to objectify chronical time. It is a condition necessary to the life of societies, and to the life of individuals in societies. This socialized time is that of the calendar." Based as we have seen on calendar time, this time of our shared cultural experience of history would thus have the rhythm given by a regular computation based on a point of origin coinciding with a founding moment in the community's past. And in the perspective adopted by Benveniste, this counted time not only does not integrate into its linearity the cyclical occurrences from which calendar time is also made, but it is placed in opposition to "linguistic time," which is linked to the exercise of the word. There would be a contrast between calendar time and linguistic time to the extent that, obviously, the axial point of the latter, stemming from the putting-into-discourse, coincides not with the point of origin, but with the very moment of enunciation, a "now" which defines itself concomitantly with a "here" in a new intermingling of temporal and spatial parameters. These discursive indices recalling time and space of communication combine with the pronominal forms of "I" and "you" to constitute what Benveniste in an almost contemporary study calls "the formal apparatus of enunciation."[22] From this linguistic and enunciative *hic et nunc*, the position varies with the place, the moment, and the actors of the putting-into-discourse itself.

A surprising paradox, this opposition between calendar time and linguistic time, for the person interested in representations of time and space. It seems indeed that the configurative capture of time and space implies, on

---

[22] Benveniste 1974:71 and 76–78; "formal apparatus of the enunciation:" 79–88. See on this the reflections of Culioli 1999:166–173, who insists not only that we construct verbally from the absolute spatio-temporal origin an "origin of locution," but also that "the 'I' enunciatory subject as origin of the referential can present itself (and be presented as) mobile and current over time." On the relationship between "discourse" (as distinct from "history") for the "formal apparatus of enunciation," see the critical remarks by Adam, Revaz, and Lugrin 1998 and Calame 2005b:122–128. On references to different types of *comput* based on a moment of origin, see Molet 1990:257–261.

the contrary, a combining of calendar or chronical time and linguistic time, in the complex operations of putting-into-discourse. Configuring linguistically a time which is at once smoothed, regulated, and profiled by a homogeneous system of measurement, but also accentuated by cyclical celebrations, any discursive representation of time and space orients the temporal line from the point of origin of the calendar computation toward the focal point of the putting-into-discourse. Which is to say that, by the putting-into-discourse, temporality organized by the computation from an axial point of origin (also marked out spatially) is oriented toward the "instance of enunciation"; represented grammatically by the "I" of the "speaker," this instance of a discursive and enunciative order is also the object of a spatial and temporal locating. The "performance" of the discourse makes the spatio-temporal parameters correspond with the *hic et nunc* of communication and with the different places and moments of reception. Conforming to a particular chronology, the putting-into-discourse of time (and of space) that the writing of history constitutes is therefore oriented equally by an enunciative logic!

As it relates to the operation of putting-into-discourse of time, together with its spatial corollary, the tension which exists between the two focal points of any discursive temporality, between chronological point of origin and instance of enunciation in the *hic et nunc* of communication, implies a twofold passage: from social reality to the order of discourse, then, conversely, from discourse to this reality; from the extra- to the intra-discursive, then from the intra- to the extra-discursive, if we may be allowed this admittedly artificial operative distinction. From the temporal point of view, one thus moves from the scale of measure of socially organized and configured time to the discursive and enunciative assumption of this scansion into the discourse, only to return later to reality and to social representations through the process of communication in its mobile *hic et nunc*. This discursive movement under tension requires that we distinguish carefully, from both a temporal and spatial point of view, two levels of a different (semiotic) nature: on the one hand, the (extra-discursive) level which corresponds to the act of enunciation and narration and which thus coincides with the empirical and historic time and space of the putting-into-discourse (and, consequently, of telling)—for instance, the choral and ritual execution of the song composed by Bacchylides to celebrate the young citizen of Metapontum; and on the other hand the (intra-discursive) level of expression in the discourse itself, by different linguistic and enunciative means, of this time and this space of the enunciation—the affirmation of the "I" of the poet and the allusion to processional chants of young people in the colonial city of Magna Graecia.

The social and historical reality (of an extra-discursive sort) must thus be distinguished from intra-discursive and enunciative spatio-temporal reality (we go so far as to speak of the *énonciation énoncée*, the "uttered enunciation"), even if the latter finds itself highly dependent on the former. For the historian, this means that, through verbal and discursive mediation, the moment and the place of his act of putting-into-discourse, of his enunciation, are integrated into the operation and into the result of the discursive configuration of time and space of the history: from the enunciative point of view, the historian is present in his own discourse. Because of the obvious permeability between extra- and intra-discursive, especially in the process of communication, historic discourse itself carries (linguistic and enunciative) traces of this enunciative tension; it is part of any putting-into-discourse, and thus of any reference by means of language.

It is thus in the very instant of the putting-into-discourse and of the enunciation, with its *mimesis* II operations, that time and space as lived and the social and individual memory come into the configuration of any discourse, especially if it is poetic and literary. They take place not only in the forms of enunciation as they relate to the *hic et nunc* of communication, but also in the rhythm of the narration (the different narrative movements which, in the melic poem of Bacchylides, permit a return to the moment of the heroic founding of Tiryns), as well as in the chronological scansion of the utterance itself (and consequently in that of the narrative—the chronological sequencing of the spatial movements which lead to the institution of choral dances in honor of Artemis in Arcadia). This last distinction between the rhythm of narration and chronological scansion corresponds to the classical distinction between *Erzählzeit* and *erzählte Zeit*, between the rhythm of recounting (and describing) and time (and space) recounted (or described).[23] It is important to notice that it is subordinated to the operative distinction made between the empirical time and space of the act of enunciation on one hand, and the temporality and discursive spatiality of the uttered enunciation, then of the narrative (if there is a narrative), on the other; the latter are the linguistic and discursive expression of the former, in the tension we have mentioned between the *hic et nunc* of the enunciation and the point of origin of a calendar time which is both linear and cyclical.

---

[23] On this distinction, see Muller 1968:269–286, Genette 1972:71–78 and 128–130, Benveniste 1966:237–250 and 251–257. On the constituent effects of the "discursive time" in the writing of history, see also Certeau 1975:104–109.

This complex combining of temporal and spatial lines is noticeable from the very first Greek historiography. At about the time of the Bacchylides poem already mentioned, we witness the passage by poets from ritual celebrations of a historic and legendary past of the community to reelaborations of the most recent past offered in prose by the first logographers, historiopoietai such as Herodotus and Thucydides. One can see in these different forms of historiography, from the point of view of narration and the scansion of time recounted, a mix analogous to that of poetry, between the linear temporal succession (still heterogeneous from a measurement point of view) and cyclical returns. If counting up the generations ensures for the history of the Persian Wars, as configured by Herodotus, a chronological depth and measure articulated along several genealogical lines (often badly coordinated), the changing of the seasons gives to the Peloponnesian Wars, as Thucydides conceives them, a cyclical scansion.[24] Through the enunciative strategies incorporated by both of these historians, time recounted and time of narration converge toward the temporality of the uttered enunciation ("*énonciation énoncée*"); and, by this enunciative means, these three temporal lines open *hic et nunc* onto the extra-discursive time and space of this new writing of history, on the present place and time where the narrative configuration finds its effect. Calendar time (with its twofold dimension already discussed) and linguistic time are interlinked in the spatial and temporal development of the poetic and historiographic discourse itself.

It will be noticed that once again, thanks to the brief examples chosen in Greek literature, we have gone from poetic configurations of time and space to configurations which we generally consider historical. There is thus no "radical" break between poetic configurations on the one hand, undoubtedly more marked by reference to a past and to a geography, both heroic, practically reactualized and refigured (Americans would say "reenacted") in the time and space of ritual, and on the other hand prosaic puttings-into-discourse focused not only on a more recent past and a nearby geography, but also more animated by practical reflections on motivations for the actions; the forces at play in the rebalancing of justice for Herodotus, intentions of domination and will to power for Thucydides. Even if neither can be called the father of modern historiography, we see the enunciative face of Herodotus assuming the profile of a judge, while Thucydides makes the (as yet nonexistent) histo-

---

[24] On this kind of narrative scansion, see Bouvier 2000. On social and configurational effects in the constituting of a "third time," and the fundamental biological idea underlying the sequence of generations, see Ricœur 1985:160–171, as well as 331–332 and 337.

rian into a moralist.[25] Undoubtedly the archaeo-neologism "historiopoiesis," proposed earlier, would be capable of accounting for the configuring activities of these first logographers: through new writing forms, they place at the service of the Greek cities the traditional poetic means used to fix in collective memory the closest great actions of men of the past and the nearest geography, by conferring on these great deeds a legal and moral meaning.

The practical effects of the historians' work of spatio-temporal configuration depend strongly on the enunciative dimension of the historiographic putting-into-discourse, in classical Greece as well as in hypermodernity.

2.5. Inescapable pragmatics

Any configuration of past time by a putting-into-discourse cannot help but reformulate a temporality already prefigured and partially configured in other forms of expression, before returning (as in any symbolic process and especially through the enunciative intermediary) to a reality already informed and from which it originates.[26] It is in this return that the fifth ambiguity is lodged in Ricœur's work, maintained by the attempt to situate the intervention of the historian and his "representance" in refiguration, and consequently to see it as *mimesis* III. In making the writing of history coincide with this interpretive and generally critical moment, there is a risk of missing the important pragmatic dimension. One thus risks petrifying the historiographic discourse into an immutable text, interpretable only through biblical-type hermeneutics. Inscribed in the historic movement from which they spring, puttings-into-discourse which coincide with operations of configuration have in return an essential impact on the very direction and profile of this movement. Animated by the enunciative orientation imprinted on the putting-into-discourse in *mimesis* II, this pragmatic return provoked by the procedures of historian configuration rightly belongs in *mimesis* III. Refiguration does not consist only in interpretive readings of manifestations of historiopoiesis, but also in social practices. Particularly through the enunciative bias, the work of temporal (and spatial) configuration and reconfiguration of the past, combined with intellectual reelaborations, thus gives rise to what is no doubt hermeneutics, but a practical hermeneutics.

---

[25] On Herodotus as arbiter and judge, see Darbo-Peschanski 1998:172–175, and on Thucydides, Loraux 1980. On Herodotus as father of history, see the references given by Calame 2000a: 112–114; for historiopoiesis, see above, section 2.3 with n20.

[26] As is natural for any manifestation which depends on the processes of construction and symbolic representation; see the remarks that I set forth in 1996b:15–68 (especially 49–54).

Between temporal and spatial prefiguration and configuration, it is essentially the linear and chronological aspect of calendar time which (on the order of "third time") facilitates the passage from the extra- to the intra-discursive in the putting-into-discourse of the temporality and spatiality of historiopoiesis. On the other hand, the practical impact of historiographic reformulations undoubtedly applies more to the cyclical aspect of calendar time, in recurrent celebrations of a memorial sort. Taking up the categories of cultural and social anthropology already mentioned, one could say that the first passage seems to belong more to the "myth" and the second to "ritual." Whatever one may think of these questionable concepts, the arrow of social time is largely organized by the dialectical movement, divided between line and circle, which passes through puttings-into-discourse and spatio-temporal configurations whose practical and hermeneutic impact is animated especially by a strong enunciative orientation.

And so it is, for example, in classical Athens: the recuperation and reformulation of the exploits of Theseus as a founder of the Athenian synoecism and democracy manifest themselves in the creation of an epic poem; the writing of this poem in Homeric diction is accompanied by the ritualization of religious honors to the new Athenian hero, an annual celebration inscribed in the city's calendar. The historiopoietic production of the *Theseid* corresponds to the creation and organization of the annual Festival of Theseus on the eighth day of Pyanopsion, at a heroic shrine whose space and iconographic decor are changed for the occasion.[27] This combination of linear depth and circular scansion through a recurrent "reenacted" discursive event is also found in our own calendar temporality. If its fundamental rhythm shows the weekly recurrence imposed by the economic and industrial organization of productive work thanks to the technical measurement of clock time, this rhythm originates from the cosmogonic narrative of the Creation in *Genesis*, reread in the ecclesiastical context. Modern calendar time is also accentuated both by celebrations linked to important episodes of the biography of the heroic founder of Christianity as they are recorded in *New Testament* narratives and by a series of variable anniversaries. These anniversaries generally celebrate in the same annual rhythm the "historic" events which marked the past and which continue to orient the present of communities which have become national, in the same dialectic between circle and line![28]

---

[27] For details on the process of epic and religious intervention surrounding the heroic figure of Theseus in Athens at the beginning of the fifth century, see Calame 1996b:153–156 and 398–443.

[28] Crosby 1997, in dating around 1250 Western Europe's passage from a qualitative perception of

3. Interlude: Between places and acts of memory

In ancient Greece as in many traditional cultures, moments of memory, moments ritualized and maintained by the configuring work of historiopoietai, are often attached to places of memory. By their ritually organized and often cyclic rhythm, these shared moments of memory contribute to the practical orientation of the flux of historic and social time in which they themselves are integrated. Undoubtedly for us, the rapid multiplication and the extreme segmentation of those traditions on which the polymorphic culture of (post) modernity rests are combined with the orientation toward an immediate future indicated above by way of prelude.

Polymorphic segmentation and immediacy would have caused confusion which has changed the relationship between memory and history to a supposed "radical break." In this context, the structuralist stratagem of binary opposition can serve as explanation; it reduces the break to a dichotomy organized, in a rather heterogeneous way, by traits such as "plural/universal," "spontaneous/critical," "absolute/relative," "lived relationship with the present/representation of the past," "sacred/secular," "emotional/intellectual," etc. The conclusion drawn from this restoration of a sort of *Grand Partage*, as "structuralist dichotomy," seems unavoidable: "Memory is rooted in the concrete, in space, gesture, image, and object. History is attached only to temporal continuities, evolutions, and the relationships among things. Memory is an absolute, and history knows only the relative." But the same historian also reaffirms that "the need for memory is a need for history," since we must recognize that, especially because of archiving operations made possible by writing, memory relies on history.[29]

Historical memory is undoubtedly fixed in "places of memory," but it is also consecrated and maintained in the community through discursive means. Almost a century ago, the reality of different forms of "collective memory," known by our societies founded on a "verbal substrate," had been recognized. The role attributed to language in its social dimension and as an instrument of

---

temporal reality to a quantitative perception, showed the impact of new technical means of measurement on the calendar organization of social time. Molet 1990:190–238, offers a series of examples of calendar structures whose cycle is devised either according to the changing of the seasons or by astronomical measurements.

[29] The supposed "break" between history and memory was traced by Nora 1984:xix and xxiv; it has been reaffirmed by Prost 1996:298–303, and replaced into its ideological context by Chesneaux 1996:125–132.

comprehension sends us back to attempts at discursive configurations by historians and at transformation of isolated accounts, of singular documents and individual consciousness of time, into a temporality to be shared in a collective temporality. We must remember that in the Egypt of the Pharaohs, the temple of Hathor at Dendera, a work of the god of writing, Thoth, celebrated by Plato in the *Phaedrus*, was conceived as "a three-dimensional monumental transposition of a book which has all the signs of a canon." Architecturally, the temple is a realization of a basic plan; from the epigraphic point of view, its iconographic decor corresponds to a program; on the religious level, it is the place where ritual rules are carried out; and socially it provides space to the respect of ethical rules guaranteed by the divinity.[30]

If it is true that the places of memory, in antiquity as well as in (post) modernity, work only as signs—*sēmeîa* in Thucydides' meaning of this term which we shall take up later (4.2)—they are on the one hand the object of ritualized celebrations designed to reactivate regularly, in the present and communally, the history which they indicate and which they designate; in this, these monuments constitute spatial points of reference of the "third-time" which is calendar time, in its twofold linear and cyclical dimension, which places it between social temporalities and discursive temporalities. On the other hand, sites which evoke the past are themselves subject to a historicity which transforms them and replaces them as the memorial relationship with the group concerned with its own past is modified. In their geographic organization, places of memory bring a determining spatial and visual contribution to the temporary fixing of representations and configurations of the past from which history is made; and so these sites constitute the material traces of the practical relationship which the work of historians maintains with the present. Interest in history, individual and community sensitivity for the past, are no doubt nourished by the erudite and didactic practices of the historiopoietai. Regular ritual celebrations centered around the places of memory which in ancient Greece were, for example, the tombs of heroes, just as the commentaries punctuating the accounts displayed in the museums and monuments of our modernity are there to ensure, despite any dichotomy, the hermeneutic and practical relationship between plural representations of the past constructed by historians and a collective and uttered memory to maintain and adapt to the circumstances of an ever-changing present moment! That is the reason why the historian must also double as an anthropologist, especially when he turns his attention toward different communities.

[30] Halbwachs 1925:40–82; Assmann 1992:177–185.

4. From the time of historiopoiesis to historic space: Herodotus

Anyone who speaks of places of memory speaks also of memorial monuments, inscribed in a symbolic geography but also in calendar time and social time. Reciprocally, it goes without saying that constructed spaces are integrated into puttings-into-discourse done by historiopoietai. Indeed, our apprehension of the natural and cultural spaces which form our geographic-social ecology are obviously subject to the same procedures of representation and configuration as our individual and collective perceptions of physical time and social time, to be restored to the interpretive virtualities of refiguration.

4.1. A spatio-temporal investigation

At least in the European tradition, with Herodotus historiographic investigation is supposed to begin to offer itself as a joint exploration and putting-into-discourse of time and space. The discursive configuration proposed by *historía* is made up of the intercrossing of forays into the temporal depth of the past of different cities or cultural groups and of multidirectional travels in the field of the geography of the world inhabited by communities of men. In Herodotus, the spatial transgression of limits assigned by justice to the political power of sovereigns proves to be one of the essential motives of history; from that, the chronological progression exploring the causes, which are also wrongs, of the origin of conflicts confronting Persians and Greeks, feeds on incursions into space inhabited and civilized by the protagonists of the historic action. Far from being diverting digression, these "ethnographic" developments of the *Investigation (Historía)* by the historian of Halicarnassus are inserted organically into the timeline of narration which organizes and assumes narrated time.

On an etiological level, this temporal scansion of the *erzählte Zeit* by the *Erzählzeit* is itself supported by the time of the (uttered) enunciation; thus, through interposed enunciative interventions, it is subject to the judicial time which orients the unfolding of history. Indeed, Herodotus assumes in his own discourse not only the role of investigator, but also that of judge. His anthropological descriptions are thus subject to a principle of comprehensive explanation. In an integrated spatio-temporal perspective, this principle guides the listeners and later the readers through the exposition of historic causes put forward as first causes, and the spectacle of the geo-political makeup of the Persian Empire. It guides them toward the time and space which are roughly

27

those of the uttered enunciation, and thus toward the extra-discursive *hic et nunc* of communication: Athens just after the Persian Wars.[31]

Herodotus' *Investigation* ends, from the point of view of recounted time and space, at the moment when the Persians are thrown back onto the Ionian coast, thus leaving Athens full latitude to develop its maritime power and its political domination in the Aegean Sea. The historical geo-political itinerary proposed by the investigator is thus matched, in the course of narrated time, with movements ascending toward the time of heroes and geographic incursions all the way to the ends of the inhabited world. It is perhaps this spatio-temporal complementarity in the historian's work which Plutarch felt at the moment he began his historic biography of such a hero as Theseus the Athenian.[32] Confronted with a domain dominated by poets and mythographers and which offers neither proof (*pístis*) nor transparency, the historian says that he finds himself in a position analogous to that of the geographer who, having reached the end of the inhabited world, can only write on his map generic labels such as *Dark Marshes* or *Sea of Ice*. However that may be, for the work of this "archaeologist," the prevailing criterion is verisimilitude (*tò eikós*), the only criterion capable of submitting the fictional (*tò muthôdes*) to the historian's argumented discourse.

4.2. Pragmatic aspects of enunciation

The main concern of the Halicarnassian investigator is "progress in his discourse" (*probḗsomai es tò prósō toû lógou*) in order to "denounce" (*sēmḗnas*) whoever was at the source of acts of injustice against the Greeks. The metaphor of forward progress indicates that the point of reference for the investigation by an interpreter of clues who sets himself up as a judge—as we have seen—is spatial as well as temporal. "To me" (*ep' emeû*): this focal point fulfills very precisely the three parameters of the "formal apparatus of enunciation"—actual time, actual space, speaker.[33] But this inaugural declaration recalls that, from an enunciative point of view, historiopoietic discourse especially is traversed by the phenomenon of deixis.

---

[31] See especially research by Payen 1997:249–280, and additional references to be found in Bichler and Rollinger 2000:27–42, 158–159, and 165–169.

[32] Plutarch *Theseus* 1.105. See Calame 1996a:44–46.

[33] Herodotus 1.5.3–4; on the utterance of the famous programmatic enunciation, see my references in 2000b:151–153, and on the enunciative position of the judge, see n25 above. On the "formal apparatus of the enunciation," see n22 above.

Well before Benveniste's reflections on enunciation and its formal apparatus, the German linguist Karl Bühler had recognized that the point of origin of any discourse consists of a series of spatial, temporal, and "personal" points of reference. Composed of indications of *here*, *now*, and *I*, this set of enunciative reference points corresponds to what could be thought of as the "instance of enunciation." And this *Hier-Jetzt-Ich-System* proves to have a remarkable mediatory ability, as much from the point of view of the relationship between intra- and extra-discursive as from the perspective of the operative divide between "history/narrative" and "discourse." Particularly on a spatial level, a demonstrative such as *hóde* in Greek may refer (by anaphora or cataphora) to what has just been said or what is going to be uttered in the discourse, as also to an element of the external situation of enunciation and of reference of the discourse. The *deixis* which such a demonstrative permits is thus divided between *Deixis am Phantasma* and *demonstratio ad oculos*. Working on the intra-discursive creative and symbolic capacities of the language and thus calling on the imagination, the anaphoric and cataphoric procedures of the *Deixis am Phantasma* can be combined with those of the extra-discursive demonstration which is the *demonstratio ad oculos*.[34]

The operations of the deixis can thus establish a correspondence between the enunciative and textual position of the *persona loquens* (the "speaker") and the biographic person who really pronounces the discourse. They can relate (intra-discursive) enunciated time with the (extra-discursive) moment of its enunciation; and concomitantly, they link space constructed in the discourse to the space of the very instant of communication. It is essential to take into account this system of spatio-temporal coordinates of the instance of enunciation with its deictic extra-discursive references, if we wish to follow the discursive development of practical concepts of time and space: spatio-temporal concepts which can only fulfill their pragmatic function on condition of outlining an enunciated and textual time and space related to the actual space and time of their enunciation. It is exactly this movement that we witness in Herodotus' *Investigation;* its spatio-temporal deployment ends at the very moment of the present geopolitical event which confronts his public: the extension of Athenian power throughout the Aegean basin.

---

[34] Bühler 1934:79–82, 107–140, and 385–392, with the refinement, as it applies to Pindar's poetry, offered by Felson 1999:1–12; see now Calame 2005b: 122–128.

5. A historiographic semiotics of indices: Thucydides

The simultaneously spatial and referential aspect of discursive temporalities has thus led us back to places of memory, which is to say downstream from the putting-into-discourse appropriate to historiopoiesis. If we go back upstream, we find ourselves confronted with prefigured natural and constructed spaces; they are configured in the historical discourse, to be shaped into and transformed by the putting-into-discourse of the historiopoietic operation. From this spatial point of view, the work of the *historiopoietes* is largely based on material indices which are conventionally understood as traces; by their concrete and tangible nature, the traces correspond to meaningful spaces, spaces on which interpretation of the indices confers a temporal dimension.

5.1. About traces

In modern historiography, the trace proves to have a special and paradoxical status. In the eyes of contemporary historians, the trace is that which permits imagining the document in its material aspect. This is the case for Marc Bloch: "Whether it is bones walled up in the ramparts in Syria, a word whose form or use reveals a custom, or a narrative written by a witness to an ancient or modern scene, what do we mean by 'documents' if not a 'trace,' that is to say a mark, perceptible to the senses, left by a phenomenon which is itself impossible to grasp?" Or, in a more positive definition, Michel Foucault: "To reconstitute from what the documents say—and sometimes just hint—the past from which they emanate and which has now disappeared far behind them; the document was always treated as the language of a voice now reduced to silence,—its fragile trace, fortunately decipherable." As a discipline now charged with working out the documents themselves, historiography includes traces. By documentary work on their material nature, history transforms these different forms of social "persistence" into veritable "monuments."[35] Thus it is that Ricœur borrows the trace from historians to attribute to it a meaning (*signifiance*) and, from that, an indisputable capacity for return to the past. As a vestige, the trace would be an element of mediation between the *hic et nunc* and the reality of things past; as an index, it would constitute the material place of the semiotic reference to the past, and at the same time the operand of the historiographic research and deciphering that it prompts.[36]

---

[35] Bloch 1964:21; Foucault 1969:14–15.

[36] Ricœur 1985:171–183; see also 1998:18–27. On this mediating position of the vestige, see Kitani 1999:25–27.

Once again, Ricœur's return to the dull ideological and rhetorical heaviness of Heideggerian phenomenology should demonstrate its emptiness, or at least point out the enormous misunderstanding maintained by the philosophical hermeneutics which is heir to it, especially through Hans-Georg Gadamer.

Certainly, in *Being and Time* one reads with interest that "signs are something ontically at hand which as this definite useful thing functions at the same time as something which indicates the ontological structure of handiness, referential totality, and worldliness." Putting aside the vague etymological redundancies and extravagances of this questionable style of writing, the thought could well be worth taking up and clarifying. But the *Dasein*, the "being-there" fundamental to the human condition, will prove to be marked from a spatial point of view by a constituent "de-distancing" (*Entfernung*). In the relationship of man to the world, this ontological condition of "de-distancing" would abolish all meaningful distance! This is why the *Dasein*, in its temporal essence, can realize its being-in-the-world only in the *ecstatic* mode. Animated constitutively and ontologically by the concern already mentioned, the *Dasein* can only be projected into the future assigned to it by its being-toward-death. Without pretending to dissipate the obscurantist cloud which surrounds such a phrase as "ecstatic and horizontal temporality temporizes itself *primarily* from the future," one can understand why historiography is condemned to follow the destiny assigned to *Dasein* and to its historicity; understood as "having-been" (*Gewesen[heit]*), historiography proves to be projected constitutively toward the future. This is the reason asserted by Heidegger to explain that "historiography by no means takes its point of departure from the 'present' and from what is 'real' only today, any more than does the historicity of unhistorical Da-sein, and then grope its way back to the past. Rather, even *historiographical* disclosure temporalizes itself *out of the future.*"[37]

This is another way of saying that the signifying role glimpsed in the document apprehended as an index, even as a trace, is completely evaded by the phenomenological metaphysics of time. The ontological philosophy of Heidegger is so careful to stick closely to the essence of a man entirely devoted to *Dasein* and thrown into the world, that it is not ready to grant the least semantic dimension either to human beings or to their productions.

---

[37] I have intentionally summarized very schematically a few considerations offered by Heidegger 1996 (1927):77 (§83), 97–105 (§104–114), 292–297 (§317–323), 391 (§427), and 360–361 (§395) (Stambaugh's translation); see on this Ricœur's inadequately critical commentaries, 1983:93–100, 1985:95–143 and 177–182, as well as 1998:20–21. I would add that it is useless to substitute an "open phenomenology of futurity" for a "closed phenomenology of being-toward-death."

Phenomenological ontology is inspired by such an obsession with essence that it is incapable of grasping man in and as a symbolic and discursive creation, which is one of the things that makes him human. This failure to take verbal creation into account is paradoxical in a philosophy developed almost entirely by creating concepts founded on etymological games evocative of opera librettos written by Richard Wagner.

One could willingly grant that the first apprehension of the past takes place only through an immediate present projected into the future, but one must add that such an apprehension cannot be lived, then recaptured as a representation, through external and internal forms of perception, forms whose status depends entirely on the theory of knowing that one accepts.[38] The necessary projection of the past into the future, through a present in constant and irreversible flux, thus escapes from immediacy to the extent that it takes place as manifested temporality (and spatiality). This temporality and this spatiality are embodied not through an *ecstasy* (*Ekstase*) whose status is just as inconsistent as the play on words which designates it, but in a construct which constitutes and determines the individual through symbolic manifestations shared with the members of the cultural community to which he inevitably belongs. A social animal and a man of culture, the individual lives, from the point of view of his shared history, among meaningful traces, genuine prefigurations of time (and space) in a semantic and "anthropopoietic" configuring function.

5.2. Greek prefigurations of time: The *sēmeîa*

Let us return from theoreticians of time to practitioners. Thucydides of Athens is not just the writer of the war between the Peloponnesians and the Athenians, as he claims while affixing his signature at the beginning of his treatise. The present Greece (*nûn*) and what is at stake in Athens' hold on the Aegean Sea cannot be understood without referring to the temporal development of both. From that stems the necessity of a preliminary trip through former times (*pálai*); from that, an "archaeology" (to use the expression of the scholiast) which starts from the reign of the eponymous hero Hellen over the land of Phthia and from the first attempt at maritime domination by Minos. This prefiguration of Athenian thalassocracy leads us through the Trojan Wars and beyond the Persian Wars to the beginning of maritime power of the Athenians themselves, in a convergence of the initial pan-Hellenic perspective and

---

[38] See on this the excellent study by Borutti 1996.

the Athenian point of view for the present: time and space! Thus it is both in the temporal development of political-military history of Greece and in its geo-political constitution that one will find the causes (*aítiai*) of the conflict which now opposes the Athenians and the Peloponnesians.[39]

For exploring these "ancient times" (*tà palaiá*), we have, according to Thucydides, *tekméria*, or marks of recognition. These identification indices can be transformed into proofs (*písteis*) by the argumentation of their interpreter. Among these marks and indices, most are verbal. But, as the very etymology of the word *tékmar* indicates in referring to vision, some are also visual. This is the case, for example, with the present (*nûn*) size of Mycenae, which could not be used as an "exact index" (*akribès sēmeîon*) of the size of the city at the time of the Trojan War. These few visual and spatial references can corroborate or invalidate, for this distant past, what the verses of epic poets such as Homer are likely to "reveal" (*hōs Hómēros toûto dedélōken*); so it is also for the example of the role played by the maritime power of Agamemnon in the conduct of the expedition to Troy.

In the often contradictory combination of present visual indices and verbal indices transmitted by tradition (*ho lógos*), the work of observation (*skopeîn*) and of evaluation (*nomízein*) on the part of the writer are essential. The mistrust (*apistía*) which sight generally arouses, in contrast to the confidence (*pisteúein*) accorded to information given in Homer's epic verses, depends on him. These considerations certainly seem to reverse the terms of relationships of confidence which link a historiographer like Herodotus to sight rather than to hearing! We note nonetheless in Thucydides the consciousness that indices of the past offered by a Homer came from the poet's work of fabrication (*poíēsis*), and that in this respect the narrated actions are certainly, in their organization, the object of a definite embellishment (*kosmêsai*). For the *arkhaîa*, the search for the truth (*alétheia*) consists of evaluating the actions of mortals, starting from indices whose semiotic and poetic dimension, designed to charm an audience, must lead to an attitude of critical mistrust. In view

---

[39] Thucydides 1.1.1–1.2.1 and 1.23.4–1.23.6. Note the circular development, complemented by chiasmus, which evokes in the initial passage and once again in the concluding passage of the "archaeology" (according to the expression used by the scholiast) the conflict between the Peloponnesians and Athenians. On the oral tradition concerning the thalassocracy of Minos, see Hornblower 1991:18–20. Murari Pires 2003:84–92 has shown that the inaugural signature of Greek historiographers, as well as the prelude to great epic poems, included information that is axiological (elements worthy to be narrated), teleological (the utility of the narrative), onomasiological (the enunciative position of the speaker), methodological (relating to the truth of the discourse), and archaeo-etiological (the role of origin as an explicative principle).

of the *muthôdes*, in view of the fictional element of poetry, it is appropriate, for speeches pronounced by men as well as for their deeds, to reformulate these "sayings" and these "deeds" based on the often divergent memory of the protagonists of the war itself.[40] Thus not an objective history, not a purely referential history, but a form of configuration which "collects through writing": "he has collected through writing" (*sunégrapse*) says Thucydides in the initial signature of his treatise about the war between the Peloponnesians and the Athenians.

Because it is itself constructed and because it belongs to the fictional, the visual and auditory trace, raised to the rank of a recognition index, is the object of a work of rewriting. Because it is enunciatively oriented, the account, which is based on memory (*mnémê*), requires the historiographer to intervene with a demand for accuracy (*akribeía*). And so after all these centuries there is a lesson to be drawn from the methodological remarks formulated by Thucydides on the profession of historiographer: it is impossible for the man who sees the marks of the past in their disparity, not as a philosopher but as a practitioner reformulating it as history, to avoid a semiotic putting-into-form. Between prefiguration and configuration, this fabrication transforms every trace into an index or, to use a term sacred to the discipline, into a document calling for reading and interpretation. In this context, speaking of trace proves a misleading metaphor, even if one agrees to endow the trace with a vague *signifiance* ("signifying"). Foucault reminded us that constituting the traces of the past in documents is an integral part of the work of elaborating history, of its *poieîn*.

Thucydides himself does not hesitate to rehabilitate sight (as related to *lógos*) as soon as the spatial disposition of the history's scene furnishes an index which is not misleading, but direct from earlier times. When from Mycenae and from the time of the Trojan War we pass on to Athens and the beginnings of the Peloponnesian War, the sanctuaries raised at that time on the Acropolis do not represent a simple index, but a true mark of recognition: no longer a *sēmeîon*, but a *tekmérion*. But a proof of what? These sanctuaries in fact recall the action of Theseus which goes back to the most ancient times (*apò toû pánu arkhaíou*). After the first legendary kings who ruled over the territory of Attica, it is indeed Theseus who founded the city of Athens; there

---

[40] Thucydides 1.1.2; 1.9.2–1.10.3; 1.20.1–1.21.2 and 1.22.4; for the hermeneutic relationship which the Greek historiographer maintains with the *palaiá* and consequently with the past of his own community, see the references I gave in 1996a:38–41. For the dialectic of sight and hearing (*ópsis* and *akoé*) in Herodotus, see Hartog 2000:5–7, and 2001:23–29 and 395–411, as well as Calame 2000a:120–121.

he regrouped the inhabitants of Attica around a single council and a single prytany. In this political act of founding, the statesman of the age of heroes also demonstrates his quality of discernment (*súnesis*) which he shares with the nearly contemporary historians, Themistocles and Pericles. As for the relationship between past and present whose establishment the *tekmḗrion* allows, it is ensured by ritual celebration. Indeed, just as the synoecism of Theseus is reactualized in the popular feast of *xunoíkia* organized for Athena "still now" (*éti kaì nûn*), so also the permanence of ritual cults and practices which take place in the witness-edifices adjoining the Acropolis, ensures the relationship between ancient times and the present, between the *arkhaîa* or *palaiá* and the *nûn* with its space of realization.[41]

These are thus rites which, through their recurrent and cyclic rhythm, institute the sanctuaries of the gods and the heroes as places of memory; they are religious acts which add to the linear unfolding of calendar time the cyclical dimension which makes of them a true "third-time"; and they are rites which weave the historic relationship between the founding of an institution and its reenactment into a continuity which extends to the present. For Thucydides, this is the case for the Anthesteria celebrated in the sanctuary of Dionysus in the marsh, "as is the custom even still" (*éti kaì nûn*), as well as for the Ionians, themselves natives of Athens; so it is also for the ritual of lustral water which one goes to get at the fountain to prepare for a marriage ceremony, a custom practiced "still now and since ancient times" (*kaì nûn éti apò toû arkhaíou*).[42] A cyclical rhythm in the one case, a linear succession of steps in the individual life in the other. In this context, the index of spatio-temporal *deixis* which the pronoun *hóde* represents is capable of actualizing Bühler's twofold, intra- and extradiscursive reference which we described, and of sending us back not only to that which has just been uttered in the discourse, but also to the very place and moment of enunciation, of communication. Thus, because of the synoecism begun under the intelligent initiative of Theseus, the Athenians designated the Acropolis with the simple noun *pólis*, maintaining the custom up to the present day (*éti mékhri toûde*): the moment and place of enunciation. In a clearly etiological perspective, it is the combination of the linear dimension and the cyclical or occasional dimension of calendar time which is at the base of the index value of a *tekmḗrion* which is both spatial and temporal, offered as a witness to the hermeneutic historian!

---

[41] Thucydides 2.15.2–3; cf. Hornblower 1991:261–269 as well as 25 with references to several passages where *sēmeîon* is practically used as a synonym of *tekmḗrion*. Cf. also n43 below.
[42] Thucydides 2.15.4–6.

5.3. Sight and hearing: Recent history

In the case of a *tekmḗrion* which goes beyond visual index value to become proof, sight seems once again to prevail over hearing. That in any case is affirmed by the Athenians sent as ambassadors to Sparta, in a speech recreated by Thucydides, in the hope of turning the Lacedaemonians away from war with their rhetorical arguments (*ek tôn lógōn*): "Events of truly ancient times (*tà mèn pánu palaiá*), what good is it to evoke them, those events whose witnesses (*mártures*) are accounts entrusted to the hearing (*akoḗ*) rather than to the sight (*ópsis*) of the listeners(!)? But for the Persian Wars and everything that you yourselves have seen and lived (*xúniste*) ... it must be spoken of." In the context of a search for guarantees implied by the word *mártus* and its derivatives, in a context where sight is again favored over hearing, it is the barbarians who must bring proof (*tekmḗrion*) of the new maritime power held by the Athenians; a proof delivered by the defection and flight of the Persians at the end of the Battle of Salamis. In confrontation with the Spartans, the *lógos* of the Athenians offers itself as testimony (*martúrion*) and revelation (*dḗlōsis*) of the merit of their own city! The intention of their speech is indeed to "signify" (*sēmênai*) their strength. Attributed both to the oracle at Delphi by Heraclitus and to his own discourse by Herodotus, this signifying function must both contribute to reminding (*hupómnēsis*) the oldest what they knew from having seen it and to telling the youngest what they cannot have experienced. When the more recent past is involved, one must have recourse to the testimony of those who experienced the event visually. But for the sophist Thrasymachus, when it is a question of constituting the fathers, we must be satisfied, for what is outside our experience, with hearing the older narratives (*lógoi palaióteroi*); later, one can have recourse to information given by the elders, and based on sight.[43]

One can of course try to attribute a simple function of relationship and questioning to the "signifying" (*significance*) of traces, as Ricœur does.[44] But in so doing, one overlooks that the indication role assigned to the trace presupposes a form, and more precisely a symbolic form. It presupposes a figure which, both by its contiguous relationship with that which caused it and by its spatial orientation, returns semiotically to both the action and the actors which gave rise to it. From the first, this figure carries not only the dynamic process which it evokes, but also the polysemy appropriate to any semiotic

---

[43] Thucydides 1.72,.1–1.73.5; Thrasymachus fr. 85 B 1 Diels-Kranz. The meaning of *mártus* as guarantor is clarified by Hartog 2000:6–7. On the meaning of *sēmaínein*, see Heraclitus fr. 22 B 93 Diels-Kranz and Herodotus 1.5.3 (see also n41 above).

[44] Ricœur 1985:176–177 and 182–183.

composition. It gives rise to and calls for interpretive work. When historiography is involved, or more generally any constitution of a representation of the past, the trace proves finally to be only a metaphor situated between the prefiguration of a past action and its interpretive reprise in configuration. It returns finally to the different indices that positivistic historiography in the nineteenth century thought it could stabilize and objectify in documents, whether the documents had been archived or not.

The first Greek historiography can throw some light on this point concerning a preliminary putting-into-form of indices of the past by way of prefiguration. The index aspect of the past is particularly visible thanks to the distinction that Greek historians of the classical period made between ancient acts (*tà palaiá*) and "new" acts (*tà kainá*). Let us go back with Herodotus to the moment when the Athenians, facing the Tegeans, claim the place of honor in the battle order for the future Battle of Plataea, in 479. To the ancient wars fought against the Heraclids, against the Amazons, or during the expedition to the Troad, the Athenians add the great deeds done at the very recent Battle of Marathon. Sharing between the distant past and recent past in defining the field of history is coupled with a distinction between its actors: individual heroes such as Minos, Agamemnon, or Theseus in the "archaeology" of Thucydides on the one hand, civic communities of Athenians, Peloponnesians, and barbarians on the other. But more than a century after the end of the Persian Wars, when Demosthenes again takes up the same distinction between ancient events (*arkhaîa kaì palaiá*) and recent events (*kainá*), the temporal limit separating the latter from the former has naturally moved. And so, in the argument on the necessity for Athens to maintain a fleet, the Battle of Salamis, at the time of the Persian Wars, is moved to the *palaiá* side while the very recent surrender of the Thebans thanks to the intervention of Athenian triremes in Euboea obviously belongs to the *kainá*. Moreover, one must add that for Demosthenes the distinction between distant past—glorious though it may be—and recent past, redraws the line of demarcation which Herodotus himself traced, concerning the methods of his inquiry, between hearing and sight. Among the orator's audience, if knowledge of the city's past "which time itself cannot efface from memory (*mnémē*)" is based on *akoé*, hearing, their knowledge of the recent event is based on "what all of you have seen (*heōrákate*)."[45]

---

[45] Herodotus 9.27.1–6 and Demosthenes *Against Androtion* 12–15: see Calame 1996a:39–43. After a passage of "archaeology" which Thucydides devotes to the synoecism of Athens (1.16.1; see also n41 above), the historiographer himself is led to divide into three periods the temporal space extending from the moment of Athens' founding as a city to the present war: *tà arkhaîa, tà hústeron, mékhri toûde* (!) *toû polémou*.

5.4. The *historía* and the role of images

What this ancient concept of historic time suggests to us is thus a permeable division between a past distant enough that we know it through *lógoi*, by accounts transmitted through the (generally oral) tradition, and a recent past to which the historiographer and public have been eye witnesses. Verbal formulations on the one side, images evoked on the other. When the written tradition becomes the guarantor of the city's memory, prefiguration of the distant past will depend on the putting-into-discourse implied by the verbal document, while the prefiguration of more recent history will continue to rest on eyewitnesses, who will take it upon themselves to translate into verbal and oral form the images supplied by their memories. In regard to this division between ancient history and recent history, the increase in the number of media has placed modern historiography in a delicate position.

This is the case especially in the debate on the extermination camps and their sinister political premises. For the moment, this point of no return in European history belongs to what the Greek historians would call a *kainón*. The determining role is played by eyewitnesses and, through intervening images, by visual witnessing. But what will happen when the *kainón* becomes *palaión*? The new intervention of photography, of filmed archive and the recording of oral testimony, allows us to suppose that the role of the visual will continue beyond the deaths of the last survivors of this plan of annihilation, conceived in a manner all the more systematic and cynical in that it took advantage of the new technologies of the industrial era. Some of those same technologies have subsequently permitted us to maintain visual and aural memory.

Despite its orientation toward the place where it was conceived and established, the Holocaust Memorial Museum in Washington provides an illustration of a new form of practical history, mixing material traces, archival documents, oral and visual testimony fixed in image and writing, or animated by films and recordings. The convergence and metamorphosis of different index marks into a historiographic configuration is done not only by the commentaries which clarify them, while also situating it all in a chronology and in the logic of a political and social movement, but also through their spatial organization within the architecture of a museum. Conceived as a sort of initiatory trip into historic and moral awareness, since each visitor wears for the time being the identification card of a victim of the Nazi camps, this three-dimensional historical configuration increases the pragmatic element of any historiographic operation. The path down which the visitor proceeds, whatever his speed and his reading, can only lead to a refiguration into individual memories, strengthened by a collective memory.[46] But this refiguration is even more oriented by the *hic et nunc* of this hermeneutic visit, in that it is not accompanied in Washington by a comparable museographic reading about African slavery or the genocide of North American Indians. In any case, the analogical relationship of equivalence that the Greek historiopoietai establish between the distant past and oral narrative on the one hand, the recent past and visual witnessing on the other, finds its terms largely blurred. This is because still and animated images can now be transmitted over time, but also because of a historic memory which, individually and collectively, in both its configurations and its refigurations, is constantly fed and animated visually by the images selected and disseminated by means of extremely powerful media: daily papers, magazines, television news, internet sites ... Largely integrated into the document-testimony, the visual is now included in the "museographic putting-into-discourse."

Whatever the semiotic status (perhaps the cognitive and neuronal status) of images often expressed in verbal terms, the strategic moment is indeed the moment of passage from the different ways of prefiguration (through sight and hearing) of painful episodes of the past, to its pragmatic configuration by configurational procedures used by historiographers and historiopoietai. In thinking about this transition, we can once again take inspiration from Greek terms and concepts. Thucydides—as mentioned—bases his research of indices which are intended to become proof (*tekméria*) on witnesses and testimony: *mártures* and *martúria* understood as guarantees. But Herodotus sees his own work of narrative re-elaboration and descriptive rewriting based on the discourses (*lógoi*) of others as a work of investigation (*historía*).

Often questioned, the meaning of the term *hístōr* refers to the idea of guarantee offered by the one who collects the testimonies rather than that of

---

[46] These refigurations underlying visitors' reactions to the Washington *mnêma* are probably the best response one could provide about the pragmatic aspect of any historiographic configuration, to the ethical and philosophical contortions regarding the Shoah recently taken up by both J.-L. Nancy, " La représentation interdite," and by J. Rancière, "S'il y a de l'irreprésentable," in *Le Genre Humain* 36, 2001:13–40 and 81–102. "The forbidden representation of the camp is exactly that representation which I have attempted to call 'forbidden,' to understand the putting-into-presence which divides presence and opens it to its own absence (...): suspension of the 'being-there' to allow sense and ab-sense (*absens*) to get through," or "to claim the existence of the unpresentable in art, on the scale of the unthinkable of the event, one must first make this unthinkable completely thinkable, completely necessary according to thought. The logic of the unrepresentable is supported only by a hyperbole which finally destroys it ..."; antidotes to this especially in Vidal-Naquet 1995:271–291. On the different kinds of museographic configuration as historic memory, see Maffi 2008:125–157.

eyewitnesses which the root of the word would seem to imply. We know that the etymological basis for history, through the root *vid-, evokes Latin *videre* as well as French *voir*. If the *mártus*-witness is indeed the guarantor of what he has seen, the *hístōr*-scholar is capable of arbitrating between several testimonies that he guarantees. Such is the enunciative status of Herodotus in his own discourse: often reporting several narrative versions (*lógoi*), the historian of Halicarnassus rarely takes a position on them.[47] Herodotus is an investigator and a guarantor before being a judge. This is why, while assigning to his investigation the memorial objectives which are those of epic poetry, he gives up on presenting a discourse on truth inspired by the Muse, as the Homeric singer would have done. In most cases, he prefers to hide his enunciative authority behind the generally anonymous or plural third-person "one" of accounts by others. Herodotus thus leaves it to his listeners to take care of the (moral) judgment of veridiction, in the hermeneutic moment of refiguration!

5.5. Return to "poietics"

With putting-into-discourse through the witness of visual memories and their understanding, as well as their discursive reformulation by the guarantor and arbiter, we have gone from prefiguration to configuration, from *mimesis* I to *mimesis* II, to return to concepts borrowed from Aristotle and developed by Ricœur. And it is Aristotle who in his *Poetics* shows which aspects of fabrication belong to any narrative representation, whether dramatized or not. The poet is thus conceived of as an artisan of "plots" (*mûthoi*). Is there not in this a contradiction with the well-known and often-cited distinction between poet and historian, outlined in the same chapter of the *Poetics*? At the beginning of an important development dedicated to po(i)etic art, Aristotle draws a clear line between *poieîn* and *légein*, between "creating" and "relating." In contrast to the mimetic and representational aspect of the poet's art, doesn't the author of the *Poetics* give to the investigator (*ho historikós*) the duty of simply "telling" what happened (*tà genómena*)? Quite apart from the rhythmic or non-rhythmic form of diction, it would thus fall to the historian to say what happened, but to the poet to tell things "as they might happen." The former

---

[47] The meaning of *historía* and the enunciative positions which stem from discussion of it are taken up by Marincola 1997:3–10, Calame 2000b:115–125, and Hartog 2001:24–35 and 407–411 (see also 2000:6–7, on the semantic difference between *mártus* and *hístōr*); on the meaning of *historía* in general, see Nagy 1990:255–262 and 303–316. Judicial aspects of Greek historiographic discourse have been clarified by Darbo-Peschanski 1998 (cf. n25 above), and Prost 1996:288–293, extended the reflection to the writing of history in general.

would be reserved for the particular (*kath' hekástou*), and the latter for the general (*kathólou*). To the historian the actions of men, identified by proper name, who really acted or suffered by the acts, such as Alcibiades; to the poet human actions which, though sometimes attributed to individuals, are more on the order of verisimilitude or necessity.[48]

Nonetheless, by including any operation of *mímēsis* as the effect of *poieîn*, Aristotle invites us to expand to other forms of putting-into-discourse the modes of representation attached to the narrative and poetic emplotment. As such, poetic art, as we all know, applies to the possible (*tà dunatá*) and consequently to that which could happen on the level of verisimilitude and necessity. But Aristotle does not fail to add that the artisan of plots (*tôn múthōn poiētés*) who is the practitioner of the poetic arts can also fashion past actions (*genómena*): "And so it seems that the poet (*poiētés*) must be the fashioner of plots more than of rhythms. If he is indeed a poet, it is by representation (*mímēsis*) and what he represents are actions (*práxeis*). If he should sometimes fashion (*poieîn*) actions which really happened (*genómena*), he is nonetheless a poet. There is no reason that some among past events could not be in the order of verisimilitude (*eikós*) and of the possible (*dunatá*), and by intermediary this man is their poet."[49]

Without claiming to add a proper commentary to a chapter so frequently commented on, one cannot help but recognize that Aristotle's concluding remark is rarely mentioned. This omission is hardly surprising, since such an affirmation tends to erase the hackneyed distinction between historic investigation and poetic creation, between relating the singular and representing the general. Whether or not one shares Aristotle's opinion on the relationship between what really happened on the one hand, and the possible, plausible, and necessary on the other, the past too can be the object of a poetic elaboration, in the etymological sense of the term. Herodotus and Thucydides are there to show us that logographers are also historiopoietai. The "poietic" creation of a possible world from prefigured reality in the necessary sequence, leading to the construction of a verisimilitude (*vraisemblance*), corresponds all in all to the modern concept of the "fictional." Not in the sense of creating a fictive world provided with an autonomous semantic existence (corresponding to the American meaning of *fictional*), but in the sense of fabricating a possible world from tangible and shared experience of the natural and social

---

[48] Aristotle *Poetics* 9.1451a36–b 11, as reread by Ricœur 1983:57–84.

[49] Aristotle *Poetics* 9.1451b27–32 (adapted from the French translation by R. Dupont-Roc and J. Lallot), where the expression kaì dunatà genésthai is sometimes athetized by modern editors.

world, by exploiting the semantic potential of any language, to return to this world of social practice. Let us remember that Thucydides himself states that the speeches with which he punctuates his narrative are reconstructed according to the words probably required by the situation of the moment, and with respect for the words really pronounced, as far as the opinions expressed are concerned.[50]

Of course history rests neither on the universal nor on the singular, but on the specific, which alone can be understood insofar as it refers to a plot. That is at least the definition proposed by Paul Veyne. If it is also true that emplotment allows establishing elements necessary for comprehension and that consequently "the sequencing of texts expresses the real intermingling of causes, conditions, reasons, and consistencies," then historiopoiesis is also answerable for the work of representation and fabrication indicated by the Aristotelian notion of poetic *mimēsis*,[51] except that historiography represents the actions of men or social groups, not as they could or should happen, but as it thinks them plausible and intelligible after they have happened.

In relation to verisimilitude, the intelligibility of historiography is ensured largely by a series of semi-empirical concepts capable of inscribing configured actions in a comparative series, and in the intellectual paradigm on which history's audience depends. "It is only with concepts able to cover a certain duration of time, capable of a reiterated application and used empirically, thus with concepts endowed with a structural content, that the way is opened which permits knowing how a history formerly 'real' can today appear to us possible and representable," said Reinhart Koselleck thirty years ago.[52]

We must add that because of their operative nature, these notions situated between the figured and the abstract constitute precious instruments of translation between cultures—translation between the past and the present, as far as the historian's profession is concerned.

So the modern historian brings into play motives, intentions, goals, and circumstances to place into sequence selected actions, schematized using

---

[50] Thucydides 1.22.1. The difference between a "fictional world" and a possible world created by poetic means is very well redefined by Edmunds 2001:95–107; see also the remarks and references which I attempted to give on this subject in the studies cited in n20; concerning history, we must add the observations of Borutti 1996:240–248.

[51] Veyne 1971:75–76, partly reprised by Prost 1996:237–262 (256 for the quotation) in a good chapter entitled "Emplotment and narrativity."

[52] Koselleck 1990:133–144 (quotation translated from 141). To say intelligibility is also to say knowledge (*connaissance*); on this subject, see for example Chartier 1998:87–107. On the role of semi-figured concepts in comparison as well as in translation between cultures, see the references given in section 6 below.

semi-empirical concepts and categories. Inscribed in spaces which are themselves schematized, these actions are returned to intelligibility in the present. Thus the historiographer abandons the singular to make himself both the *poiētḗs* and the interpreter of the past. This is one of the essential goals of the work of historiographic configuration. Beginning from a past referent, already prefigured, from prefigurations materialized in indices, the pragmatic impact of historical writing of time and space and the discussion it causes about human systems of spatio-temporality depends on the ability to manage these different procedures of mimetic and poietic schematization.

6. For an anthropological historiography

As we have said, when it comes to the might of Agamemnon and his capacity to organize a naval expedition prefiguring the maritime might of Athens, Thucydides does not hesitate to base his work on the testimony of the poet Homer. The epic poem of the Trojan War must be considered as capable of providing indices, and thus proofs (*tekmēriôsai*). But to go back farther in time and to understand the causes of Agamemnon's might, it is best to follow a genealogical path. Through Atreus, the king of Mycenae, we reach Pelops, the founding hero who gave his name to the Peloponnesos. In this quest for an axial point, from both a temporal and spatial point of view, the historiographer has no choice but to leave the Homeric poems and turn to what we would call "tradition." From an enunciative point of view, this tradition corresponds to a collective account analogous to the "they say" or "one says" so frequently used by Herodotus. These statements depend on the *lógoi* of the ancestors (*parà tôn protérōn*); statements of logographers, nonetheless, capable of transmitting the most obvious facts; statements which in the end are based on memory (*mnḗmē*)![53]

Implicitly focused on Athens, this memory is not really attached to specific places where it would be the object of ritual commemoration. Isolated from any liturgy, the shared memory is integrated here into the procedures of putting-into-discourse and of spatio-temporal configuration of the community's past. Despite the work of writing (*suggráphein*), despite the secular and critical aims which animate it, the intellectual effort of memorial configuration offered by Thucydides produced a monument which strongly resembles

---

[53] Thucydides 1.9.1–1.10.1; cf. n40 above. Modern readers of Thucydides think that the historian bases his work mostly on the works of his contemporary Hellanikos of Lesbos: cf. *FGrHist* 4 F 157, and Hornblower 1991:31–32.

"the testament that no human community, even without writing or historians, has failed to write or at least to think, where the use of the past in an argued form is devised."[54]

6.1. Interfering temporalities, converging approaches

If tradition may be considered a form of (discursive and figurative) argumentation based on a shared cultural memory, it seems that anthropologists and historians too should share their approaches. The very nature of their object invites them to collaborate in the comparative understanding of configurations and discursive representations of the past which prove to be less heterogeneous than one would have liked to think. From the outset, in exotic cultures as well as in the Western historical tradition, the configurations of past time which attract the attention of scholars all present a number of common narrative, descriptive, argumentative, and pragmatic characteristics. These analogies lead to a comparatist attitude and to an exchange where anthropologists and historians are naturally called to critical dialogue. This is especially true for the eye that we can cast beyond the centuries, in an academic comparison relying on our own ways of writing history, on the historiopoietic practices of a Herodotus or a Thucydides.

But it happens also that historic temporalities and social spaces belonging to an exotic culture on the one hand as well as to our own cultural tradition on the other find themselves in competition, necessarily leading the historian's view to intersect the anthropologist's view. So it is that the European system of dating and measuring time could guarantee historic chronicles which allowed the English to demand the mortal remains of Captain Cook, sanctified in a final blaze of glory. At the same time and in the same place, the oral narratives of the Hawaiians tell of the resurgence of the captain's bones from the watery depths, legitimizing integration into the cyclical time of the economic and political rite of Makakiki, for the god Lono to whom the illustrious English explorer had been assimilated by the natives.[55] We end up with the configuration of two regimes of temporality and spatiality from the same event. Spatio-temporal simultaneity and interference here require the comparative view.

---

[54] The words of Lenclud 1994:43, in a study which tries to lessen the great divide between societies of "orality," attached to a fluid tradition constantly modified, and writing societies invited to set down a tradition from which they may distance themselves; this as an indirect response to the "break" sketched by Nora; see n29 above and Kilani 2003:231–238.

[55] On the "apotheosis of Captain Cook," whose death is recorded by the English chronicles on February 14, 1779, see the documents and narratives mentioned by Sahlins 1979, as well as 1981:9–32, with commentary by Marcus and Fischer 1986:103–105.

Plural representations of time and the past from traditional societies and those of Western societies may also mix together, often brought together because of the progressive integration of traditional societies into calendar time and Christian biblical time, and later into the market economy.[56] Temporal intermingling and integration into a single spatial context can replace competition between representations of time which depend on different cultural paradigms. It may be that the time shared by the native community opens onto the civilized political time of a society organized along Western lines, as is, for example, the case in the (auto-)biography of Papua-New Guinea Prime Minister Michael Somare (even the combination of an indigenous last name with an Anglo-Saxon first name is significant and anticipatory ...). Or it may be the other way around, and the spatial intervention of western temporality can reorient native time: the return to Papua of an American anthropologist contributed, for instance, to a millenarian reversal of ancestor worship, after the "wasp" was first integrated into traditional time by assimilation with Baingap, the cultural hero of the Arapesh community of Ilahita. Or it may even be that the local and universal (Islamic) genealogical temporality relies on a purely fictional written document; on such a fictive chronicle depends, for example, the identity of the El Ksar oasis in the south of Tunisia; it finds its identity confirmed in the procedural time of research by the Swiss-Tunisian anthropologist working on site.[57]

Adding to these different modes of real integration, through spatial coincidence, of native temporalities into the Western spatio-temporality which is that of the research historian or anthropological investigator, shared ways of writing add another invitation to collaborate. The convergence of historians' and anthropologists' views of temporal configurations intersecting in space is often reflected in the ways of putting-into-discourse proper to both fields, and consequently in the monographs they produce. The historical (re)configuration undertaken by both groups readily takes on a holistic aim, like novelistic fiction. This desire for narrative coherence brings together, for example, Marcel Griaule's *Dieu d'eau* (Paris: Chêne, 1948) and Georges Duby's *Dimanche de Bouvines* (Paris: Gallimard, 1973), especially in the rhetorical and novel-like

---

[56] Different ways of integrating whites and their economic system into Papua temporalities through biblical time and the story of the sons of Noah are discussed by Kilani 1994:119–136.

[57] On the syncretic temporality which flows through and organizes Michael Somare's autobiographic odyssey from his native village to the Port Moresby palace, see my study from 1998:342–349; for a very nearly opposite route by a Western anthropologist, see Tuzin 1997:126–156; the example of reformulation of Muslim political temporality through contact with an anthropologist is studied by Kilani 1992:21–48, 95–126, and 261–317.

relationship with the narratives of the sage Ogotemmêli in the one and the chronicles of Guillaume le Breton in the other.[58]

But in the prefiguration phase, a precondition for any putting-into-discourse whether historiographic or anthropological, practitioners in the field of history and explorers of ethnology have similar contingencies regarding accounts and witnesses. Both are confronted with the dialectic between sight and hearing. Despite the specific opportunity of "participatory" observation granted him, the anthropologist's eye is oriented by his intellectual training and his academic preconstructs, in his spatial distance. The historian adopts a point of view just as oriented by his academic context, and besides, because of his temporal distance, his perspective depends on the conceptual and discursive intermediaries to which sight images and the visual memory of witnesses and accounts are always subject. In both cases, in direct observation as well as in the apprehension of traces and accounts, prefiguration depends on a rhetoric of the eye. Along with its own characteristics and in the perspective of the *enárgeia* already mentioned, it implies a prior putting-into-form of significant "material" to reelaborate.[59] But above all, historians through time and anthropologists through space are confronted, as was Herodotus, by *lógoi*, statements and narrations by native informants for anthropologists, by verbal forms of the documents for historians; both of them imply the schematizing effects, polysemic depth, and enunciative orientation which is the result of any putting-into-discourse.[60] Prefigurations are involved for both the historian and the anthropologist, but configured prefigurations!

For that matter, practitioners of history and masters of the field of anthropology came together when cultural and social anthropology agreed to abandon its structure of working in pure synchrony. Not only are historians and anthropologists from that point on confronted with the historicity of the object they are building and which they must rebuild every time they

---

[58] On the novel-like aspects of anthropological monographs, see the numerous studies mentioned by Kilani 1994:27–39 and 46–62, and on the narrative dimension of monographs produced under the "Ecole des Annales," see Carrard 1998:62–79 and 207–214.

[59] On observation and the rhetoric of the eye, refer to Affergan 1987:137–162, and to Fabietti 1999:33–71.

[60] Criticism of anthropological discourse, even sharper in the Anglo-Saxon world than in France, as well as attempts to found a dialogic anthropology created by the interaction between two cultures which any ethnological study must necessarily confront, have marked research in the past three decades: see the summary chapter in Marcus and Fischer 1986:45–76, referring to the work of Vincent Crapanzano, Clifford Geertz, and Paul Rabinow, among others; see also information on this given by Malighetti 1998 and by Fabietti 1999:41–46 and 232–238.

return to the field, but among the representations which form the foundation (prefigured but also already configured by their own procedures for putting-into-discourse), a choice position is indeed held by the community's different conceptions and often narrative representations, of the past and more generally of time and space.

These convergences invite historiographers to embark on a comprehensive *historía*, inspired by the semiotic modes of understanding cultural and social anthropology. Centered on symbolic manifestations and on meaningful practices, anthropology is always quick to fit a particular spatio-temporal situation into the system of representations relative to the culture concerned. But these convergences also invite historians to adopt the new critical consciousness of anthropology regarding configuring procedures inherent both in its own operating concepts, its own peculiar discursive modes, and in its academic rhetoric. Finally, these convergences outline a commitment to do what I shall try to do here in a limited way, to confront several practical concepts of time and space within a particular culture comparatively, in the course of the history of one civilized community, or in the contact of one civilization with other cultural systems and models.

6.2. Possible worlds and historicity of belief communities

Through anthropological and representational procedures of putting-into-discourse, the work of temporal configuration thus implies procedures of *poíēsis*, of mimetic crafting in the sense Aristotle uses in his *Poetics*. To this extent, the possible world thus created may indeed be inscribed within the logical coherence implied by the necessary, or of the moral verisimilitude which underlies the believable. So it is that the discourses of historians presents themselves to us as configuring representations of space and time by means of selection, conceptual schematization, spatial focalization, chronological sequencing, emplotment, and modeling description, causal and argumentative logic which place the event in a multi-faceted situation, discursive rhetoric, and, finally, in a "showing" (*faire voir*) which probably coincides with the images evoked by individual and collective memory. From this observation, the wish would be that the writing of history could adopt the ways of an anthropology anxious to explore the most symbolic aspects of the situation, marked as it is by the cultural actions of men.

But like the work of anthropologists henceforth conscious of the historicity of their objects, discourses produced by historians are themselves subject to historicity and to spatial referencing, by the enunciative spatio-temporal implication which we have described! They craft possible worlds which in the spatio-temporal dimension are themselves taken up in the factual flux brought about by the flow of physical or cosmic time and by the local interventions of men and their cultural and social communities.[61] Because of these very practical consequences already mentioned, inherent in any representation and especially in putting-into-discourse, because of the effects of knowledge and of conviction implied in a somewhat paradoxical manner by the historian putting-into-discourse, the verisimilitude and coherence of the possible world built by verbal means find validity in a particular belief community and in the system of representations which it shares; a belief-community and a culture located in space and time; a belief-community and tradition which are themselves dependent on cultural localization and historicity.

This awareness of concomitancy between on the one hand the community's configurations and conceptions of time and space in their practical aspect, and on the other hand the individual refigurations and representations which flow from them in a cultural context which is itself subject to history, corresponds to what Maurice Halbwachs said so well nearly a century ago: "We can remember only by finding the place of the events that interest us in the framework of collective memory ... But the forgetting or deformation of certain of our memories is explained also in part by the fact that these frameworks change from one period to another. Society, depending on circumstances and according to the time, imagines the past in various ways: it modifies its conventions."[62] We must add that the social and individual impact of configurations of time and space which are collectively accepted in the moment of refiguration (thanks especially to the historian's job of putting-into-discourse) contributes in turn to modifying those representations, in a dialectic and dynamic movement, which we can hope is critical. Thus, if we consider the refiguration of time which takes place at the moment of reception (in *mimesis* III), the act of historiopoietic putting-into-discourse and its discursive and configuring results show some striking analogies to the operations of repatriation of knowledge and native cultural practices which anthropological putting-into-discourse definitely does: integration of distant perceptions and knowledge, beyond temporal distance, into the norms of Western academic

---

[61] Fabian 1983:30–35, 156–165, insisted on the historicity of simultaneity presumed by research on other cultures; he criticizes "a persistent and systematic tendency to place the referent(s) of anthropology in a Time other than the present of the producer of anthropological discourse." (31).

[62] Halbwachs 1925:278–279.

knowledge, a parallel to adapting geographic distance to the same norms. In each case, through time as well as across space, we witness a transcultural translation which in turn has an impact on both systems of representations thus brought together.[63]

From this point of view, the several studies proposed here can be considered as postmodern representations of Greek configurations of time in their practical aspect! These studies are an attempt at transcultural translation of poetic and practical concepts and configurations of temporality and spatiality, across temporal and spatial distances. They are thus an attempt at transposing indigenous ways of conceiving, speaking, and practicing organic space and cosmic time in its social prefigurations, into categories generally recognized by the French-speaking academic community, and if possible the Anglo-Saxon as well. If the historian's work is located within *mimesis* II (to take up once again the categories re-elaborated by Ricœur) in efforts to (re)-configure the past, then the efforts offered here belong more properly among the refigurations of *mimesis* III, in their perspective of critical readaptation![64] But these readings of Greek configurations of temporality are themselves inscribed, obviously, in a temporal and hermeneutic flux marked by a singular (academic) culture. That is to say their relative character as regards a cultural paradigm situated in a precise history and geopolitical space, their reference to a changing time and place in the academic community. To this extent, these readings can only lead to other readings, brought about by the polysemy of any symbolic manifestation, as well as by the necessity for constant critical and interpretive readaptation to the paradigms of a present in the flux of time and the mobility of space!

6.3. Regimes of historicity and logics of temporality

It is within this dynamic dialectic of configuration and refiguration, and of hermeneutic readaptation to constantly changing paradigms, that the notion of "regimes of historicity" becomes fully pertinent. This recent semi-empirical category was devised in a rare collaboration between a historian and an anthropologist. It allows us to focus less attention on the obvious fact that

---

[63] On cultural repatriation and the critical attitude it requires, especially in its meaning for "cultural studies," see for example reflections by Marcus and Fischer 1986:133–157, Kilani 1992:311–317, and 1994:11–26, as well as Remotti 1990. Prost 1996:444–453, describes very well what is at stake academically in the *repatriement* of the past by historians. On the question of transcultural translation, see references given in Calame 2002:67–77 and n74 below.

[64] See above, section 2.5.

communities of men and their cultures are inscribed in the flux of (cosmic and social) time, or on their manner of living a historicity independent of the oral or written nature of their tradition, and more on the representations that these men create of it for themselves. To this extent, "the regime of historicity would define a culturally limited and conventional form of relating to the past"; so "historiography would be one of these forms and, as a genre, one symptomatic element of an inclusive regime of historicity."[65] This means that the operational category of the regime of historicity would include both communitary and cultural prefigurations of time, and their configurations by the more specialized crafting of a *historiopoietes*, finally becoming an agent of comparison. So it would probably be suitable to substitute "temporality" for "historicity," and "logic" for "regime," since it is true that the thought of history refers communally and restrictively to the configuration of the unique past, especially since the past is reformulated only in tension toward the future, through the *hic et nunc* of elaboration and the enunciation of a symbolic manifestation, usually assumed more or less collectively because of its internal logic. The obvious correlation of the *nunc* with the *hic* warns us that every regime of temporality is interwoven with a "regime (or logic) of spatiality"; it localizes the corresponding configuration of time, pinpointing it in a space which is also shared between natural and cultural ecology and symbolic construction.

And so, between prefigurations and configurations of physical, organic, and social time, regimes and logics of temporality spring from a singular factual and cultural situation and in turn act upon this situation, in combination with a regime and logic of spatiality. If one perceives the event and its contingent nature clearly from the first, through the inherited categories of one's own background and one's own culture, suggests Marshall Sahlins in discussing what he calls "mythopraxis," in turn "every reproduction of culture is a change, to the extent that the categories which organize the world at a given moment acquire a new empirical content when in action."[66] We must add that the work of the symbolic process which takes place especially through the (semi-empirical) categories of the culture produces new configurations. Because of their pragmatic aspect and because they are accepted by a given

---

[65] Definition given by Hartog and Lenclud 1993:26, with comments by Hartog 2003:17–22 and 26–30; see also, on an ancient Greece immersed in modernity, Detienne 2000:61–80.

[66] Sahlins 1985:50–84 and 142–161 (149 for the quotation), especially as reread by Hartog and Lenclud 1993:34–36, and by Hartog 2003:38–47. On the social effects of symbolic social representations, especially through what we call rites, see Calame 1996b:49–54 and 165–173.

belief community and inscribed in a collective memory, these configurations not only condition the social reading of the past into different configurations, they also orient action in the past and in the immediate future, and determine the very apprehension of the present and the future. One can see from President Clinton's statements in the introduction that for a free enterprise society, constantly worried about the renewal of perpetual youth, historiopoietic models have largely been replaced by the incitements of advertising in all its forms, in postmodern communities: incitements to action and to appearance, in management and in economic behavior, as well as in symbolic manifestations and consequently in cultural orientation.

Despite this neo-modernity, it is the possibilities of reception and refiguration by the community from which they spring, and for whom they are intended, which makes these logics of temporality and spatiality into "regimes of truth": truths which answer to the configuring criteria of the plausible and of poietic and fictional coherence; truths which act upon the world from which they spring; practical and relative truths, located in space and in time as collective memories; truths which consequently rest on symbolic representations and paradigms which vary in history and in the geography of cultures; but truths which depend on possible worlds related to one another, in that every symbolic and cultural creation is founded on transitivity and on communicability.[67] If the very notion of a "regime" implies the idea of practical management of a shared representation or a cultural model, the plurality of regimes of truth as memories could not possibly have as its corollary an epistemological position of absolute relativism: their interaction and their translatability forbid it.

6.4. Enunciation and regimes of identity

The institution of a logic of temporality and spatiality which corresponds to a particular regime of truth passes through a semiotic putting-into-form which is generally discursive. Founded on the resources of fictional creation proper to any *langue* ("natural language"), if not to any *langage* ("semiotic system"), temporal and spatial configuration is thus a semantic construction, through the procedures of putting-into-discourse already mentioned. This means that it is normally formulated in polysemic terms which call for the multiple readings, the multiple refigurations which its pragmatic aspect gives rise to

---

[67] Between reliability and suspicion, Ricœur 1998:17 is aware that "truth in history thus remains unresolved, plausible, probable, questionable, always in the process of re-writing."

in both time and space.[68] But to speak of a putting-into-discourse implies accepting enunciative responsibility for the various utterances (*énoncés*) which configure time and space. While contributing to emphasizing the polysemy of the spatio-temporal world constructed in the text and to attracting the hermeneutic and critical activity attached to reading and to refiguration, the utterance of the enunciation (*énoncé de l'énonciation*) organizes and orients this possible world from a focal point represented by the "instance of enunciation," an instance already mentioned when discussing the axial point of the narrative putting-into-discourse, with its pronominal and spatio-temporal coordinates: *I, hic, nunc*.[69] It is especially through this enunciative bias, whose impact on the narrative and discursive organization of temporality and spatiality we have seen, that the pragmatic dimension of verbal and textual production becomes apparent. The *I/we* can be constructed enunciatively in the time/space configured in the discourse only in relation to the discursive *thou/you* which refers to the actors and actresses of hermeneutic reading and of critical refiguration, both intellectual and practical.

From a temporal point of view, projection into the future of the discursive construction of past time, with its practical aims, rests precisely on these enunciative procedures.

After all is said and done, it is an identity being built, through represented and uttered time and space, as well as in the spatio-temporal process of the placing-into-discourse and of the enunciation themselves. This enunciative identity is based on the interlacing of a configuring representation (narrative, descriptive, or argumentative) of time and space with the temporal and spatial logic which organizes the progression of the discourse. This enunciative identity is thus built first in the putting-into-discourse, and later acquires through collective memory the (provisional) stability which is the condition of its being instituted as a regime of truth. But because of its very discursive (and consequently polysemic) nature, this configured identity contains

---

[68] Let us remember that Benveniste 1974:222–227, while attributing to the linguistic function a double modality of (semiotic) meaning and (semantic) communicating, asserts that polysemy "is only the institutionalized sum, so to speak, of contextual values which are always instantaneous, continually capable of being enriched, of disappearing, in short without permanence, without consistent value."

[69] I will limit myself to reaffirming here the essential operative distinction between situation and (extra-discursive) process of communication, (intra-discursive) textual traces of this process (enunciation uttered by means of the "formal apparatus of enunciation"), and the enunciation itself (assertion, narrative, description, etc.): see n22 above and Calame 2000a:18–34 for reflections based on an ample bibliography; on anthropological discourse, see also Affergan 1987:213–223.

within itself, within its temporal and spatial parameters and in its enunciative element, the premises for new transformations. To state it once again in a
reformulation of Ricœur's terms, used in the intermediate step of his twofold
study of time: from a core of *idem*-identity, this psychosocial "sameness"
(*mêmeté*) with its spatio-temporal reference changes to an *ipse*-identity. By
progressively acquiring consistency through discourse, this "*ipse*-ity" (*ipséité*)
ends up reaching the appearance of a new "sameness" (*mêmeté*); but because
of its very discursive and enunciative nature, the identity of this new idem is
ready to change into new metamorphoses, through intervening *ipse* refigurations in interaction with others.[70]

By its generally discursive character and by its enunciative form, the
regime or logic of time and of space can in some ways serve as an envelope for
an *ipse*-identity, but an identity which tends toward the *idem*. Far from referring back to a psycho-philosophical "self" (*soi*), this discursive identity, with
its fluidity marked by moments of stability, is part of the collective and the
cultural. "History is played out there, on the limits which connect a society with
its past and the act of distinguishing itself from that past; in lines which sketch
the face of current affairs while distancing itself from its other, but which the
return of the 'past' constantly modifies and blurs," said Michel de Certeau.[71]
As a symbolic product, this historical identity is active, through the pragmatic
aspect of any discursive configuration; and so it contributes to orienting the
time and space of the past toward a *hic et nunc* which is itself in tension with
the future. For any cultural community, discursive representations of time and
space are also ways of conceiving itself symbolically, of speaking to and acting
upon itself, of organizing its spatio-temporal environment in the flux of physical and social time and in the space where it is practiced.

So the transformation of a logic of temporality and spatiality into a
regime of practical truth and memory is achieved by the voice of authority
which carries the discursive configuration, be it oral or written, individual or
collective. This metamorphosis is also accomplished through rules of genre
which, together with language rules, ensure its social foundation. But because
of the polysemy already mentioned, a symbolic manifestation related to identity has in itself potential for its challenge and transformation, in the dialectic
of the collective *ipse* and *idem*. In this, we must not forget that not one of the

---

[70] See Ricœur 1985:352–358, and 1990:11–35 and 60–72, relying on "personal identity," on the
Cartesian *cogito*, but also on the "subject of enunciation."

[71] De Certeau 1975:49–50. The transition from an individual identity to a collective identity
through historical and cultural tradition is well described by Assmann 1998:130–144.

discursive and identity-related representations of the heroic Greek past which we call "myths" can be grasped in its "essence" except perhaps as mythographic plot. These fictional and symbolic configurations show themselves to us in different versions informed by the historical and ritualistic conditions of particular instances of putting-into-discourse, by an individual enunciative orientation, and by precise genre rules which insure their expected community effects and pragmatics.[72] The identity-related polysemy recognized in representation, as well as the recognition of its irreversible cultural historicity, can serve as valuable antidotes to overly massive ideas such as the collective consciousness, (primitive) mentality, or even the social framework of memory![73]

7. Comparative triangles

The few exercises in refigurative reading offered here concerning different regimes of temporality and spatiality in ancient Greece are intended as exercises in transcultural translation, both transcultural and transhistorical translation. In cultural and social anthropology as well as in comprehensive history, the approach to and understanding of manifestations of a different culture and a distant past can be achieved only through repatriation of an indigenous knowledge which is itself the result of prefigurations and configurations, perhaps even refigurations! Glimpsed in some of these practical and discursive exercises, this knowledge is reconstructed on the basis of our own cultural prefigurations and preconstructs. It is thus transformed by the process of schematization and rhetoric which are proper to the academic discourse discussed earlier, designed to be read by an academic audience which refigures it: when all is said and done a fictional and polysemic knowledge because of the mimetic and semantic procedure of putting-into-discourse. A knowledge which shows the enunciative orientation of any discourse, especially when instituted as a regime of truth; knowledge built and founded on a relationship which is constitutionally marked by asymmetry. Just like knowledge produced by anthropologists, the knowledge of cultural historians of Greek knowledge is determined by the thematic and

---

[72] Cf. Calame 1996a:25–55 and 2000b:47–51.

[73] The notion of "identity-related polysemy" (*polysémie identitaire*) could serve as an answer to the well-founded objections that Lloyd 1990:135–145 presents, concerning the notion of "mentality": the impossibility of realizing several mentalities in a single individual and the lack of any principle to explain sudden changes in a mentality.

epistemological interests of the moment, situated in academic time and space. Its placing into a configuring and discursive form depends on the questions that we ask the documents and the accounts we have built and on which it is based.[74]

In the anthropology of the ancient world, temporal distance apparently forbids any form of direct apprehension of the ethnographic context by a "participant observation." Since one cannot respond to the requirements of a dialogic anthropology facing Greeks whom the irreversible flow of time has reduced to silence, comparison may in some measure fill the documentary gaps. Marked by their semantic putting-into-form and by their own enunciative perspective, neither texts, nor figured representations, nor even archaeological vestiges can directly answer the questions we would like to ask them ...

Certainly, in this proposal to "revive" the comparative method, we must avoid the pitfalls recently denounced by some French-speaking representatives of anthropological Hellenism: "Greek man" constituted in otherness within proximity; an idealizing focus on general laws and common cultural themes to erase differences; Hellas definitely compared to itself alone in an enclosure inspired by nationalism.[75] Animated by internal polemics, these criticisms have done little but touch on the obvious idealization to which efforts to open expressions of Greek culture to the outside have led, a culture which, when all is said and done, is incomparable! But what is at stake from now on are the operators of comparison themselves: on the one hand the basic categories of cultural and social anthropology, and on the other the rhetorical procedures of putting-into-discourse and of textualization of repatriated indigenous learning. Among the former, ideas such as the opposition of "nature/culture," the tribal initiation rite, and the "myth/rite" pairing, have often been elevated to universals despite their historical and semi-empirical nature; and the latter are now the object of historical and critical attention which has revealed their modeling impact.[76] These pernicious effects of structuralism have tipped a number of the human sciences into a historicism which must be refounded, and into a form of relativism which must be mastered.

---

[74] What is at stake in transcultural translation is well explained by Borutti 1999:170–202 (interactive research, interpretive construction and possible world through the fictional workings of writing), and also by Fabietti 1999:227–260 (indigenous categories, cultural hermeneutics, prototypes and forms of lives, metaphorization); see also Malighetti 1998:205–215 and Calame 2002:67–77.

[75] See especially the criticism by Loraux 1996 and by Detienne 2000:9–13 and 41–59.

[76] See Calame 2002:69–72.

Comparative methods have definitely lost nothing of their vitality. But they can maintain it only by becoming less centered on differences and contrasts than on similarities which can only be the result of the formalizing construction of the anthropologist or the historian. Comparison of the cultural and symbolic manifestations of ancient Greece either with those of another civilization closely related in space and time, or with those of an exotic modern culture with an analogous profile in its traditions, is essential. But to animate its critical and reflexive dimension, comparison must also be nurtured with an oblique look, on our part, at our own cultural practices. From this, there flows the necessity of a comparative and critical triangle which I hope will not be disavowed by the most committed representatives of "Cultural Studies," such as Stuart Hall: *comparandum, comparatum*, but also *comparans*.[77]

Discursive and poetic representations of time and space are instituted as spatio-temporal logics and as regimes of truth. And so it is not a question of claiming to explore and determine, through some genealogy of interpretations, "the" meaning of a few discursive practices of temporality and spatiality located in ancient Greece. But it is right to clarify those aspects which seem pertinent to our preoccupations of the moment, by contrast with and as an echo of analogous regimes occasionally found in other cultures—fully conscious of the transitory nature of explorations subject to preconstructions and transformations, in the flux of the history of our own cultural space and of our own academic interests. Since time and space are two of the conditions at the foundation of communication itself, the historicity and spatial orientation of our refigurations of the configurations and spatio-temporal logics of other cultures and other eras offer all in all a guarantee of their pertinence for the present. What makes it interesting, when all is said and done, is not just the possible semantic core which allows one, through the different procedures of simplification, schematization, and abstraction which are part of refiguration, to ensure stability and coherence of a meaning across cultural milieux and generations. Interest is not aroused solely by (supposed) universals, nor by archetypes (as reassuring as they might be ...), but rather by the effects of specific meanings in particular natural, cultural, and historical contexts. Within the dynamic dialectic and irreversible temporal flux of configuration and refiguration, these continue to produce highly semantically dense manifestations and symbolic and discursive practices.

---

[77] See the introduction to Grossberg, Nelson, and Treichler 1992:1–16; "Academic disciplines often decontextualize both their methods and their objects of study; cultural studies properly conceives both relationally."

Each of the four studies which follow will thus have as its object a discursive representation of time as related to the space where it developed. Each of them will be about a particular textual configuration. In addition, each of the proposed readings will attempt to combine a wide anthropological perspective with an enunciative sensitivity that relates back to the context of enunciation. This will provide an opportunity to bring forth each time something about method relative to transcultural translation. In each case, we will also conduct a limited contrastive comparison with one or two analogous regimes of temporality and spatiality. Finally, we will proceed—as already mentioned—to a brief return to one of the paradigms which, in human sciences, have strongly influenced research on the ancient Greek world in the course of the past four or five decades: structuralism, gender studies, new philosophical idealism, neo-mysticism.

II

THE SUCCESSION OF AGES AND POETIC PRAGMATICS OF JUSTICE

Hesiod's Narrative of the Five Human Species

W HAT HAS NOT BEEN SAID OR WRITTEN about the "myth of the races?" Inserting Hesiod's didactic *Works* poem into a specific time and space, this narrative in Homeric diction is the best example of a text which periodically inspires and focuses interpretive controversy among philologists sorely in need of a new topic. Throughout the different readings the text has inspired, with few exceptions, these hundred lines have been viewed as an autonomous narrative ensemble, cut off from its discursive context, and also cut off from its enunciative situation. The narrative has been reduced from discourse to text. The double structural interpretation from which it benefited in the 1960s contributed to this double isolation, reinforced by the tenacious modern belief in the existence of the myth in itself. Comparison to parallel Eastern versions could have led to an opening up, but due to this universalizing ideological context, it led instead to *aporia*.

1. Object and method: From structural analysis to discursive study

Through a simple sin of omission, an entire series of obvious points about the discursive reality of the "Hesiodic myth of the races" has generally been forgotten.

> If you wish, I shall recapitulate another story (*lógos*), correctly and skillfully, and you lay it up in your spirit: how the gods and mortal human beings came about from the same origin.
>
> Hesiod *Works and Days* 106–107 (trans. Most)

The use of a native category mentioned at the very beginning of these introductory lines (lines 106–107) demonstrates an essential point: these lines do not represent a "myth," but a *lógos*: and so it is a tale, a simple narrative, a simple telling. Next, because of the numbered order of succession in which this *lógos* presents them, the *géne* do not correspond to "races," but this term recalls generations of ancestors, that is to say groups of humans. These groups, five in number, are marked in each case by a special birth, by a spatial-temporal extension, and are marked collectively by an order of linear succession; this is why instead of referring to the myth of the races, we shall substitute the designation of the narrative of five families or narrative of the five ages or even the narrative of the five clans or of the five human species. From the enunciative point of view, the narrative of the five families is introduced without any invocation to the Muse by use of a form of the perfomative future *ekkoruphôsô* (line 106); "I am preparing to achieve"; directly assumed by the "I" speaker, who thus relates it strongly to the narration of the preceding account which tells of the creation of Pandora. Similarly, the *lógos* of the five ages leads into a narration of the fable of the nightingale and the hawk, by means of a similar performative form (*eréō*, line 202: "I am going to say").

The narrative of the five clans, far from being isolated, is in the middle of a sequence of three *lógoi* , which is itself inscribed in the larger intra-discursive context set out in the lines at the very beginning of the *Works*: address to the Muses of Pieria to sing praises to Zeus and to put into place the semantic line of justice and the administration of law which will run throughout the entire first part of the poem; evocation of Perses and then an address to the prodigal brother, to introduce by the apologue of the two Disputes the isotopy of productive work (lines 10 and 27) which underlies the semantic development of the second part of the composition; allusion to the conflict which opposes the speaker-*I* and the interlocutor-*you* (Benveniste calls this discursive figure the *allocuté*) and which can be resolved by a judgment reestablishing the equilibrium of fair sharing under Zeus; and, by the utterance of that judgment, introduction of a third isotopy, that of the poetic word in its efficacy.[1] Finally, and still on the enunciative level, the sequence of the three narratives leads to a number of exhortations to Perses, interlocutor or addressee of the *I*-speaker, urging him to keep to the ways of justice in the city; then, in a progressive enunciative slide through more general invitations addressed particularly

---

[1] The three isotopies articulating the content of the *Works* into three interlaced lines of semantic development were defined by my essay in 1996c, where there are also a number of references to various studies illustrating this idea.

to kings, the poem of the *Works* focuses finally on the prosperity which the advice given to a general *you* is supposed to produce.

While ensuring the coherence of the ensemble of the composition, the polymorphic construction of these different enunciative addresses and interventions, through procedures to which we shall return, poses a question about which genre this poem in epic diction belongs to; and the rules of genre which organize this heroic composition themselves lead, in a transition from the intra- to the extra-discursive, to questions about the enunciative circumstances and the poem's function! Since it may avoid the interpretive omissions already mentioned, attention to the marks of enunciation that analysis of discourse offers should allow us to trace out the regime of temporality (and of spatiality) at the basis of the narrative of the five ages as it is set out in the *Works*, while at the same time illustrating the discursive and poetic effects of a didactic spatial and temporal configuration. In a brief comparative return to what has become the Semitic paradigm, we will ask questions about the intra- and extra-discursive functions of a poetic representation of time past, spatially oriented toward the future, before drawing from it one possible lesson in the context of postmodernity.

The interpretive controversy brought about by readings of the narrative of the five ages was deeply marked by the principles of structural analysis in the second half of the twentieth century.

It is to Classics philosopher Victor Goldschmidt that we owe the break with the traditional reading of the narrative as intended to account for the progressive decadence of humanity, gradually given over to injustice. It is also to him that we owe the earliest structural paradigm. Mostly taken up in France, the idea is a brilliant one: through narration, tracing a genetic line establishes a static structure. This narrative procedure makes it possible to demonstrate that the succession of "races" in its decline leads finally to a hierarchic order which assigns distinct places to gods, demons, heroes, and finally to the dead. In reconsidering the reading of the Hesiodic narrative, Jean-Pierre Vernant systematized structurally the fundamental function of a "myth" which he considers "genealogical": grasped in synchrony, the final differentiated order results from the successive birth of entities which the structure organizes, in the diachronic narrative: golden "race," silver demons, men of bronze, race of heroes, men of iron, leading to the order of the world assured and controlled by Zeus. His conclusion about the Hesiodic narrative of the ages: "The succession of ages in time reproduces a permanent hierarchic order in the universe."[2]

---

[2] Goldschmidt 1950:33–38 (unification of two different traditions, the "myth of the ages" and the

But to this structural perspective, structural principle itself must be added; it hypothesizes that values composing systems are organized in a sequence or a hierarchy of binary opposites. From that follows the interpretive reorganization of the "myth of the races" into a succession of three couples of *géné*, symetrically opposed to one another, within a structural opposition presented as a distinctive semantic trait: *díkē/húbris*, "justice/violence." In this hermeneutic perspective, the men of gold represent the reverse of the men of silver in the exercise of sovereignty; the brutal violence of the men of bronze contrasts with the courageous justice of the heroes in the area of military activity; and the iron age is divided structurally into two contrasting periods of justice and decline from the point of view of productivity of agricultural labor. By reorganizing diachrony into synchrony, the structure ends up fitting into the tri-functional model attributed to the Indo-Europeans.

Numerous attempts were made subsequently to avoid the different reading distortions implied by this coincidence established between the diachronic succession of structural oppositions and the synchronic architecture of the tri-functional ideology. These efforts were generally reduced to modifications of the arithmetic economy of the structural schema: "Gold vs. Silver (utopian reference)/ Bronze and Heroes 1 vs. Heroes 2 (Homeric reference)/ Iron 1 vs. Iron 2 (political reference)," or "Golden Age—Silver Age—Bronze Age (process of decline)/ Age of Heroes (recovery)/Iron Age 1—Iron Age 2—Iron Age x (new decline, with hope of recovery)," or even "gold—silver/ bronze—heroes (organized as a tetrad which closes on itself, as a chiasmus, the process of decadence then improvement/present race (iron)."[3]

Among these three attempts to reconcile the principle of genesis leading to structure with the anomalies of a text which, for example, introduces heroes in a sequence of metallic ages, this latter model has a decided advantage; it takes into account the singular status assigned to the iron age by its particular enunciative presentation. Without really drawing all necessary consequences from such an observation, it has been noticed of late that the introduction of the last age was marked by a strong enunciative interven-

---

narrative of the "separation of divine beings," where the former becomes an etiological myth of the latter), in an analysis taken up by Vernant 1960:24–30 (25 for the quote); for details of the controversy over attempts to apply the principles of structural analysis and what each of the two authors brought specifically, see particularly Couloubaritsis 1996:479–485 (see also references given in n7).

[3] In order, cited are interpretations by Carrière 1996:419, Couloubaritsis 1996:517–518, and Crubellier 1996:453.

tion of the speaker or narrator, an "I" whom we have good reasons to identify with Hesiod (as "author-function.")[4] In this passage from "history" (or "narrative") to "discourse," it is actually both narrated time and the time of narration of the narrative of the five families which come to coincide with the time of the uttered enunciation (*énonciation énoncée*), and consequently with the enunciation of the poem. The moment is located in the utterance itself by the forceful insertion both of the "I" of the speaker-narrator (line 174) and by the *nûn* (line 176) which relates the *génos* of iron to the present moment, temporally.

> If only then I did not have to live among the fifth men, but could have either died first or been born after-wards! For now the race is indeed one of iron.
>
> *Works and Days* 174–176 (trans. Most)

In abandoning the structural paradigm which imposes artificial divisions in order to reconstruct binary oppositions, it is essential to follow carefully the spatial-temporal development of the narrative. Beyond simple recounted time, attention must be turned both to the temporality of the narration which transmits its own rhythm to the succession of ages, and to the time and space of the uttered enunciation, marked by the intervention of the speaker-narrator; in this way, attention will be drawn to the temporal lines which organize the narrative and which give it coherence. Such a perspective is even more important since on the one hand the "myth of the races" shows only a very small part of the principle of explaining structure by genesis, and on the other hand it does not constitute a real genealogical narrative where the final taxonomic order is determined by the progressive engendering of the different entities which compose it. The men of bronze, for example, disappear forever into Hades and assume no function under the sun of the enunciative *nûn*; they no longer exist at the moment and in the space in which the speaker situates his poetic word.

Also, contrary to the principle of the genealogical narrative where a third entity is born from the union of two first entities, the *génē* are created

---

[4] Credit for pointing it out belongs to Neschke 1996:473–477; see also Crubellier 1996:440–442, Most 1997:111–114, and Sourvinou-Inwood 1997:4–5. The relevant reading of Neschke results in organizing the ages into two triads: gold/silver/bronze, heroes ("before us")/iron ("now")/iron 2nd phase ("after us"). The identity of the speaker or reader with Hesiod is whispered to the listener/reader by lines 22–25 of the *Theogony*; Stoddard 2004:1–33, has just completed a good study on the controversial question of the autobiographical value of the "I" of the Hesiodic poems, and prefers the notion of "implied author" (34–59).

by an all-powerful god who does not place them in a system characterized by the genealogical tree. The groups of humans replace one another in a precise chronological order. This means that the *géné* do not correspond to "races," but rather represent sets of human generations, "human species," or, more precisely, groups of ancestors.[5] Which is why (as we suggested earlier) it is better to substitute the terms family, clan, species, even age if one takes into account the chronological aspect of the succession of the five groups.

2. Narrative development: Enunciation and argumentation

Before concentrating on the structure of the narrative itself, before taking up the question of its narrative context, then of its possible extra-discursive reference, we must first look at its enunciative presentation and at its argumentative insertion in the immediate context. As we have just said, the narrative of the five human families is situated between the story of the creation of Pandora (lines 42–105) and the fable of the nightingale and the hawk (lines 202–212); it is thus inserted in a narrative triad which is strongly articulated (*gár*, line 42) with a first development of the two rivalries and the necessity of resolving the judicial conflict (*ténde díkēn*, line 39) between the poet and Perses. This argumentative dimension springs less from the double narrative and narrated time of the story than from the uttered enunciation and from the enunciated line of the poem in which the *lógos* of the five ages is inserted. This poetic line of argument calls for five observations.

2.1. A narrative and poetic prelude

The first observation relates to a point already mentioned. As will also be the case later concerning how best to designate narratives inserted into Attic tragedy, development on the five families is qualified as *lógos* (line 106) where one would expect to see *mûthos*. Although the context gives no precise indication, it is not impossible that *lógos* is a semantic slide; this polysemic term could designate not just an ordered and pragmatic speech, the semantic value which *mûthos* generally assumes as used in poetry of what is called the "archaic" period, but also the seductive narrative which it sometimes designates in the same period.[6] Let us repeat:

---

[5] Concerning the semantic distinction between *génos et geneé*, cf. n30 below.

[6] On the meaning of *lógos* as opposed to *mûthos* in Hesiod's poems, see Lincoln 1997, and additional references given in n7.

> If you wish, I shall recapitulate another story (*lógos*), correctly and skillfully, and you lay it up in your spirit: how the gods and mortal human beings came about from the same origin.
>
> Hesiod *Works and Days* 106–107 (trans. Most)

Whatever term one chooses to designate it, the narrative of the five ages is introduced by a brief prelude. Brief though it may be, it calls for a second set of remarks. It divides its enunciative procedures between the address of one character to another character, just as we see in the dialogues of epic poetry, and the address of a poet to his intended audience, just as we find in the different forms of didactic poetry. The appeal to the wishes of the hearer "if you will" (*ei ethéleis*, line 106), for example, evokes Glaukos' address to Diomedes in the *Iliad*, while the performative future implied by the form "I am going to relate," "I am about to tell the essentials" (*ekkoruphósō*, line 106) evokes the affirmation of the poet's voice, in its enunciative authority. At the end of the proem of the *Works* itself, after calling on the presence and the authority of the Muses who will sing of Zeus, the speaker-narrator strongly affirms the realities of which he plans to speak (*ke muthēsaímēn*, line 10) to his interlocutor: "And I, Perses, would tell of true things."[7]

Despite its generalizing value, this "thou" to whom he speaks has a name: it's Perses. So it is to the prodigal brother that the entire passage, including the three narratives, is addressed. Starting in line 27 and taken up again in line 213, the direct address to Perses closes the sequence of three narratives on itself, in a remarkable "ring structure," the better to take up the argumentative development on justice.[8] It is also necessary to observe that this double address to Perses is combined with a secondary address to kings; these *basileîs* are evoked in the passage which introduces the three narratives (lines 38–40), and they finally become the hearers to whom the fable of the nightingale and the hawk is addressed (line 202). We must add that by the place and the interplay of pronouns, Perses, in his double enunciation, is confronted with the poet addressing him in the proem to the ensemble of the poem as well as in the brief prelude to the narrative of the five clans: the expression *toi egṓ* in

---

[7] *Iliad* 6.150; see also *Iliad* 20.213. I studied the enunciative profile of the prelude to the *Works* (1996c:170–175); analyses of these ten introductory lines are also indicated: in Antiquity, their authenticity was questioned. Wakker 1990:88–90, suggests for *ekkorupháō* the meaning of *kurz erzählen, skizzieren*.

[8] On the triple interlocutor to whom the *Works* is addressed (Perses, the generic *you*, and kings) see my remarks in 1996c:174–181 (and n29), as well as Schmidt 1986:29–79. On the structure of the entirety of the poem, see Hamilton 1989:47–84.

line 106 ("to you, I") echoes the *túnē egṓ* in line 10 (despite the modern punctuation which underscores the fact that the "thou" pronoun refers in this case to Zeus).

Third (technical) observation: the sentence in the prelude to the narrator represents a transformation of the utterance which one finds in a number of Homeric dialogues: no longer "I am going to tell you another (argument)" (*állo dé toi ereṓ*) as in the *Iliad*, but in a more precise translation, "I am preparing to give you the essence of another story" (*héterón toi egṑ lógon ekkoruphṓsō*, line 106).[9] By comparison with this metamorphosis, and insofar as it also corresponds to a Homeric formulation, the second part of the prelude's utterance (*sù d' enì phresì bálleo sêisin*, "you, put this in your heart," line 107) no doubt also undergoes an expansion. And so the famous line 108, which gives content to the *lógos* yet to come by assigning to gods and to men a common ascendancy, would be "authentic." As a complement to the recommendation made to Perses to carefully record the *lógos* which the poet is reciting, the role of this line would also serve to indicate, as in any prelude, the theme of the narrative to come: the anger of Achilles for the *Iliad*, the tribulations of Odysseus for the *Odyssey*, the birth of immortal gods for the *Theogony*.[10] The narrative of the ages as it is set forth in the *Works* would thus be centered on the question of the common origin of gods and mortals; this accords with line 59 which presents Zeus as the father of both men and gods, and is in harmony with line 112 which attributes to all men of the gold *génos* a way of life similar to that of divine beings. We shall return to this question.

Fourth observation: the declaration of the speaker-narrator's intent regarding the narrative whose substance he will draw forth is matched with a reference to the poet's technical know-how. Whether adverbial (*epistaménōs*, line 107) or adjectival in form, for us this poetic ability corresponds to that of Odysseus, who knows how to sing like a bard, to that of the servant and messenger of the Muses, evoked by Theognis, who posesses a wisdom which is his to share in a didactic way, or to that of the poet Solon who, as recipient of the Muses' gifts, knows "the full measure of seductive wisdom" (*himertês*

---

[9] The required parallels are proposed by West 1978:177–178, and by Carrière 1991:65; see especially Xenophanes fr. 21 B 7 (Diels-Kranz): *nûn aût' állon épeimi lógon* (note the *aûte* which indicates the recurrent addition).

[10] All details of the controversy concerning line 108, which is commented in the scholia, can be found in Carrière 1991:63–72. On the structure of the Homeric proems, see especially Pucci 1998:11–29.

sophíēs métron epistámenos).[11] The *lógos* proferred in the *Works* to enumerate the four generations of men leading to the age of iron is truly that of a sage. It implies a narrative technique which recalls the knowledge of the Homeric poet, and even more recalls the know-how of the elegiac poet, with its didactic and pedagogical aims which coincide precisely with the poetic intention animating the *Works*—as we shall see.

Finally, the narrative of the five human species is not just strongly linked to the narrative of Pandora's creation which precedes it and to the fable of the nightingale and the hawk which follows it, as indicated by its presentation as second narrative (*héteron lógon*, line 106); but the sequence of three narratives is itself attached by an argumentative *gár* (line 42, "indeed") to the first development of the poem, dedicated to the present conflict that opposes the speaker-narrator to his principal addressee, Perses. In its discursive logic, this means that the narrative triad makes up the first part of the argumentation intended to re-establish the balance of the *díkē*, which is to say intended to resolve the dispute with the prodigal brother. The enunciative form assumed by the group of lines which precedes the triple narrative is unambiguous: by a form of the imperative subjunctive which includes in the first person plural both the "I" and the "thou" (*diakrinōmetha*, line 35), it is to put an end to the rivalry which opposes "us," by one of those righteous judgments which come from Zeus; by that very act "we" will set aside those "bribe-swallowing" kings who intend to resolve (*dikásai*, line 39) "this" case (*ténde díkēn*), which is to say both the lawsuit of which we've just spoken and the present case—in the double procedure of anaphoric and monstrative deixis, both intra- and extradiscursive, described by Bühler and discussed in the first chapter.[12] This means that from a semantic point of view the three narratives responding to the poetic intention of a performative order are intended to once again take up the three isotopies developed in the prelude and in this first part of the poem. They are—I repeat—the semantic line of balance of *díkē*, dynamically matched to the poetic necessity of re-establishing its balance; next the thematic line of the *bíos*, which is to say the production of life resources which form the conditions for the realization of justice in the city; and finally the line of the proferred (poetic) word and its effectiveness especially in the area of the *díkē* ...

---

[11] *Odyssey* 11.368; *Theognis* 769–772; *Solon* fr. 1:51–55 (Gentili-Prato).

[12] On the enunciative phrasing of this groups of verses, see the analysis presented in 1996c:178–181; on *deixis*, see chapter I, section 3.2 with n33; on this passage, cf. Calame 2005b: 122–125.

2.2. The concern of the beginning: Between *Homeric Hymns* and historiography

From the "now" of the repeated address to Perses, with no other transition, the *lógos* of the five ages moves on to the narrative itself. From the time and space of "discourse" with the recommendation to the listener to accept in good spirit the proferred (poetic) word, we thus pass to the time and space of the "story." By coinciding here with the beginning of narrated time, the initial development of the time of narration forcefully indicates which is the axial moment , the moment of origin of narrative temporality. Indeed the adverbial expression *prótista* ("at the very first," line 109) immediately gives an origin to the past where the form of the aorist situates creation (*poíēsan*, line 110) of the first *génos* of "terrestrial" men (*méropes*, vers 109). Through this time of narration, the narrated temporal line receives a reference of a chronological sort, or of a "calendar" sort, as Benveniste would say.

The moment of origin has a name: the reign of Kronos; and it has a place: Olympus. This process of engaging the narrative using parameters of time and space recalls the one marking the narrative conduct of certain *Homeric Hymns*. After the prelude which presents the arrival of the young Apollo in the dwelling of Zeus, the bard of the *Hymn to Apollo* wonders how he will sing the praises of a divinity as widely praised as the god Phoibos; the narrative will begin at the beginning, at the birth of the god at Delos; a beginning both temporal and spatial.

> How shall I match the hymns already sung in your honor?
> For everywhere, Phoibos, the field of singing is your domain,
> both on the islands and the mainland which nurtures heifers.
>
> ...
>
> Shall I sing how first Leto bore you, a joy to mortals,
> as she leaned against Mount Kynthos, on the rocky and sea-girt
> isla]nd of Delos ...?[13]

> *Hymn to Apollo* 3.19–21 and 25–27 (trans. Athanassakis)

The syntactic relation between the question *pôs* in line 19 and the (hymnic) relative adverbe *hós* in line 25 relates the performative future form *humnḗsō* ("I am going to sing") not only to the first verbal form of the narrative (*téke*, "she will engender"), but also with the temporal referent of origin (*prôton*,

---

[13] *Homeric Hymn to Apollo* 3.19–21 and 25–27; see also 207–216. On the meaning of the term *méropes*, see section 2.3.1 below with n17.

"first of all") and with its spatial referent (Delos). Thus, mediated by the usual procedure of the hymnic relative and in the form of a rhetorical question, the time of the uttered enunciation (the immediate and intentional future of reciting the poem) and the time of narration come to coincide with the axial moment of time recounted: the spatial-temporal beginning of the biography of the god being sung. The narrative of the Pythian part of the *Homeric Hymn to Apollo* begins in exactly the same way: the performative question concerning the modalities of praise is answered, in relative form, by the beginning both of the narrative and of the time and space narrated; mediated by a hymnic *hōs*, the question *pôs s' humnḗsō* (line 207, "how am I going to sing you?") corresponds to the points of origin both spatial (*Olympus in Pieria*, line 216) and temporal (*prôton*, lines 214 and 216) of the founding of the oracle of Delphi by the god Apollo: no longer the moment of the god's birth, but that of his first contact with men. Several hymnic compositions express in their first lines this same concern of beginning at the beginning, in order to integrate it into the *evocatio* of the divinity being sung. "I begin to sing of Demeter ... and her daughter taken by Hades ..." chants the bard who begins the recitation of the long *Homeric Hymn* dedicated to the goddess of Eleusis and to her daughter. And again, the very brief *Homeric Hymn* 13, also dedicated to Demeter, shows a significant echo between the initial declaration of the bard and the request which concludes the poem: the performative intention of beginning to sing (*árkhom' aeídein*, line 1) is answered by the prayer addressed to the goddess to "begin" the song (*árkhe aoidês*, line 3), while also directing it, (with a play on the double meaning of *árkhein).*

> Of Demeter, the lovely-haired and august goddess,
> and of her daughter, the fair Persephone, I begin to sing.
> Hail, O goddess! Keep this city safe, and guide my song.[14]

Homeric Hymn to Demeter 13.1–3 (trans. Athanassakis)

The concern of Herodotus the logographer is not very different from that of the Homeric bard, as far as the beginning is concerned. In the very forceful enunciative intervention that concludes the prologue of his *Histories*, the historian speaker declares that he knows who first (*prôton*, 1.5.3) gave impetus (*hupárxanta*, from *árkhein*) to acts of injustice toward the Greeks; this contrasts with the *lógos* attributed to the Persians who date back to the Trojan wars the beginning (*arkhḗ*, 1.5.1) of their animosity toward the Greeks.

---

[14] *Homeric Hymn to Demeter* 13.1–3; for the figure of Arche, particularly in the field of poetry, see Deienne 1998: 114–120.

In this enunciative declaration by Herodotus, a simple article matched with a participial form (*tòn hupárxanta*, "the initiator") has replaced the hymnic relative to introduce the subject of the action which is about to be narrated. But just as in the *Homeric Hymns*, and even if the corresponding spatial referent is suspended for the moment, the three temporal lines which we have already mentioned run through the narrative discourse: the time of the uttered enunciation actualized in the form of the future perfomative *probḗsomai*, "I am going to progress"; the time of the narration implied by the mention of the "narrative," and its progression (*es tò prósō toû lógou*); and finally the time recounted whose origin is given by the start of the reign of Croesus (1.6.1), the steadfast actor of the first narrative of the *Histories*! From then on, Croesus can appear—"from what we ourselves know" (*hēmeîs ídmen*; 1.6.2)—not only as the ruler of a kingdom bordering the regions of Asia inhabited by the Ionians, the Aeolians, and the Dorians, but also as the first (*prôtos*) of the barbarians to have subdued (in the bard's form corresponding to narrative time) some of the Greeks. The reign of the king of Lydia thus constitutes the spatial-temporal *arkhḗ* of Hellenic misfortunes. The three temporal and now spatial lines which organize the discursive logic of Herodotus' *Histories* are anchored in this unique point of origin.[15]

And it is not vastly different for Thucydides himself. After the "archaeology" which makes the history of the formation of Greece into a prelude to his treatise, and in one of the very rare enunciative interventions found in his work, the Athenian historian directs his attention to the question of the temporal beginning (*ḗrxanto*, 1.23.4) of the war between the Athenians and the Peloponnesians and to the implicit location between Athens and Lacedomonia. On this he declares: "Concerning why they broke the treaty, I have recorded the reasons previously in writing (*tàs aitías proúgrapsa*), in the first place (*prôton*)" (1.23.5). Despite the movement of prolepsis that the earlier narration of causes represents, as it relates both to recounted time and to this enunciative intervention, the problem is indeed the problem of the beginning of this narrated time in concomitance with the beginning of the narration and the moment of the uttered enunciation. But the search for the spatial-temporal origin coincides here with the investigation of "the truest cause" (*tḕn alēthestátēn próphasin*). In a chronological movement analogous to that which Herodotus followed and which dates Croesus' ascendancy back to the heroic time of Herakles, concern about the spatial-temporal *arkhḗ* in Thucydides becomes an

---

[15] Herodotus 1.5.1–1.6.2; on the question of *arkhḗ* in Greek historiography, see especially Darbo-Peschanski 1995:19–26.

etiological search; it leads to a quasi-judicial investigation into causes, responsibilities, even guilt, for the historical action, in accord with the hierarchically organized meanings assumed by the term *aítios*.[16]

2.3. Spatial-temporal structures and logics

Hesiod's narrative of the succession of the five human families, placed as an axial point, will begin by the appearance of the first *génos*, associated with gold.

2.3.1. Men of gold: Guardians of mortals

In relating how it came to be, the beginning description of the clan of golden age men in the *Works* leaves not the least enunciative ambiguity.

> Golden was the race of speech-endowed human beings which the immortals, who have their mansions on Olympus, made first of all. They lived at the time of Cronus, when he was king in the sky; just like gods they spent their lives, with a spirit free from care, entirely apart from toil and distress.

> *Works and Days* 109–112 (trans. Most)

Use of the aorist (*poíēsan*, line 110) situates the creation of this first species in a general narrative past; it is coupled with a temporal mark which fixes this act at the extreme moment of origin (*prṓtista*, line 109). This moment not only coincides with the beginning of the narration, marked by the introductory *mén*, with its emphatic value so frequent in Homeric poetry; it is also dated, in a way: it is the reign of Kronos. Right from the start, and well before any distinction through sacrificial practices, the difference is set out: the immortal gods who have their home on Olympus are distinct from men who, in their legal determination, can claim Merops, an ancestral figure born of the earth. To this extent, mortal men are the result of a process of successive creations distinct from the process of theogonic generation which caused divinities to appear, even if the affinities of these first humans with gold brings them closer to the gods.[17] For mortal men, the creative logic of *epoíēsan* substitutes

---

[16] Thucydides 1.23.4–1.23.5; the relationship that Herodotus establishes between the beginning and the cause in both an moral and legal sense because of the polysemy of the term *aítios* has been elucidated by several studies which I cited in 2000a:151–153 with n14 and n16; see also Vegetti 1999:276–279, and chapter I, section 4.3 above.

[17] The relationship between *méropes* (*ánthrōpoi*) and the eponymous hero of Cos, Mérops, is detailed by Chantraine 1968:687. Brown 1998:392–394, showed that objects made of gold are more often the prerogative of the gods of Olympus than attributes of the royalty.

for the theogonic and genealogical *egéneto*! Mortal men were not engendered, they were created.

Nonetheless, without being explicitly hooked to it, the succession of the families and ages of man is inscribed within the genealogical line which runs through and organizes the narrative of the birth of the gods in the *Theogony*. We must remember that while the generation of Kronos (when the men of gold were created) immediately precedes the birth and reign of Zeus, this generation is itself preceded by the other descendants of Heavens and Earth. And the very birth of Earth goes back to Chaos, posited as the very first entity (*prôtista kháos géneto*, line 116), in an enunciative procedure analogous to the one we have just discussed. Indeed, at the end of a very long proem, the bard of the *Theogony* asks the Muses to tell him "from the beginning" (*ex arkhês*, line 115) who, among the immortals, was born first (*prôton géneto*, see also lines 108 and 113). Through this plea, he begins his geneological and theogonic narrative by making the moment of his poetic enunciation coincide both with the beginning of narration and with the axial moment of the time recounted![18]

Only an implicit spatial reference corresponds to this temporal way of dating the beginning of the succession of ages, making it coincide with the reign of Kronos and referencing it to the genealogical time of the theogonic beginnings. If the gods have their home on Olympus, men (in their relationship with Merops and with a soil granted divine fertility) inhabit the earth. Thus after a death resembling a deep sleep, the men of gold remain present as "demons" and guardians of mortals, on the earth in general (*epikhthónioi*, line 123). From a temporal point of view, assigning this functions as guardians on the earth transports us toward the reign of Kronos' successor; indeed, it is Zeus who gives this guardian function to the men of gold removed underground by Gaia, the homonymic divine power. But it also moves us toward the moment of the poem's enunciation, since the guardians are still present (*eisi*, line 122).[19]

2.3.2. The men of silver: Blessed chthonians

The temporal position of the silver *génos* is described three different ways in the line that introduces it: the initial *deúteron* (line 121) introduces this *génos*

---

[18] On the genealogical temporality of the *Theogony*, see West 1966:31–39.h

[19] The status of the *daímones*, heroes living on or under the earth, is well defined by Nagy 1979:152–155, as related to respect for *díkē* by mortal men. This status is probably specified in a comic fragment attributed to Aristophanes fr. 322 (Kassel-Austin); cf. Parker 1983:243–245. See also the specific status given to the daimons by Empedocles, fr. 31B 115, 1–8 (Diels-Kranz): cf. below chap. IV n3.

as the "second" species in a numerical succession reinforced at the end of the line by the adverb *metópisthen* ("following") which is evoked at the end of this development, in a ring structure, when it is taken up again in line 142; the succession is more like a substitution, since this second family of men is once again created (*poíēsan*, line 128; in the narrative's time) and once again by the divinities of Olympus in general; finally the comparative *kheiróteron*, "worse," sets this second clan in an order of moral degradation where it appears inferior to the family which preceded it.

> Afterwards those who have their mansions on Olympus made a second race, much worse, of silver, like the golden one neither in body nor in mind.

> *Works and Days* 127–129 (trans. Most)

Time of narration and recounted time thus coincide once again in the presentation of this species whose own internal temporality merits mention; a particularly long childhood, since it extends to the end of adolescence over a period of a hundred years, followed by an adulthood shortened by the excess, violence, and impiousness which lead these men to disappear quickly.[20]

> Then Zeus, Cronus' son, concealed these in anger, because they did not give honors to the blessed gods who dwell on Olympus. But since the earth covered up this race too, they are called blessed mortals under the earth—in second place, but all the same honor attends upon these as well.

> *Works and Days* 138–142 (trans. Most)

This disappearance of the silver species is due to the will of Zeus, the "son of Kronos" (line 138). This geneaological description seems to confirm the fact that between the birth of the men of gold and their reappearance on earth a change has taken place in the temporal theogonical line that organizes the birth of the different gods. From the reign of Kronos, we are now in that of Zeus, and the mention of altars in line 136 perhaps presupposes the institution of sacrifice. However that may be, the men of silver, created by the Olympians and hidden by Earth just like the men of gold, have a second life not on the earth but under it (*hupokhthónioi*, line 141), as opposed to their predecessors who have become *epikhthónioi* (line 122), as "guardians" of mortal men. In

---

[20] On the rhythm of this biography-type, see the parallels cited by West 1978:184–185.

this localizing, which once again refers to the entire extent of the inhabited earth, the "subterranean" beings share with the gods the quality of "blessed" (*mákares* in line 241: compare to lines 136 and 139). Without being assimilated to the gods, these men of silver end up having a form of immortality, perhaps corresponding with the common origin indicated by the controversial line 108! As such, they nonetheless enjoy some of the honors which they themselves refused the gods of Olympus. To this extent, they enjoy a status which recalls that which the *Odyssey* gives, for example, to the Dioscuri: both of them were covered by the nourishing earth, before receiving from Zeus the honor of a subterranean life alternating between life and death.[21]

From an enunciative point of view, the narration of the men of gold and their move underground as "blessed" is marked by a temporal passage from the aorist to present tense forms. At the end of the narrative about the second *génos* of mortals (the silver men), recounted time and time of narration once again coincide with the time of the uttered enunciation. Indeed, this second family of human beings (*deúteroi*, in line 142, a chiastic echo of line 127, as we have mentioned), with its particular descriptive, is still honored in the present of the poem's recitation. We must add that in this same perspective of coincidence of time of the utterance of the enunciation, description of the men of silver during their long childhood as *mégas népios* ("big child," line 131) recalls the description of Perses himself at the end of the poem's section concerning respect of justice (line 286).[22]

2.3.3. The men of bronze: Self-destruction and anonymity

Zeus alone is responsible from now on for the succeeding families of mortal men. And so it is to him that it falls to create the clan of men of bronze, the third, says the poem, in a formulation very close to that describing the birth of the first family.

> Zeus the father made another race of speech-endowed human beings, a third one, of bronze, not similar to the silver one at all, out of ash trees—terrible and strong they were ...
>
> *Works and Days* 143–145 (trans. Most)

---

[21] See *Odyssey* 11.301–304, with commentares by West 1978:186–187. The paradox of the *timé* granted by Zeus to the men of silver when they themselves offered none to the gods of Olympus is marked by the chiasmus at lines 138–142, as well as by the expression *kaì toîsin* in line 142. See Schmidt 1986:31–40 and 49–52.

[22] See Schmidt 1986:31–40 and 49–52.

The *génos* of bronze is thus created from ash trees, probably alluding to a (for us) much later legend which has the human race born of these trees, just as other versions of the birth of men have them springing from oak trees. Going beyond what the text of the *Works* proposes, we can once again try to bring the creation chronology sketched by the narrative of the ages closer to the narrative line which organizes recounted time in the genealogical narrative of the *Theogony*. We then notice that in the previous summary of the theogonic process which the poet placed in the mouths of the Muses, humanity appears after the birth of Zeus, at the same time as the "generation of powerful Giants." Also, in the theogonic narrative itself, the ash Nymphs are born at the same moment when the Giants spring fully armed from the earth, fertilized by the blood which sprang from the genitals of Ouranos, castrated by his son Kronos.[23] Through the Nymphs, the *Works'* men of bronze would also be born from the earth, but in a time situated after the end of the reign of Kronos and after the arrival of Zeus, who was thus by implication born (as we have shown) at the end of the time of men of gold!

Even if it is said to be "in no way equal to the silver age" (line 144), the *génos* of bronze shares with preceding men enough traits to place it in their succession, both temporally and semantically. Like the men of silver, the men dressed all in bronze demonstrate madness and excess which make them turn their violence against themselves. The brute force of these men, exercised especially in war, is such that there is no need for Zeus to intervene in order to bring about their final disappearance.[24] In addition, impiousness is replaced with a diet based on agriculture, in Hesiod's description of the bronze family. And so, in a completely negative way, the profile of the men of bronze is inscribed in two of the three great isotopies which run through the poem to ensure its semantic coherence: administration of justice and production of *bíos*. We could also recall here that violent excess as opposed to balanced justice, piety toward the gods, and consumption of bread are some of the criteria of the yardstick used to measure the more or less savage beings whom Odysseus and his companions meet during their return voyage to Ithaca.[25]

---

[23] *Theogony* 41–51 and 183–187; cf. scholia on *Theogony* 187 (Di Gregorio 1975:40). On tree nymphs, see references given by West 1978:187; according to Nagy 1979:158–159, the wood of the ash would refer to the shaft of the lance of Homeric heroes, with its bronze spear head.

[24] Note that lines 148–149, reappearing at *Theogony* 151–152 and in the Shield 75–76, are unnecessary to the semantic economy of the passage; this is perhaps an interpolation; see West 1978:188, and, more generally, Carrière 1986:200–203.

[25] As is the case of the Cyclops in the *Odyssey*, for example: see *Odyssey* 9.105–115 and 172–176; on this see especially Vidal-Naquet 1983:48–60.

Their weapons were of bronze, bronze were their houses, with bronze they worked; there was not any black iron. And these, overpowered by one another's hands, went down nameless into the dank house of chilly Hades: black death seized them, frightful though they were, and they left behind the bright light of the sun.

Works and Days 150–155 (trans. Most)

Because of the warlike violence they used against one another in internal conflicts, the men of bronze disappeared through their own efforts. That is probably the reason why not the least trace of them remains to be attached to a name and to a reputation: they are *nónumnoi*, "without name" (line 154); but, in what is probably an etymological pun, they are also deprived of songs of praise (*húmnos*) which would perpetuate their memory.[26] They thus enjoy no form of immortalization and have only an ephemeral existence under the sun. To this extent, one cannot attribute to them any function whatsoever in the Indo-European ideology within the hypothetical synchronic structure which apparently underlies the temporality of the succession of the five ages!

Concomitant with this absence of any heroic identity indicated by an *ónoma*, and according (negatively) with the isotopy of the preferred and effective word which runs throughout the poem as a third line of semantic coherence, the time and space of the men of bronze cannot be related to the *hic et nunc* of the enunciation in the way that the preceding generations were related to it. On the other hand, the brief allusion to the absence of iron places the bronze family in the perspective of the fifth *génos* and consequently in the fifth period, the one to which the *I*-speaker of the poem indicates that he himself belongs. Seen from this angle, the chronological cohesion of the narrative is nonetheless preserved, once again by the coincidence of the temporality of narration with time recounted, and corresponding to the time of uttered enunciation. As for the way in which space is organized, Hades is now added to Olympus where the gods live and to the surface of the earth lit by the sun and where men live, a more precise localization than the earth under which the men of silver are interred, but still active as "blessed."

---

[26] On *nónumnos* meaning "without glory," see *Iliad* 12.70, 13.227, or 14.70, in contrast to the hope of heroines and heroes to become *aoídimoi*, subjects of bardic song, such as Helen and Paris at *Iliad* 6.358; see Carrière 1986:203.

2.3.4. The Age of Heroes: Marked space and time

The introduction to the *génos* of heroes appears generally heterogeneous: it breaks the succession of metals apparently organized in a decreasing scale of values culturally attributed to them. Nonetheless, from the point of view of narrative and discursive temporality as well as spatially, this new family fits perfectly into the sequence begun by the three preceding families. All of the spatial and temporal marks used to organize the syntax of these introductory lines work together to establish this continuity.

> When the earth covered up this race too, Zeus, Cronus' son, made another one in turn upon the bounteous earth, a fourth one, more just and superior, the godly race of men-heroes, who are called demigods, the generation before our own upon the boundless earth.
>
> *Works and Days* 156–160 (trans. Most)

Besides the regular usage of the aorist which prolongs the reference to past time in the narrative, the succession order of the family of heroes as related to the *génos* of bronze is underlined by a temporal subordinate. This utterance recalls the disappearance underground of the men of bronze, while a *kaí* which means "equally" (line 159) underlines the relationship with the two preceding families, in a reprise of line 140. If the place of the clan of heroes within the succession of *génē* is indicated by its ordinal number (*tétarton*, "fourth"), its creation by Zeus fits into the reiterative movement, marked by the use of *aûtis*, ("once again") and by the use of *éti* ("still").

Semantically, this *génos* of heroic men is inserted into the hierarchy of values which sets up the chronological order of the preceding families, as well as describing them. The heroes are indeed judged by the yardstick of justice and the first isotopy which runs throughout the first part of the poem. From this point of view, this family is "better," perhaps concomitantly with its heroic quality which breaks from the degradation linked to representations through the metals.[27] Spatial location of the heroes on a "boundless" earth (line 160) is also placed for the first time in explicit relationship with the productivity and food production role of the earth, in contrast to the men of bronze who "work" (the earth?) with bronze, but nonetheless do not eat bread. From the point of view of the second great semantic line of agricultural production which runs

---

[27] The impact of inserting the clan of heroes into the succession of families designated by metal is taken up and commented especially by Carrière 1996:411–413, and by Couloubaritsis 1996:492–500 (even if the order of succession of the families has nothing to do with genealogy!).

through the *Works*, the organization of space coincides gradually with what men of the present know: Olympus where the immortals live, the productive and fruitful surface of the earth for the mortals, Hades for the dead.

Whatever its comparative quality, this *génos* is no longer composed simply of human beings (*ánthrōpoi*), but of humans of the male sex (*ándres*, line 159), men who nonetheless share with the gods a part of their divine origins (*theîon*, perhaps a reference to line 108!). To this extent, and in contrast to the preceding families, the *génos* of heroes is described immediately as is their due in the current enunciation: not guardian *epikhthónioi*, nor blessed *hupokhthónioi*, not "nameless," but *hēmítheoi* (line 160), less "demi-gods" than men half-divine by their ancestry; such are, for example, the Argonauts in Pindar, Proitos' companions of the "bronze shield" in Bacchylides, or the Hippocoontidai of Sparta in Alcman.[28] When the Catalogue of Women attributed to Hesiod mentions Zeus' wish to destroy men by provoking the Trojan war, he subsumes them in the "family of mortal men"; these mortals are "demi-gods" because they are the children of the blessed gods who lead a separate life from these "human heroes."[29]

The designation of "semi-divine" is referenced to the time of the enunciation by the present *kaléontai* ("they are called," line 159; see also line 141). This reference changes to a real focal point, from the present moment on, by use of the adjective *protérē* (line 160). The *génos* of heroes represents the fourth species, as concerns the axial point of time recounted with its objective chronological measurement, but only the "preceding" one as seen from the temporality of the (uttered) enunciation, referenced in the *hic et nunc* of the poems' recitation. This double temporal focalization shows the tension between the point of origin of measured time and the reference point of linguistic time, as we discussed in the introduction! And this human species is no longer only a *génos* among others, but a *geneḗ*, which is to say that it (finally!) constitutes a true "generation." It is thus the generation of heroes which immediately precedes the generation to which the speaker-narrator belongs, a generation whose localization also covers the entire world.[30]

---

[28] See Pindar *Pythian* 4.12 and 4.211; Bacchylides 11.62; Alcman fr. 1.7 (Davies 1991); additional useful references in West 1978:191.

[29] Hesiod fr. 204.95–119 (Merkelbach-West). On the Homeric meaning of *hḗrōs* as "young warrior" belonging to the epic past, but with no allusion to a heroic cult, see West 1978:370–373.

[30] The genealogical meaning of *geneḗ* is discussed especially by Crubellier 1996:439n27, and by Most 1997:111–114; on combining reference points of (recounted) time and time of discourse, see chapter I, section 2.4.

Evil war and dread battle destroyed these, some under seven-gated Thebes in the land of Cadmus while they fought for the sake of Oedipus' sheep, others brought in boats over the great gulf of the sea to Troy for the sake of fair-haired Helen. There the end of death shrouded some of them but upon others Zeus the father, Cronus' son, bestowed life and habitations far from human beings and settled them at the limits of the earth ...

Works and Days 161–169 (trans. Most)

Just as was the case for the men of bronze, it is not Zeus who consummates the disappearance of the generation of heroes, but the activity which they themselves engage in: no longer *stásis*, but *pólemos*, no longer the mutual violence of internal conflicts constantly condemned in classical Greece, but outside war carried on in two specific places: seven-gated Thebes in the land of Cadmus, and Troy reached by ship over the great sea gulf. To these two suddenly specifed locales are added two proper names, in contrast to the anonymous destiny of the men of bronze. Presented as the causes of two warlike expeditions, Oedipus and Helen appear rather like synecdoches of these two epic wars narrated in the two great cycles of Homeric poetry.[31] From now on, time and space are described, and have a more and more precise face.

Even in the papyrological tradition, the overall syntactic structure of this passage was the object of a number of manipulations and interpolations. But if we remember that in the *Odyssey* itself, because of their excesses those who participated in the Trojan war had destinies differentiated by death, difficulties of reading can be ironed out. A brief grammar exercise will allow us to observe that the whole set of men of the race of heroes devote themselves to war (*toùs mén*, in line 160, just as in lines 122, 137, and 141), but are divided into two categories depending on whether they fought at Thebes (*toùs mén*, line 162) or before the walls of Troy (*toùs dé*, line 164). This temporal and spatial movement is taken up again in the adverb *éntha* ("in that place," and "at that time"), introducing line 166, which some readers thought they could do away with, even in Antiquity. Marked by a forceful enunciative modalization (*ễ toi*, "in truth"), this line brings chiastic closure to the allusion to the heroes' general disappearance due to their warlike acts, but it also introduces a new distinction: some (*toùs mén*, line 166) were enveloped not by the earth, but by death in its fulfillment (just like the men of bronze); others (*toîs dé*, line

---

[31] On the two great epic cycles, see West 1978:191–192, and Nagy 1979:161–166.

167) were placed by Zeus at the ends of the earth where they henceforth lived a privileged life. That is to say that some disappeared into Hades, including Achilles, Agamemnon, and Ajax whom Odysseus met during his descent into hell as told in the *Odyssey*, while others were sent to the Isles of the Blessed, following the example of Menelaus in the same Homeric poem. We can end this grammatical reading right here: just as in line 161 *toùs mén* combined with the connector *kaí* takes up again the category of semi-divine heroes that has just been introduced, so in line 170 the combining of *toì mén* with *kaí* takes up again the sub-category of privileged heroes which has just been defined to describe the particularly productive space reserved to them up to the present of the enunciation.[32]

Just as for the preceding human groups, description of the (twofold) destiny reserved to the family of demi-god heroes thus leads if not to the hic, at least to the *nunc* of the uttered enunciation. After their settlement by Zeus at the edge of the inhabited earth, the privileged heroes stay (*naíousin*, line 170) near the Ocean river which borders the most distant lands; there are found the Isles of the Blessed, easily identified with the Elysean Fields heralded by Menelaus in the *Odyssey*. In chapter V, discussing gold lamellae, we shall come back to this concept of an afterlife split between humid darkness in Hades and heroic light bathing the green prairies of an eternal springtime.[33] This return from the time of narration and from recounted time to the time of enunciation is underlined by the description of these men as "blessed heroes" (*ólbioi hḗrōes*, line 172): the form of the apposition calls to mind the particular form of general address called *makarismós*; the formula "blessed are those who," is intended precisely to praise the happiness of mortals who in death achieved a form of immortality which brings them closer to the gods.[34]

> ... and these dwell with a spirit free of care on the Islands of
> the Blessed beside deep-eddying Ocean—happy heroes, for whom

---

[32] The construction of this difficult passage, in combining the *mén* and the *dé*, is detailed by Carrière 1991:97–99. On the individual destiny of Achilles, shared between Hades and the Elysian Fields depending on the version of the heroic legend, see Nagy 1979:165–173 (cf. chapter V, section 2.3.2. below).

[33] *Odyssey* 4.561–569, with commentary given in chapter V, section 2.3.1 (with the reference as given at notes 51 and 53.

[34] The most beautiful example of *makarismós* is given in the conclusion of the *Homeric Hymn to Demeter* 2.480–489, which twice promises to those mortals who take part in the initiatory *órgia* proposed by Demeter to Eleusis a better life after death; see also Pindar fr. 137 (Maehler), accompanied by the contested fr. 133 (Maehler), which makes of mortals favored by Persephone beings who "for the rest of time are called (*kaléontai*) pure heroes (*hḗrōes hagnoí*) by men"; cf. chapter V, sections 2.1.5 and 2.3.2 below.

the grain-giving field bears honey-sweet fruit flourishing three times a year.

Works and Days 170–173 (trans. Most)

Is this then a return to the golden age, in a cyclical concept of time relating the destiny of the blessed heroes to the way of life enjoyed by the men of gold? Not entirely, since even if the evocation of the Isles of the Blessed does indeed permit a return to the isotopy of well-being that results from agricultural abundance, there is nonetheless a twofold slide between the golden age and the age of heroes.[35] A temporal slide first of all, since the abundance of an especially fertile earth refers to the past in the lives of the golden men, whereas it marks the present post-mortem destiny of heroes living on the Isles of the Blessed; a semantic slide also, in that, beyond the ring structure which seems to relate lines 172–173 to lines 117–118 (especially by reiterating the formulaic expression *zeídōros ároura*), flourishing three times a year has replaced the spontaneous production of the age of gold. If the golden age is traditionally attributed to the utopian reign of Kronos, the other is typical of particularly fertile lands cultivated by mortals, such as Cyrene in Libya. This difference in the absence of cyclic return did not escape Plato himself; in the etymologizing commentary on the Hesiodic narrative which Plato gives in the *Cratylus*, Socrates relates the family of heroes to the men of gold; but while the latter are sensible beings to the extent that *daimones* must be compared to *daémones*, "learned," the former are *hérōes* because, through *eírein*, "do say," they are skillful rhetoricians ...[36]

2.3.5. The men of iron: A prophetic future

It must be obvious by now that if one narrative ought to be shielded from the structural principle of textual immanence, that narrative must be the "myth of the races!" The structural position assumed by the fifth species, the men of iron, is indeed incomprehensible if one does not know that it is situated from the very beginning in the perspective of the speaker or narrator, consequently

---

[35] A return to the golden age which would order the four first "generations" into a cyclical representation corresponds to the hypothesis set forth by Nagy 1979:169–171; see also, in an image integrating genealogical order, Couloubaritsis 1996:492–500 and 517. Consideration of line 169, which attributes reign over the Isles of the Blessed to Kronos, seems to confirm that time is a closed circle; but line 169 reappears as the first line of a new explicative sequence (lines 173a–e), probably an interpolation and given only in two papyri; cf. West 1978:194–196, and Carrière 1991:86–97.

[36] Plato *Cratylus* 397e–398d. Concerning the fertility of Cyrene's soil, see Calame 1996a:145–147.

in the perspective of the one singing the poem of the *Works*. This displacement of the narrative point of view to an enunciative point of view, the passing from the level of "narrative" to that of "discourse," is so pronounced that the intervention of "I" is substituted for the expected description of the creation of this iron species.

> If only then I did not have to live among the fifth men, but could have either died first or been born after-wards! For now the race is indeed one of iron. And they will not cease from toil and distress by day, nor from being worn out by suffering at night, and the gods will give them grievous cares.

> *Works and Days* 174–177 (trans. Most)

By expressing a wish to be excluded from a "now" that coincides simply with the existence of men (*ándres*, line 175) who belong to the age of iron, the poet imposes his own enunciative temporality on the time of narration and of time recounted. From the grammatical point of view, the axial point of this present time, contrasting with the *prõtista* of line 109, is signified by the connector *nûn gàr dé*, "because now exactly," placed in a strong position in line 176.[37] That is to say that it coincides from now on with the axial point of the time of enunciation (as uttered in the poem), a point which itself coincides with the unnamed point in space from which the speaker speaks. This correspondence creates a strong tension, which can already be felt in the introduction of the generation of heroes, between the *hic et nunc* of enunciation and the *prõtista* at the beginning of the narrative, which marked the axial point of time recounted; this narrative and chronological beginning coincides semantically with the creation of the men of gold, in a space not yet well defined.

Unless we allow the insertion of lines 173a-e, fragments proposed in two papyri and which serve to explain and normalize the passage from the fourth to the fifth *génos*, men (*andrásin*, line 175) of the age of iron were not the result of an act of creation by Zeus. Temporally and spatially, their existence is referenced to the *hic et nunc* of the enunciation, that is to say in relationship to the I (*egõ*, line 173) of the speaker and narrator, the enunciating authority. This enunciative situation recalls the one that concludes the poem's prelude: the I of the poet is substituted for Zeus, and sets himself resolutely facing Perses (named in the third person!). It is as if the family of iron were now within the

---

[37] Vernant 1960:26, interprets Hesiod's regret at not dying "before" or "after" (the race of iron) as an indication that the sequence of the ages represents a "renewable cycle."

province of the one who assumes enunciative authority! This is what Socrates seems to have understood intuitively in the quoted passage of the *Cratylus* when, with an inclusive "we," he associates his contemporaries with the species of iron as it is described by Hesiod, in contrast to the *génos* of gold.[38]

From now on death (*thaneîn*, line 175) and birth (*genésthai*), in inverse order will no longer be those of the human species, but of the *I*. This new temporality of the poetic enunciation is thus made up of a "before" and an "after": a "before" (*prósthe*, line 175) which could situate the poet's wish to have disappeared in the time and space of the heroes (corresponding perhaps with the *protéré* of line 160), and an "after" (*épeita*) which implicitly follows the present period of the men of iron.

If the act of creating the species of iron is not mentioned, its destiny is described at length. In a first moment, the destiny of this family made up of men attached to the earth (through the use of the formula *génos merópōn anthrópōn* in line 180 just as for the species of gold and bronze in lines 109 and 143) is presented as an uninterrupted sequence of sorrows and worries, sent by the gods by day and by night. The good being inadequate to make up for the bad, this species too will end in ruin initiated by Zeus (*Zeùs d' olései kaì toûto génos* , line 180; in a verb form which will henceforth be in the future). From this first incursion into the future of the iron species to foretell its ruin, the temporal movement impressed on the narration is far from indifferent. The future moment of the destruction of this generation of men through the will of the son of Kronos is announced by a phase of complete breakdown in social relations: the failure of reciprocal trust within the family, in the political community, and toward the gods. This can be seen as the poet's way of linking negatively to the isotopy of administration of justice, or even with that of agricultural abundance in refusing to feed one's parents, but also with that of the just word which is placed in the prelude to the poem. Not only will the men of iron end up entrusting the equilibrium of justice to physical violence (*díkē d' en khersí*, line 192), behaving like men of bronze, but they will give themselves over to malicious reproach (*mémpsontai*, line 186), and by their twisted speeches (*múthoisin skolioîs*, line 194) they will ensure the triumph of the bad over the best (*areíona*, line 193; echoing the description of the species of heroes in line 158).

This situation of complete social confusion is marked by a series of states nearly all of which are introduced negatively by the conjunction *oudé*. Seen

---

[38] *Cratylus* 398a. On the structure of lines 9–10 of the prelude to the *Works*, see Calame 1996c:170–175. On the status of lines 173d–e, see n35 above.

from the point of view of the narrative's time and narration, this sequence leads to the point of no return marked by *tóte*, "at that moment," in line 197. Zeus' destruction of the men of iron announced at the beginning of the description of them leads us to expect its repetition here, in an echoing ring arrangement. But really, the temporal referent *tóte* sends us back to a stage preceding destruction; it refers to the moment when Aidôs and Nemesis will abandon men and earth to rejoin the immortals on Olympus.

> Then indeed will Reverence and Indignation cover their beautiful skin with white mantles, leave human beings behind and go from the broad-pathed earth to the race of the immortals, to Olympus. Baleful pains will be left for mortal human beings, and there will be no safeguard against evil.
>
> *Works and Days* 197–201 (trans. Most)

Reverence and Indignation, powers that ensure respect and reknown through words, leave mortal men alone with their evils, and with no means of defense, consummating the separation between humans and gods.[39] The disappearance of the iron species and its destruction by Zeus are simple and implicit consequences of the future conduct of the men of iron.

This is to say that, unlike the brief episodes telling of the destiny imposed on each of the four preceding human species, there is no negative or positive narrative conclusion here. The structure and its logic are not completely realized. This incompleteness is explained naturally by the generally recognized prophetic turn of phrase assumed in narrating the iron species:[40] the destiny promised men living in the speaker and narrator's present is only one possibility. This is underlined by the use of the optative in lines 187–188. Seen in terms of narrative logic, the *lógos* of the *génē* thus remains open. Corresponding as it does to the projection into a probable future of recounted time and narrative time, from the axial point of the time of the uttered enunciation, this narrative has neither a logical nor a semantic conclusion.[41] In semio-narrative terms, this means that it does not lead to a "Sanction" phase. It is true that the poet foresees the complete and final separation of mortal men (*thnētoì ánthrōpoi*, line 201) from the tribe of immortals (*athanátōn phûlon*, line

---

[39] For the meaning of *aidós* in this context, see Schmidt 1986:60–66.

[40] See for example West 1978:176 et 198, and Carrière 1996:424–427.

[41] Calame 1996c:181–189. The operative concepts of "Lack" and of (semio-narrative) "Sanction" used in this brief visit to narrative and argumentative analysis are defined in chapter III, section 2.1. below.

199), within the absolute reign of evil which extends implicitly to the entire inhabited earth (cf. line 197); but the destruction of the iron species by Zeus is not taken up again, thus canceling the expected Ringkomposition effect! The future remains open. Its orientation depends on the power and efficacy of the poet's word.

The narration of the *lógos* thus places all five *génē* in a single temporal and logical sequence; it leads the hearer or reader from the first axial point introducing the time and marking the space recounted (*prōtista*, line 109), to the possible future (*éssetai*, line 201), foretold from the axial time and space of enunciation (lines 174–176). This enunciative moment also corresponds to the time of the performative speech act which signals the beginning of the narration (*ekkoruphṓsō*, line 106: "I am going to state"), and which has already been mentioned. The narrative's temporal and logical suspension thus restores to the speaker, and so to the poet, the power to conclude the narrative as he wishes. The same applies to the two narratives which surround the *lógos* of the five human families. The spatial-temporal logic of this *lógos*, along with its incompleteness, can be understood only in this larger narrative context.

2.4. Narrative and poetic context

Just like the *lógos* of the five families of men, neither the Pandora narrative which precedes it, nor the fable of the nightingale and the hawk which follows it, closes with a real phrase of narrative Sanction.

2.4.1. Narrative of Pandora and the jar of Hope

I have attempted elsewhere to show that the conclusion of the Pandora narrative in the *Works* isn't really in narratological terms a logical conclusion. In this version which differs in narrative logic from the one given in the *Theogony*, Zeus' rage is doubled, indirectly represented by taking the spontaneous *bíos* away from men, and in reaction to Prometheus' ruse to steal fire for men. The double "Sanction" given in this first narration of the *Works* could correspond to Zeus' doubled rage: the creation of Pandora and the gift of this deceptive misfortune (*pêma*, line 82) to men "who eat bread"; and through the presence of woman, diffusion of evils among men on land and sea, diseases, and sorrows (*kḗdea lugrá*, line 95). Spatially, the divide is now complete between the gods on the one hand, "all" (*pántes*, line 81) of whom live on Olympus, and who are thus involved in the etymology of Pandora's name ("gift of all"), and men on the other hand who live on the earth (*epì khthoní*, line 90) that they cultivate. But the presence of Elpis at the bottom of the jar from which these sad afflictions came indicates that the narrative state (reached after the creation of Pandora and after the jar is opened) is far from stable; even less so since Zeus himself wanted the *píthos* to be closed before Hope could escape.

Related to the potential for later narrative action development embodied in the dynamic figure of Hope, the time sequence of the Pandora narrative in some ways anticipates that of the *lógos* of the five ages. The narrative has its departure point (time of narration) in a present state: the gods do not hold (*ékhousi*, line 42) the resources of life at man's disposal. From this present state, the time of narration leads us etiologically toward the origin of recounted time. If the gods have hidden the *bíos* from men, it is because of the wrath of Zeus, triggered twice by Prometheus' ruse. The resentment of the king of gods is provoked first by an act which isn't even mentioned, although it offers both the situation of "Lack" likely to set off narrative action and the axial point of the entire process of temporal-spatial separation between immortals and mortals.The version of the narrative given in the *Theogony* allows us to identify this initial moment with the creation of animal sacrifice. Then the wrath of Zeus is revived by the theft of fire which the god had hidden from men while contemplating inflicting sorrows (*kédea lugrá*, line 49) on them for the first time. The consequence is the creation of this "great evil" which proves to be Pandora, for "future men."

But that is not all, since in order to reiterate the sorrows promised to men and to spread those sorrows among them, Pandora, now a woman, had to open the jar which contained them. All evils escaped, except Hope. A return to the present is assured by consequences of the sequence of three narrative acts, intended by Zeus (concealing of fire, creation of Pandora, opening then closing the jar of evils) and all told in the mode of the aorist: from now on, the sinister evils (*lugrá*, line 100) wander (*alálētai*, in the perfect as a resulta-tive!) among men, and the earth and the sea are full of them. From a verbal and semantic point of view, this return to the present is underscored particu-larly by the return of an expression "(Zeus) imagined sorrows for men" as a ring structure (*anthrṓpoisin emḗsato kḗdea lugrá*, line 95), then by inserting the term *lugrá* in the present of the enunciation.

In its narrative progress, recounted time thus leads us to the present, a present corresponding to the reign of Zeus, as indicated by the judgment which closes the narrative ("Thus, there is no way to escape the will of Zeus," line 105), but a present which is also that of the enunciation, since the begin-ning of the narrative implies a *you* which takes up and expands the address to Perses (line 27), to an anonymous enunciative interlocutor, and thus addressed to a generic someone. This more general you is also the one to whom the narrative of the five ages is addressed, preceding the fable of the hawk addressed to kings.[42] Like the gods hiding the *bíos*, the speaker here lets his interlocutor glimpse briefly, in the potential mood, a life practically free of productive work. And, specified as it is at the beginning of the *lógos*, this more favorable way of life not only evokes the subsistence of Hope, but it also relates to the state preceding the opening of the jar; before Pandora intervened, all tribes of men lived apart from the evils and diseases which bring death faster.

In its use of formulaic diction, and by exploiting the variations it permits, this absence of ills and fatigues (*nósphin áter te kakôn kaí ... pónoio*, line 91) anticipates the description of the golden age that begins the succession of the five *génē*; men did indeed live like gods in the time of Kronos, quite apart from pain and misery (*nósphin áter te pónou kaì oizúos*, line 133). By contrast, the near future of the iron species as the poet imagines it is marked by constant fatigue and misery (*kamátou kaì oizúos*, line 177). The first state of easy work imagined at the beginning of the Pandora creation narrative evokes the condition that men of gold in the following *lógos* will enjoy, and evokes it even more strongly in that the spontaneous production (*ároura automátē*, line 118) that characterizes the golden age contrasts with the spontaneity of diseases (*autómatoi*, line 103) resulting from the instability which is the end result of the Pandora story! Through these correspondences and verbal repetitions, the precarious situation caused by opening the jar and leaving Elpis alone in the Pandora narrative recalls the highly uncertain future prophesied for the men of iron.

Taken as a theme in the sequence of gifts and deceptive counter-gifts given to man by Zeus, a true lesson in reciprocity and in reestablishing legal balance, the isotopy of justice thus combines with that of productive work, giving the Pandora narrative both its semantic depth and its etiological purpose concerning the condition of mortal man. The temporal movement of this version, stretched between a point of origin characterized by friendliness with the gods and the present of the enunciation with its situation of imbalance, leads to a precarious state, just as its narrative conduct does; like the narrative of the five ages, it calls for a complement, if not for a "Sanction" in narrative logic.

---

[42] On the question of the interlocutor and thus the receiver of the *Works*, see n8 above.

2.4.2. The fable of the hawk and the nightingale as argument

The need for this narrative complement weighs heavily at the end of the other narrative enclosing the *lógos* of the five species of men. This is the well-known fable (*aînos*, line 201) of the hawk and the nightingale, specifically addressed to the third of three alternate successive interlocutors of the poem of the *Works*: first Perses, then a generic you, and now "kings." The apologue is told in the mode of the aorist, and this time sends us to a past so indeterminate that it might in this particular case have only gnomic value. But the narration of the animal *aînos* is referenced to the time of enunciation. By the form *eréō* (line 202), it branches off the same *nûn*, the same present moment put forth by the speaker when he tries to remove himself from the iron period (line 176); it is grasped as a speech act by the same form of the performative future which begins the full narrative of the ages (line 106). It is simply a question of "telling" the fable, just as the speaker introduces the second major part of the poem dedicated to the *Works*, by showing his will to tell it (*eréō*, line 286) to Perses, and just as in the final section of the composition, where the poet announces his intention to tell (*eréō*, line 661) Zeus's designs by telling the seasons for navigation and which days are favorable.

With its reference to an "aoristic" past, unlimited in the etymological sense of the term aorist, and by putting the hawk's (or falcon's?) words to the nightingale held captive in his grip in present direct discourse, narration of the fable brings on a sort of flattening of the temporal depth shown in the two previous narratives: the gnomic past of recounted time seems to coincide with the time of enunciation, without any intermediary and without any axial point of origin apart from the start of this brief narration. In addition, as an *aînos* the fable is both etymologically and constitutionally an invitation to decipher its "enigmatic" conduct.[43] The melodic and poetic values traditionally attributed to the nightingale's song, as well as the explicit play on words which associates the *aēdōn* with the *aoidós*, lead us to identify the melodious complaint of the nightingale with that of the speaker, poet, and bard. Given this, the hawk is far from an abstract representation of an omen for Perses, and far from incarnating the vengeance of the gods as has been proposed recently, but corresponds to the audience of the fable's speaker, the kings (at least temporarily).[44]

---

[43] The narrative and pragmatic status of the *aînos* was well defined by Nagy 1990b:147–150 and 309–313.

[44] None of the interpretations of the fable proposed in those studies I cited in 1996c:188n50, is satisfactory in this; see also the bibliographic information given by West 1978:204–205.

Indeed, the fable includes no "Sanction" phase either in its narrative logic nor in its moral. A consequence of the *húbris* shown by the violent power of the hawk-king, the narrative imbalance caused by the initial injustice is never set right. In his plaintive moan which calls to mind the owl song of the young girls reciting one of Alcman's *Partheneia*,[45] the nightingale-bard makes no articulate reply to the brutal words of the bird of prey. Claiming the power either to eat or to release the poor nightingale, the hawk appropriates the prophetic future to himself; he alone gives a moral, which he draws from his own formulation of the survival of the strongest: pain will come along with infamy (*aískhesin álgea*, line 211), for whoever tries to answer back. This is a discrete but obvious echo of the end of the age of iron, when Decency and Indignation depart, leaving mortals to their "sad sorrows" (*álgea lugrá*, line 200).[46] So neither the narrative of Pandora's creation, nor the series of the five ages, nor even the fable of the hawk and the nightingale finds the expected narrative and ethical Sanction. On the other hand, it is as if the Pandora narrative illustrates the isotopy of productive work, the *lógos* of the five ages, the isotopy of the balance of justice, and the fable the isotopy of the ordered and effective poetic word! Once again we are brought back to the three semantic threads woven and interlaced from the beginning of the poem.

2.4.3. Poetic efficacy, between justice and life resources

The reestablishment of narrative balance of the three linked *lógoi* is finally done by the poem itself, the poem taken up by the voice of the speaker-bard. A new imperative invitation assumed by the speaker and addressed to Perses is substituted for the expected reply from the nightingale-bard. Once again the verbal echoes are striking: by its formulation ("O Perses, as for you, listen to right and do not harbor violence"; *ô Pérsē, sù d' ákoue díkēs, méd' húbrin óphelle*, line 213), this address returns to the double (positive and negative) invitation that marks the start of the poem ("O Perses, as for you, lay up these things within your heart"; *ô Pérsē, sù dè taûta teôi enikátheo thumôi*, line 27). While framing the set of three narratives, the new address on the one hand associates Perses with the kings as an underlying figure for the "enigmatic" mask of the hawk in the fable, and on the other hand it is formed as a recommendation about respecting *díkē* and refusing *húbris*. In so doing, it brings the narrative

---

[45] Cf. Alcman fr. 1.85–87 (Page-Davies), with the complementary parallels mentioned by West 1978:207.

[46] Sufferings which recall the *kédea lugrá* which result from opening the jar in the Pandora narrative cf. lines 49 and 95, as well as section 2.3.1 above.

sanction and expected moral back from the three narratives to the poem itself. The recommendations made to Perses in line 213, and to the kings in line 218, thus complete the discursive and ethical logic of the three linked narratives.

This reestablishment, this discursive and enunciative rebalancing, takes place on the semantic level as well as in the temporal dimension, if not in the spatial dimension. From a semantic point of view, the recommendations to Perses in the assertive mood of the judgment reestablish contact with the isotopies of right and of productive fertility placed in the prelude and in the opening part of the poem. Briefly, and to avoid repeating what I have already said elsewhere on the function of the *Works* as an ethical judgment, but more especially as a judicial judgment, I will only point out that in contrast to the hubristic law of the strongest (*pròs kreíssonas*, line 210) uttered by the hawk at the end of the *aînos* dedicated to him, the speaker and narrator shows the "stronger" way (*kreíssōn*, line 217) which leads to just acts and which allows right to triumph over excess, over hubris, in the end (*télos*, line 218, in contrast for example with the beginning of time told in the narrative of the five human species).

Just as Epimetheus in the Pandora narrative only realized his error (*enóēse*, line 89) once the evil was accepted, the naïve person (*népios*, line 218; see line 40) recognizes his error in judgment (*égnō*, line 218) only by experiencing the triumph of justice. And in contrast with the barely-glimpsed end of the age of iron, marked by the retreat to Olympus of Decency and Indignation, the present victory of right signifies the presence of Oath and Justice; it also signifies the blooming of the city kept away from war on an earth which produces abundant harvests (*polùn bíon*, line 232), under the watchful eye of Zeus, who rights wrongs. This state of flourishing and peaceful plenty for the *pólis* once again evokes the golden age;[47] and it is even more strongly and explicitly opposed to the state which announces the eventual disappearance of the men of iron in that it is characterized by the resemblance between children and parents (line 235), which became blurred at the prophesied end of the age of iron (line 182)! The three narratives do indeed take on a semantic and argumentative function in the poem seen as judgment. From a narrative logic point of view, they get their narrative Sanction in the utterance of advice given by the narrator and assumed by his poetic voice.

---

[47] On the affinities of this privileged flourishing with the golden age, see commentary by West 1978:214–216; see also Crubellier 1996:462–463.

2.5. Enunciative polyphony and the voice of the poet

Instituting the abundant production of a quasi-golden age through the reign of justice controlled by Zeus thus requires mediation. Mediation between the isotopy of the administration of justice and the isotopy of production of the *bíos* is accomplished by the effective word, in both its positive and negative effects. This mediating voice develops in the first major part of the *Works* into a contrasting polyphony: the word of Zeus who is asked to decree (*íthune*, line 9) from the beginning of the prelude the rules of law customary in the prologue to "straighten the curve" (*ithúnei skolión*, line 7); the word of justice which must cut through the conflict that opposes the speaker-bard to Perses, through righteous judgments (*itheíēisi díkēis*, line 36); the voice (*phōnḗn*, line 79) that pronounces deceptive and untrue narratives, offered to Pandora but refused to the evils which she sets loose; twisted words (*múthoisin skolioîs*, line 194) and the false oath by the bad thrown into the face of the best to discredit him during the breakdown of social relationships at the end of the iron age; the hawk's word (*mûthon*, line 206) of violent authority in the fable regarding the nightingale-bard; and finally, in the call to justice addressed to Perses, a return to the word of the Oath and *Díkē* to set straight any twisted judgments (*skoliēîsi díkēisin*, lines 219 and 221, then lines 225–226, 230, 250, 258, 262, 263–264 and 280!), and thus ensure prosperity to the *pólis*.[48]

2.5.1. The poet's word of authority and hope

As a third isotopy running throughout this first part of the poem, the first word of authority is the poet's, prudently asserted in its power before Zeus at the end of the proem (line 10). Quite beyond the contrasting polyphony mentioned, and through the poem itself, the voice of the poet's authority is capable of resolving "this conflict" (*tḗnde díkēn*, line 39). *Díkē* describes both the present, historic legal dispute that opposes Hesiod to his brother Perses, and the display of justice as the poem describes it (*tḗnde díkēn*, lines 249 and 269) intended for kings. A judgment for the present conflict, the poem extends its field of action to the city in general, oscillating between the extra-discursive reference and the intra-discursive reference permitted by the use of deictic

---

[48] In lines 252–253, the "thrice numerous immortal guardians" who help Zeus watch over the acts and judgments pronounced by mortals recall the guardian *epikhthónioi* (line 122) which the men of gold became, through the will of Zeus; West 1978:181–183, 219–220, and 223–224, gives a series of Indo-European parallels to these divine figures watching over mortals, while positing a probable interpolation between the two passages.

hóde as described in the introductory chapter.[49] From the particular (extra-discursive) situation offered by the conflict with Perses, the poem extends the domain of administration of justice which it develops from the fictional *pólis* created in the poem to the "universal" space and time of the ideal *pólis*.

The voice of the speaker and poet is thus capable of alternating positive and negative developments in the balance of law; these take the enunciative form of invitations addressed to Perses (lines 213 and 274, a ring structure) or injunctions addressed to kings (lines 248 and 263, again a ring structure); but in terms of the universalization just mentioned they also take the form of general warnings, truths for you and one, valid throughout the space of the *pólis*. It is in the name of these principles that kings are called upon to straighten their speech (*ithúnete múthous*, line 263).[50] And so we arrive at the end of the first major part of this poem, devoted to justice; it is distinguished from the lengthy development dedicated to work and to bios through a new call to Perses (in line 286, through the intermediary of the performative future form *eréō* already mentioned).

In this provisional sense, the poet ends by expressing hope (*éolpa*, line 273) for the realization of justice, a striking correspondence to the figure of Hope which alone remained at the bottom of Pandora's jar. Accepted henceforth by the speaker with his poetic voice of authority, hope thus remains that despite everything the justice of Zeus may be realized (*teleîn* in line 273, echoing the *es télos* of line 218). After once again affirming the interdependence of the word of justice with happiness (*ólbos*, line 281) through the will of Zeus, the first major part of the poem ends like the narrative of the five ages, on a prophetic, even oracular, future: the progeny (*geneé*, line 284) of the perjurer will wither away, while that of the man faithful to his oath (once again *geneé* in line 285!) will prosper.[51] This is hope, now uttered by the voice of the poet himself:

> But whoever willfully swears a false oath, telling a lie in his testi-
> mony, he himself is incurably hurt at the same time as he harms

---

[49] According to the indications given in chap. I n33 and here n21, following the German linguist Karl Bühler who shows cases of possible combination of *demonstratio ad oculos* and *Deixis am Phantasma*; cf. chapter I, section 3.2., as well as n12 in this chapter.

[50] The complex structure of this part devoted to the lesson about justice drawn from the three narratives is analyzed by Hamilton 1989:53–66; see also West 1978:49–51 (on the text of line 263, cf. West 1978:222), and Calame 1996c:185–189.

[51] West 1978:228–229, noted the ocular value of using the adverb *metópisthe*, "in the future," in lines 284 and 285. Notice also the use of the term *geneé*, "the generation," and no longer *génos*, "species," just as in passing from the age of bronze to the age of heroes (line 160): see n30 above. On the role played by hope for the ephemeral humans facing Zeus' power, see also Semonides fr, 1, 1–10 (West²).

Justice, and in after times his family is left more obscure; whereas the family of the man who keeps his oath is better in after times.

Works and Days 280–285 (trans. Most)

From that comes the effectiveness of the poetic word, as capable as prophecy of reestablishing order controlled by Zeus, a mediator between *díkē* and *bíos*, between the balance of justice on the one hand, material and moral prosperity on the other. Ending as it does on a dynamic future, the conclusion of this first major part of the *Works*, in its putting-into-discourse, once again takes up the temporal movement of the narrative of the five successive species of men. The *lógos* of the five ages does not close time upon itself; its narrative movement does not close recounted time as a circle. But just as in the other two accounts in the narrative triad, this dynamic temporality arranges the preceding species into a sequence with an argumentative value, a pragmatic line which makes its lesson active in the present of the enunciation and in the space of the city.

A paraenesis opening on the near future of social and political time, this lesson in justice drawn from the narratives places the *Works* in the large genre of didactic poetry.[52] From that stems the twofold call to Perses through the poetic voice of authority supported by Zeus, to listen to the lesson of justice (line 275), and in the immediate future to work (line 299) in accordance with the three isotopies of reestablished justice, agricultural production, and the effective poetic word which ensures the semantic coherence of the whole of the poem with its two constituent parts!

2.5.2. Communication, poetic genre, and the city

While contributing internally to giving a civic and universal meaning to the advice concerning justice offered by the *Works* in its two constituent parts, the various enunciative indices which punctuate these hexameter verses in epic diction also point to the external and historical communicative situation. Along with the question of the argumentative insertion of the narrative of the five generations of men into the intra-discursive context of the poem, the poetics of its enunciation also poses the question of its extra-discursive context. The enunciative indices mentioned send us back to the conflict between the speaker and narrator (which the *sphragís* of the *Theogony* allows us to identify as Hesiod) and his brother Perses. These two figures thus appear not simply as discursive

---

[52] On this, see information given by Neschke 1996:477–478 (with n22).

creations, as "poetic persons" in particular enunciative positions; they also correspond on the one hand to poetic functions such as that of the bard who can later take up Hesiod's verses, and on the other hand to historical subjects. These individuals have the civil and civic identity which a proper name confers, and they are involved in a specific family situation which other indices allow us to glimpse.[53] But through its fictional powers the poem has transformed a historical dispute about an inheritance in a particular city into a general situation, valid for any *pólis* where the power of arbitration is in the hands of "kings," whether the heads of aristocratic families or the elders meeting in council, who represent the authority of Zeus on earth and in the city.[54]

In transforming an individual conflict into a discursive situation through the fictional powers of poetic practice, the I of the speaker who corresponds to Hesiod has become a bard whose voice has a particular pedagogical and prophetic authority. And the *you*—Perses—has been transformed into the generic receiver appropriate to the different Greek forms of didactic poetry: "Cyrnos" for the poems collected in the Theognidea, "Pausanias" for Empedocles, but "our city" for Solon.[55] Moving from the intra- to the extra-discursive sends us finally beyond the instance of discourse (and its "partner") to the rules of the poetic genre, often ignored when discussing the *Works*. A possible subject for another study, which should also propose a rereading of our sparse information on the historical, institutional, and social development of the *pólis*, the political community between the eighth and seventh centuries.

3. The hazards of comparison: "Comparing the incomparable"?

Probably due to the serious gaps in our historical knowledge of the civic communities to which Hesiod was speaking, interpreters of the narrative of the five human families turned to comparison to find possible confirmations of their readings in parallel narratives from other cultures. For anyone

---

[53] The controversy concerning the identity of Hesiod as *persona loquens* or as biographic figure has been the object of a recent study by Stoddard 2004:1–33; concerning both the poetic and historical identity of Perses, see n8 above, and additional information on the figure of "Hesiod" given in Calame 2000a:96–100 (and in n20 and n23); in general, see Calame 2005a:14–21.

[54] An attempt to reconstruct the historical and social context relative to the policy of establishing justice through the abundance of production extolled in the *Works* can be found in Carrière 1986:229–236. On the controversy concerning the identity of the *basileîs*, sometimes compared to the *big men* of Papuan communities, cf. Carlier 2003:13–23, in which he returns to his thesis of 1983, unfortunately without addressing Hesiod directly.

[55] The didactic goal of the *Works*, reestablishing justice under the control of Zeus, was very well explained by Nagy 1990a:63–74.

who hopes to enrich the interpretation of Greek texts whose universe of reference has largely disappeared due to cultural and temporal distance, the comparatist's route offers two privileged ways of proceeding, first proposed through historical and social anthropology: Indo-European reference and Semitic reference.

3.1. Comparatist incursions between Indo-European and Semitic references

Apart from the vaguely historical filiations which nineteenth-century *Geisteswissenschaften* was so fond of, it is generally now admitted that the Indo-European world is only an erudite reconstruction. Georges Dumézil himself finally recognized that the three great "functions" which in the Indo-European "family" correspond to particular institutions and statutes have only ideological reality. This transfer of the triadic structure of social reality to the symbolic level may bring with it a skeptical attitude about the line of hypothetical historical filiations to commit comparative procedures to pure synchrony. That is the prudent way taken by Jean-Pierre Vernant when he attempts to refer the three pairs of "races," previously opposed or even divided, to the three functions of sovereignty, war, and fertility, in order to reorganize them into structural pairs.[56]

Re-readers of the narrative of the five species as viewed from the perspective of Indo-European comparatism didn't need many narratological tricks to show that the Irish narrative of the catastrophic succession of five races given in Book of the Conquests of Ireland showed no homology, either logical or semantic, with the Hesiodic narrative. For that matter, in the Greek narrative itself, it has been remarked that one must "display considerable ingenuity" to assign to the men of silver and their reciprocal violence to the first function, the exercise of religious and royal power, or to place the heroes and their afterlife under just the military heading, or to split the iron family in order to attribute to it only a production function.[57] In attempting to assimilate each of the (supposed) couples of "races" to one of the functions of the Indo-European ideological model, one forgets too quickly the transitional role that the iron species plays between the narrative succession and the eventual genetic institution of the three functions, and its final situation where the speaker-poet

---

[56] The birth and development of the Indo-European concept, as well as that of "Aryan," have been retraced by Olender 1989:26–38; see also Bernal 1996:277–286 and 385–442. On the status of Indo-European "ideology," see Dumézil 1968:46–53 and 493–496 (for Greece); concerning the Hesiodic narrative of the five species specifically, cf. Vernant 1966:43n103.

[57] Carrière 1986:218–226, with n66.

himself is located. From a structural perspective which accounts for a complex state by its genealogy, the iron family should simultaneously imply both the function of production and the ensemble of the triadic paradigm, in this narrative and enunciative intersection with its spatial and temporal function!

Really, if one agrees to work in pure synchrony, forgetting any possible genetic relationships, it is to show, by differences and contrasts, that comparison can be an enriching and methodologically sound method of reading, avoiding analogies whose possible pertinence can be ensured only in their generality and abstraction.[58]

From this perspective, would Semitic reference be more productive? Since the beginning of the twentieth century, Hellenists have been sensitive to numerous narratives in Middle Eastern and ancient Indian cultures which portray a narrative or descriptive confrontation between metals of different values serving to distinguish different social states. Among these narratives, the one most reminiscent of the Hesiodic *lógos* is without question the narrative of the dream of Nebuchadnezzar as told in the Old Testament book of Daniel. The narration shows all the enunciative characteristics of a past narrative, while giving precise chronological and spatial references.[59] Even if the statue portrayed in the narrative could perhaps find a historical referent in the period of exile of the Jewish people, corresponding with the chronological index given in the text itself, it appears to be based on an oral tradition whose writing down goes back only to the middle of the second century BC.[60]

3.2. Daniel and the vetero-testamentary dream of Nebuchadnezzar

And so, in the second year of the reign of the sovereign of Babylon (which corresponds to about BC 604), the young Daniel, along with other young Judeans recognized for their knowledge and intelligence, was taken to the royal court to confront the dreams which troubled Nebuchadnezzar's sleep. Eschewing the incompetence of the Chaldean magicians and soothsayers for the wisdom and science inspired by the God of Israel, Daniel succeeded in satisfying the king's paradoxical wishes, first foretelling the dream itself, before correctly interpreting it. Calling on the authority of God, Daniel himself

---

[58] On the question of comparatism, see chapter I, section 6 above.

[59] Daniel 2:1–3, 7, pointed out by Reitzenstein 1924/5:525–527, taken up again by West 1997:312–319, who justifies the relationship of Hesiod's "Myth of Ages" with different eastern texts by saying that "its very formulation is un-Greek" (312)!

[60] The conditions under which the vetero-testamentary narrative was written, as well as its date, are the objects of a balanced study by Lacocque 1983:66–79. Thanks to Thomas Römer for this useful bibliographic entry.

recounts the dream of the brilliant and terrible statue with a head of gold, a chest and arms of silver, stomach and thighs of bronze, legs of iron, and feet made of iron and terra cotta. By destroying the fragile feet, a rock brings about the statue's collapse, and all of its elements are dispersed by the wind, leaving only the mountain born of the destructive rock.

In the kind of historical interpretation of the dream given by Daniel himself, the head of gold is identified in the narrative with Nebuchadnezzar, who through the will of God in Heaven rules over all humanity, with power, strength, and glory. Moving from the synchronic to the diachronic, the parts of the body become kingdoms which follow one another, in progressive decadence, until finally the agglomeration of iron and clay marks the arrival of a reign subject to division. This ultimate reign will be destroyed and finally replaced by the mountain, recalling the eternal kingdom of the very God who, while destroying forever all preceding reigns, also ensures the veracity of the dream and the pertinence of its interpretation!

Without going into the details of a rather complex discursive and enunciative construction, we notice that apart from a few analogies limited to the succession of metals, the Old Testament narrative presents a recounted time, and consequently a narration, centered on a precise chronological moment (second year of the reign of Nebuchadnezzar, and a defined geographic point (Babylon, the capital and the residence of the king). In this, the narrative is completely unlike the Hesiodic narrative of the five families which, rather than having a historical spatial-temporal reference, is oriented on the *hic et nunc* of the enunciation, a *hic et nunc* which is referenced neither temporally nor spatially. The temporality that runs through the biblical narrative is thus the exact inverse of the discursive time constructed in the Hesiodic narrative.

From the enunciative point of view, the narration describing the statue and its destiny, along with the interpretive narrative that it gives rise to, are not directly taken on by a speaker-narrator inspired by the Muse; rather, both are put in the mouth of one of the protagonists of a third-person narrative marked by chronological and historical points of reference, set off from any explicit enunciative intervention. Inserted into an anonymous narration, the twofold narrative about the statue made of four metals (plus clay) is thus spoken by the wise foreigner who intervenes in Nebuchadnezzar's court. But in his inserted narrative, and thus mimetically, the young Daniel is inspired by the knowledge of God; that knowledge is revealed in a vision prior to his confrontation with the king of Babylon. The indirect instance of enunciation that underlies the narrative of the statue and its interpretation is thus dual: on the one hand it relates to the "God in Heaven" recognized by the Hebrews in the kingdom of Juda, and on the other hand it relates to one of the young men chosen by the king of Babylon for a scholarly education; he enjoys superior intelligence and knowledge, especially in the interpretation of dreams, thanks to the god of Israel.

In the narrative that frames Daniel's intervention, the king's requirement that he guess the dream before correctly interpreting it also places the structure temporally before it actually happens: first the five reigns (not *géné*, or human species) in synchronic and hierarchic order assigned to them by the relative value of the corresponding metal and by their respective place in the body of the statue, then the narrative intervention of the rock which, after simultaneously reducing all parts of the statue to dust, transforms itself into a mountain. This narrative overthrow gives its temporal dynamic to the interpretive narrative which follows, transforming the classification order given by the description of parts of the statue into a succession of more and more fragile kingdoms. This sequence leads to the creation of the eternal reign of "God in Heaven," the god who gave to Daniel the knowledge and inspiration which are the very basis of the hermeneutic narrative itself.

Contrary to what happens in the Hesiodic text, the (narrative) present of the uttered enunciation of the subordinate biblical narrative is well-marked by a prior address to the king of Babylon, while being placed from the outset under the authority of the God of Israel:

> Daniel answered in the presence of the king, and said, "The secret which the king hath demanded cannot the wisemen, the astrologers, the magicians, the soothsayers, shew unto the king; But there is a God in heaven that revealeth secrets and maketh known to the king Nebuchadnezzar what shall be in the latter days. Thy dream, and the visions of thy head upon thy bed, are these; ..."

Daniel 2:27–28, King James version

This enunciative spatial-temporal referencing coincides not only with the end, but also with the beginning, with the central moment of recounted time: the head of the statue is not only the head of the king beset by visions, but it is also the kingdom of gold and consequently the reign of Nebuchadnezzar himself. The successive reigns are henceforth presented in an interpretive and prophetic future which leads them, in a conformity between time of narration and narrated time, to final destruction; a destruction which, with the advent of the kingdom of God on earth, marks the creation of a second axial point. Because of its permanent and terrestrial nature, and also because he who dominates and he who reveals through the mouth of Daniel are one and the same, the narrative time of the reign of "Great God" includes the time of enunciation while at the same time providing its meaning. Thanks to this reversal, the future and divine kingdom of the one God of the Judeans takes the place of the golden age of the present human reign as spatial and temporal point of reference; the different discursive levels and the different spatial-temporal lines of the biblical narrative all converge there.

A teleological perspective, centered on the atemporal and universal reign of divine authority, has taken the place of a focus on the time-space of the enunciation and on the effects of the poetic word. Nothing could be more foreign to the poetics of memory in "archaic" Greece; nothing could be more exotic for the Greeks, constantly preoccupied by the realization of their mortality within the civic community, in an earthly time without absolute divine finality and subject to sudden and unforeseen reversals of fortune; nothing could be farther—as we shall see in the last chapter—from the accompanying concern for a form of afterlife in an ideal world, isolated from the home of the gods on Olympus, at the ends of the inhabited earth.

4. The *hic et nunc* of a didactic poem

Despite the numerous ways of transmitting it that have been imagined recently, in trying to refer the symbolic manifestations of eighth- and seventh-century Greeks to different "oriental" influences, neither the date of the biblical text nor the ideology which runs through it will permit us to establish the slightest contact, much less any filiation, with the Hesiodic text.[61] Rather than allowing us to claim that "the myth appears entirely alien to the general Greek view of the past as reflected in the whole corpus of epic and genealogical poetry," study of the spatial-temporal structure of the narrative of the five human species reveals within the succession of their respective qualities what has rightly been seen as a progressive "historicization";[62] to this is added a more and more specific spatial focus. Indeed, if the description of violence committed by the men of bronze on the earth in general recalls

---

[61] This despite soothing remarks by West 1997:2–4 et 586–624, who in his great comparative work asserts his interest in parallels in forms of expression in ancient texts of "Western Asia," then deliberately rejects the differences.

[62] See especially Carrière 1996:411–418, and, less rigorously, Most 1997:121–127, and Ballabriga 1998:329–339, whose "historico-genetic" hypothesis is debatable, to say the least. See also Vian 1963:167–169.

the same vocabulary which often describes the heroes of the *Iliad*, related to their partial integration into the poetic "age of bronze," the mention of epic heroes who died under the walls of Troy or of Thebes evokes the religious honors accorded some of them in Hesiod's time. The gradual narrowing of the temporal gap, moving toward the historic reality of the enunciation's "now," goes hand in hand with a geographic movement toward its "here:" following the spatial reference of the first three families on the earth of men, the heroes are situated in Greek space, in Thebes and in Troy, in order to lead (along with the age of iron) to the hic of the poem's enunciation. It will be for the future, oriented by the poem, to offer from this *hic et nunc* a spatial-temporal frame valid for any (Greek) *pólis*, subject to Zeus and enjoying the prosperity ensured by the balance of justice.

Quite apart from any attempt to divide these periods occupied by each *génos* and to articulate these entities into opposing pairs, what is particularly striking in the unfolding of recounted time in the narrative of the five ages is the alternation of auspicious times of nearness to the gods and periods of impious violence.[63] This concept of the social and historical time of mortal men is reminiscent of Herodotus' famous declaration, placing his *Histories* under the reign of alternating happiness and misfortune; this alternation, under the sign of *díkē* and *húbris*, of justice and of breaking with justice, strikes the cities of men as well as men themselves. Even closer to the poetic tradition in which Hesiod places himself, this logic of temporality also evokes the image of the falling of leaves used in the *Iliad* by Glaukos to explain the succession of generations of mortal men to Diomedes! We shall return to this in the final chapter.[64] This unpredictable rhythm of prosperities and calamities, combined with an alternating succession of births and death, is much more

---

[63] This alternation has been felt successively by Carrière 1986:226–229, who proposes organizing the succession of human species along a sinusoidal temporal axis, by Couloubaritsis 1996:500–507 and 517, who imagines a narrative temporality organized according to a helicoidal rhythm, or by Most 1997:108–114, who tries to see in Hesiod's narrative the combination of three schemes: 1+1+3, 1+1+2+1, 1+1+1+2 ...; see also Crubellier 1996:453–455, who despite everything remains attached to the image of cyclical temporality. If one must choose an organizational model, one could limit oneself to locating it in the semio-narrative development of the narrative: according to the narrative logic proposed by the "canonic schema," the status of the men of gold and of silver would correspond to the phase of narrative Manipulation, then the action of the men of bronze and especially that of the heroes would evoke the phase of Competence, which would find its realization and Performance in the age of iron with the Sanction that prophetic utterance by the poet's voice represents.

[64] Herodotus 1.5.3–1.5.4; *Iliad* 6.145–149 on the base of a gnomic sentence taken over by Mimnermos fr. 8, 1–7 (Gentili-Prato) and by Simonides fr. 19 (West²); additional references can be found in Calame 2000a:85–86; cf. also chapter V, section 3.1 below.

than a succession reorganized into opposing pairs in the Greek representations of lived time. It is one of the essential elements of the mortal human condition and its spatial-temporal regime, related to the Olympians and especially to Zeus, as it is defined in the three narratives of the *Works* before being described by the poet himself.

While the very condition of the mortal precludes a cyclical return to the golden age, the narrative of man's past from its point of origin (situated in another time), as well as the evocation of the post mortem destiny granted to the generation of heroes (generation, not species: *geneé*, not *génos*) in a confined space, reinforces the spatial-temporal power of the poet's word. A temporal course and a spatial incursion are placed at the service of a poetic voice, supported by the Muses and inspired by Zeus, which maintains hope of lawful action (*action juridique*). In its poetic extension, this act of justice will place the civic community, through the development of vital resources, in a state near the quasi-divine beatitude experienced both by the men of gold at the beginning of human history and by the heroes at the ends of the earth. Quite apart from any cyclical concept of time, it is here a question of reorienting the future, through the didactic force of the epic word, and by reference to a paradise lost and a paradise to be found: the golden age and the isles of the blessed in a poetic memory oriented towards the future.[65] Only justice and work can make the "here" of the city coincide at least temporarily with these two other places that resemble the domain of the gods. The social propositions formulated in comedies from the first part of Aristophanes' career, using reversal and comic derision, are really not very different: from the Acharnians to the Peace, the civic utopia staged before assembled citizens in the theater and sanctuary of Dionysus refers to a golden age which can be realized only through the orderly workings of distinctly human institutions on which the age of iron is founded, on marriage, sacrifice, and banquet![66]

This social and temporal "elsewhere" which can be realized at least temporarily in the here and now, in civic order ensured by Zeus, can also be reached after death, through verbal and ritual practices to which we shall refer at the end of this essay. In any case, this place and time of civic utopia has nothing to do with the kingdom of God on earth, as comparison with the biblical text suggests. This is a warning against a too-hasty comparative method which touches only on narrative and thematic analogies, without

---

[65] Cf. Carrière 1991:100–105; "The golden age is a mythic guarantee of prosperity for the just men of today" (101); see also Brown 1998:401–409, for relevant parallels.

[66] On this, see the conclusions drawn by Auger 1979:72–89.

concentrating on the specific effects of meaning in particular cultural and historic contexts. More positively, it is also a plea for an approach sensitive to "indigenous" categories, while recalling that the nature of any such procedure is necessarily triangular: to the notional contrasts which point up the confrontations of two different "exotic" cultures, we must add the comparative perspective of anthropology itself. However dialogic it may claim to be, this perspective can only be interpretive:[67] "native" categories can only be perceived and reformulated through a delicate translation operation, culturally marked in space and in time, since our own (academic) culture is itself subject to historical and conceptual change.

But beyond this brief lesson in method, the didactic nature of the poetic word of the *Works* invites us to read in the profusion of obligations by Hesiod another invitation, more precisely concerned with our own relationship to our representations of the past. *Nûn gàr dè génos estì sidéreon,* "it is now the species of iron" (line 176), sings the bard reciting the *Works*, at the moment when he intervenes in his own narrative to orient the course of time toward prophecy. In relating the past enunciatively with the present, Hesiod is grounded in what will become a constant in Greek historiopoietics, both in its poetic versions and in its more historiographic forms. Herodotus' way of referring narrative events of the recent past, events which he reformulates or reports, to the present and to his own time (*es emé*) stems from this permanent concern—as we have said. From the epic poetry tradition in the Hellenistic period, we could also add Apollonius Rhodius' use of the heroes' tombs as indices (*sêma*) of the temporal relationship that unites the epic past to that which endures "there still now" (*énth' éti nûn per*); and much later it is still this same concern with relating a native heroic past to the present of Romanized Greece that inspires the constant etiological perspective of the itinerary that Pausanias proposes, to places of memory and of religious history in continental Greece.[68]

This etiological perspective is already implicitly present in the Hesiodic narrative of the five ages: the current state of breakdown in justice denounced by the poet can be explained only by abuses committed by the preceding

---

[67] Different aspects of the challenges presented in translating anthropological concepts which try to be dialogic are discussed by Borutti 1999:171–202, and by Fabietti 1999:57–71 and 227–251; concerning the question of transcultural translation, see remarks I presented in 2002:67–77.

[68] On Herodotus and Pausanias, see references given by Calame 2000a:164n17 and 241n77; for Apollonius Rhodius, see for example *Argonautica* 1.1058–1062 or 2.714–719, which contrasts with the Homeric narrative where the heroic protagonists of the epic action refer to the present of the poem's enunciation as if to a future time! Cf. Saïd 1998:16–19.

human species.[69] Across the centuries and through didactic hexametric poetry, the voice of Hesiod still reminds us of two things: he invites us to set aside the most disengaged forms of "micro-history," and also calls on us to reject the nominalism to which history leads when it is reduced to simple "forms of writing."[70] Our own relationship to a past which we (re)configure cannot help but be engaged in the present, a present which we help to orient, through the fictional and rhetorical procedures of configuration; but this relationship itself is also inspired in one way or another by an explicative causality which becomes motivation for the present. To this extent, the future is bright for what we call "social" history, despite its recent denigrations on the part of postmodern liberalism with its sophisms ...

---

[69] As stated by Brown 1998:389 ("Put together, the past bad races account for the origin of the vices which Hesiod considers to be most prevalent among his contemporaries").

[70] Rancière 1992:207. Concerning the restricted forms of micro-history, see the critical references given by Ricœur 2002:267–280; for a good understanding of it, see remarks by Vidal-Naquet 1995:217–230.

III

GENDER AND HEROIC IDENTITY BETWEEN LEGEND AND CULT

The Political Creation of Theseus by Bacchylides

GENDER IS A CONSTITUTIVE ELEMENT of social relationships based on perceived differences between the sexes," or "a primary way of signifying relationships of power."[1] Quoting definitions taken out of their contexts could hardly be said to show intellectual rigor or academic collegiality. But such quotes are certainly a practical way of introducing a reading intended specifically to show how a modern concept, stemming from the social development of industrial and technological neo-capitalist civilization can, through comparison, throw light on a representation of time and space in a poetic configuration of memory in a culture where this modern and western idea was never operative.

1. Sexual social relationships and spatial-temporal representations

By adopting this pragmatic point of view (de rigueur in discourse anthropology), and then moving on from the question of the argumentative (intra-discursive) role of a narrative spatial-temporal logic to the problem of the extra-discursive function of a poetic narrative, we propose a reading of a composition by the poet Bacchylides, with its complex spatial-temporal element, in light of recent questions about social relationships between the sexes. This poem of the classical era, performed ritually in conditions which we shall explore, tells a previously unknown episode in the heroic biography of Theseus of Athens. The poem belongs to the great genre of "lyric" poetry and takes the form of a

---

[1] Scott 1986/1989:94–95.

dithyramb. But before studying the process of fictional creation in the poem from the perspective of semio-narrative analysis and before being led to the external situation of its "performance" and its pragmatic effects in creating and maintaining a civic memory (especially given the poetic and religious genre to which it belongs), we must first give a few more details concerning what is meant by "gender," as well as concerning representations of time and space.

1.1. Enunciation of representations of gender

Why gender as grasped in the practical and discursive representations that each of the sexes creates of the other sex in given historical and cultural conditions?

It is not new to say that social relationships of sex have been one of the nuclei of academic debate in the social sciences in the past three decades. Even the section titles in major American university libraries offer evidence of this. While we witnessed a substitution of "cognitive sciences" for "linguistics" toward the end of the last century, "women's studies" have proven remarkably resistant. On the European side of the Atlantic and just as significantly, the University of Lausanne, in a rather forced collaboration with its sister institution in Geneva, and after the prudent delay always advisable in a Calvinist country, created a program in "gender studies" several years ago, and integrated it into the curriculum of students in the social sciences.[2]

This chapter employs a perspective which, resistant though it may seem to be, could also fall victim to the inevitable changes of the hermeneutic and epistemological paradigm in human sciences. But the intention is not simply to follow new trends and to allow the reader to breathe a bit of contemporary air. It is intended to show how an idea relevant to modern times can prove to be a useful instrument in transcultural translation, in this study's reflections on Greek representations of temporality and spatiality.

Decidedly instrumental, the perspective of social relationships and representations of sex must be explained within the enunciative approach generally adopted in these chapters. From a discursive and enunciative point of view, the definitions quoted as a prelude to this chapter are phrased not only in a neutral mode as simple affirmations, but in a surprisingly abstract and impersonal formulation, as if the perception of sexual relationships had no subject, as if the representation of sex differences were not itself subject to differentiation due to asymmetrical relationships. But the mutual perception of each sex

---

[2] Laboratoire Interuniversitaire en Études Genre (LIEGE), Universités de Genève et de Lausanne.

by the other, based on biological reality and on the symbolic representation of sex differences, is never symmetrical. This culturally- determined asymmetrical perception varies, of course, from one society to another, from one historic period to another, from one individual to another, and from one age to another. Neither of the two sexes ever gives itself, or concedes to the other sex, the same way of seeing itself and of seeing the other. And each of these perceptions is constructed as a representation largely in terms of language and collectively accepted discourse.

This enunciative observation should be especially relevant for a Hellenist whose attention is drawn to the specifics of Greek poetry during what is termed the "archaic" period, during the development of the *pólis*. It falls to him to account for the "lyric" poems composed by an adult male poet, under the control of a small civic community still dominated by a double monarchy, and sung by groups of young men, but also by choruses of young girls. The question posed by the relationships implied in such performances in the Sparta of the seventh century, ritual in nature and generally religious in purpose, probably cannot be reduced to a simple game of combining structural opposites, even though this arrangement of a conceptual system using binary opposites like individual/collective, adolescent/adult, and feminine/masculine is all the more tempting in that these contrasting classifications were widely used by Greek thinkers themselves!

Both the historiographic term "archaic" and the literary genre category of "lyric" are subject to epistemological criticism, but beyond that what is involved in these ritually-destined poems is the distinction that must be made between on the one hand the historic situation of communication with other social actors in a ritualized "performance", and on the other hand the fictional return of this situation in the poetic discourse involved; this external situation manifests itself, as we have seen as the "utterance of the enunciation." In the case of the Lacedaemon of the poet Alcman, we must take into account the poetic and collective expression, by a feminine plural I, of erotic feelings aroused by a more mature girl, through the intermediary of a traditional discursive form; its historic and ritual "performance" implies the choral group of adolescent girls singing and dancing the poem, as well as the young girl leading their movements, and finally the poet who composed their song and who is their music master.[3] Only the use of a ritualistic and traditionally

---

[3] I tried to address this enunciative aspect of (discursive) representation and of (collective) expression of gender in my study 1998a; see also 2000b:32–48. On the question of the discursive identity of the lyric "*I*," cf. n41 below.

poetic language can account for the paradox of an adolescent female perspective composed by an adult male poet such as Alcman in Sparta (or later, Pindar in Thebes) but assumed by a group of young female aristocrats; through the creative control of a poet working in his "author-function," the choral group under the direction of a choregos performs a danced and sung ritual, most probably with an initiatory purpose.

In the wider context of the poetics of *épainos* and *mômos*, of praise and reproach, through the intervening poetic discourse and ritual "performance," this strange discursive interference between representations and very distinct gender identities must be thought of in terms of intersection and complementarity; these relationships of reciprocal complementarity are often established by poetic and symbolic means, as we shall see. On this point, the comparison given in the conclusion of this chapter, with the social and symbolic workings of the ritual complex belonging to an exotic contemporary community, may throw light on the Greek discursive situation; the comparative approach should also confirm the social appropriateness of modern attention to the definition of "gender" and to the practical representations to which it gives rise.

1.2. Temporalities between line and circle

Sketchy as they may be, these preliminary remarks on our postmodern sensitivity to social relationships marked by gender should prove useful to the reading of temporal and spatial development in a poem composed at the end of the Persian wars by the poet Bacchylides of Keos, very probably intended for a mixed choral group; the performance of this "lyric" composition by a group of young Athenian women and men was integrated into a religious and civic celebration dedicated to Apollo. But this brief preview on ritual conditions of communication (which we shall examine from the point of view of the uttered enunciation) calls for two additional remarks about the temporalization and spatialization of an essentially narrative dithyramb.

First, as we said in the introductory chapter, Benveniste saw historic and social time, scanned in a linear chronology using a regular scale of measurement, as "calendar time" (or as "time of the calendar").[4] In so doing, he failed to think that the notion of a calendar also refers to the measured rhythm of

---

[4] Benveniste 1974:70–76; cf. chapter I, section 2.2. For the study of another Bacchylides poem from the same perspective of pragmatic temporalization shared between linear and oriented narrated time, time of narration, time of the uttered enunciation, and ritual time, cf. Calame 2000c.

the cyclical scansion of social time shared by the community. This scansion is given to calendar time by the recurrence of ritual celebrations, generally spaced out over the lunar year, following several different cyclic rhythms; this ritual scansion gives to the memory of the community a practical rhythm, belonging to a procedure of "anthropopoiesis." Especially in classical Greece, this putting-into-discourse of history gets its temporal (and spatial) rhythm by narrative means, from a combining of these two ways of measuring time: on the one hand the chronological line organized according to different calculations provided by the succeeding generations or the quadrennial list of winners in the Olympic games or the annual succession of the archons of Athens; on the other hand the circle, with its circular logic organized according to different rhythms, furnished by the annual or quadrennial repetition of great local or Panhellenic festivals and celebrations, but also from the simple circular change of the seasons.[5]

Poetic discourse, with its own narrative and enunciative temporal structures, plays an essential role in this calendar combining chronological time and cyclical temporality. Hesiod's didactic poem, with its narrative of the succession of the five human families, confronted us with a narrative that combines both a narrated time and a time of narration oriented toward the time and space of the uttered enunciation in the poem; this convergence moves toward a judicial action, along with a pedagogical effect on the (punctual) present of communicating the poem. In following the development of time and space in Bacchylides' poem 17, we shall see how integrating discursive narrated time into the linear development of narration and of the song itself leads to the cyclical time of ritual for which the melic poem is intended. From the articulation between narrated time-space and time-space of narration, then the (intra-discursive) time-space of the uttered enunciation which encompasses them, we shall move on to the (extra-discursive and festive) time-space of "performance" of the poetic composition. We may then ask our questions regarding social relationships of the sexes, in the wider political and ideological context of the religious and cultural celebration. The poetic narration of a past which leads to a present ritual will lead us finally not only to tackle the question of the relationship between what we think of as "myth" and what we consider historiographic representation, but will also lead us to explore how this discourse relationship refers to a complex historic situation.

Secondly, we shall return to the clever distinction Ricoeur made between the stability of an "*idem*-identity" (in the "sameness" of the character!) and the

---

[5] On this last point, see Bouvier 2000:120–131.

mobility of an "*ipse*-identity" (in its moral "ipseity"!). But this distinction can be introduced here, from the start, as it relates both to the poetic construction of time and space and to the social relationships of the sexes that this discursive representation implies.[6] Without taking on the psychoanalytical basis for dialectical movement between the stable core of the human identity and its possible alterations in the development of cultural and anthropopoietic construction of the individual, we must point out that, especially as regards gender, the moral *ipse*-identity is built on the individual and personal level as well as from the collective and cultural point of view. And we shall see that in the case of the poetic representation of past time and space subordinated to a ritual efficiency, the individual identity will be configured more in the recounted story (and thus in the "myth"), while the collective identity will be formed in the course of the sung "performance;" this process of creating both an individual and a collective human identity, an anthropopoietic human identity, is accomplished thanks to the temporal unfolding and the spatial localization of the ritual and religious celebration into which this complex representation is integrated. This dialectic movement between individual identity and social identity in a movement of "anthropopoiesis" through social memory offers at least a chance of giving a positive answer to the question of the aesthetic value of Bacchylides' *Dithyramb* 17, a composition which is often condemned for its apparent narrative inconsistencies.[7]

2. Narrative movements in time and space

The narrative parts of Pindar's compositions are characterized by various effects of extension, suspension, focusing, prolepsis and analepsis, numerous and often embedded ring structures.[8] By contrast, the narration of Bacchylides' *Dithyramb* 17 follows a distinctly linear development, and the narrative covers nearly the entirety of the poem. Before turning our attention to its spatial unfolding, we must first briefly explain the temporal structure.

---

[6] See chapter I, section 2.2 and chapter V, section 5.

[7] Critics have denounced the fact that the ring Minos throws overboard in his challenge to Theseus is forgotten; they have also denounced the contrast between the heroic and masculine first part, and the lighter and more feminine second part; cf. references in Segal 1979/1998:300; see also Käppel 1992:158–161. On the notion of "anthropopoiesis" as an operative category including the different processes of creation and representation of the human by various symbolic and practical means, see Affergan et al. 2003:1–16 and 41–74.

[8] These different procedures are summarized by Griffith 1993:607–609; for several specific cases, see Calame 1996a:66–78, with references to other studies on narrative temporality in Pindar's odes.

2.1. Essay on semio-narrative analysis

Bacchylides' narration follows a line so regular that its rhythm practically coincides with the linear development of recounted time. That is to say its narrative logic exactly fits the "canonic schema" of the narrative, with its sequence of four phases of "Manipulation," "Competence," "Performance," and "Sanction," confronting a (semio-narrative) "Subject," manipulated by a "Sender," and supported by various "Helpers," and an adversary set up as an "Anti-subject."[9] And so the development of narration in *Dithyramb* 17 shows a strange and rare correspondence between this logical and analytical structure and the representation of time and space on which it is based. This coinciding is based on a unity of time coupled with a remarkable unity of place. Unfolding on a ship (*naûs*, line 1) between Athens and Crete (*Krētikòn pélagos*, line 4), the narrative action takes place in a single day: a certain day on the sea, heading toward Crete, in the time of "history" or "narrative," and without the least incursion in the time (or space) of "discourse."[10] The narration starts immediately, without the enunciative intervention of the poet's *I* to be expected in any epic or melic poem, and without any invocation of the inspirational authority of the Muse.

> The ship with the blue-black prow, as it carried Theseus, steadfast in the battle din, and the twice seven splendid youths and maidens of the Ionians, was cleaving the Cretan sea, for northerly breezes fell on the far-shining sail thanks to glorious Athena, the aegis-shaker; but Minos' heart was chafed by the dread gifts of the Cyprian goddess with desire in her headband, and he could no longer keep his hand from the girl but touched her white cheeks. Eriboia shouted for the bronze-corseleted descendant of Pandion, and Theseus saw it and rolled his eyes darkly beneath his brows ...

Bacchylides *Dithyramb* 17.1–17 (trans. Campbell 1992:217)

The narrative action of Bacchylides' *Dithyramb* 17 begins with the usual situation of "Lack"; it brings on the break in equilibrium which is necessary to

---

[9] (Critical) details on the operative value of the canonic schema of narration in Adam 1991:69–95, and in Calame 1996b:55–59. To distinguish them from the semantic values they assume in each specific narrative, the elements (actants and actions) of semio-narrative syntax are written here with capital letters.

[10] To return to the two categories developed by Benveniste 1966:237–240; cf. above chapter I, section 2.4.

the confrontation of the two protagonists of the action. Both are presented at the beginning of the narration, a Subject and an Anti-subject both manipulated by a specific Sender. First Theseus borne toward Crete by the vessel itself (*naûs ... ágousa*, lines 1–2) with the help of Athena, then Minos whose heart is led astray, indirectly manipulated by Aphrodite. The victim of the break in equilibrium between the two (semio-narrative) Subjects of the narrative is the young Athenian woman Eriboia, on whom Minos, motivated by erotic desire, unjustifiably tries to lay his hands.

The Manipulation phase of the narrative begins with line 16. Because of the inappropriate gesture of Minos toward the girl, Theseus becomes the first Subject of the action. It is he, the Athenian, who provokes the hero of Crete by criticizing him for not being able to master himself. Carried away by his *thumós* (line 23), his affective force, Minos is in some ways the victim of his own emotions: by overstepping the limits, he has committed an act of *húbris* (line 41). Just as in the usual scenario of the *Iliad*, Theseus as a prelude to the duel compares his own genealogy with that of his Cretan adversary. In so doing, the Athenian hero gives the names of the principal Senders of the heroic action to come, in collaboration with the feminine divinities already mentioned. Confronted with Aegeus, the son of Zeus, and of the daughter (*kóra*, line 32) of Phoinix (which is to say, Europa) Theseus affirms his own birth from the union of Poseidon and the daughter of king Pittheus; at the same time, he insists on the previous virginity of his mother whose union with the god was honored by the gift of a veil (or a belt? *kálumma*, line 37) from the Nereids. From a spatial point of view which corresponds to opposing Zeus and Poseidon, the birth of Minos is linked to the earth since the Cretan hero was born on Mount Ida, while Theseus' genealogy is linked to the sea.

The break in narrative equilibrium and the fact that justice is at stake is alluded to by Theseus himself. In aspiring to fulfill the *moîra* (line 24) and thus to realize what is apportioned by the gods, he shows that he is conscious of the danger of "tilting the balance of justice" (lines 25–26).[11] And so at the end of his address to Minos, in a ring structure, he declares his will to respond to the violence and arrogance of Minos (*bían*, line 23; *húbrin*, line 41), as much by his own force (*bían*, line 45) as by the decree (*krineî*, line 46) of a god. Just like the tragic hero Oedipus who assumes his own action while asserting that his sufferings are inflicted by Apollo in the accomplishment of his *moîra* and

---

[11] The meaning of this expression is explained by Maehler 1997:189–190; see also Gentili 1995:57–59. For possible meanings of *kálumma*, cf. n17 below.

his *daímōn*, Theseus declares himself the subject of his own act, while at the same time claiming his divine father Poseidon and placing himself consciously within the fulfillment of the *moîra*, the force superior to the gods. Not just the "double motivation" generally spoken of when trying to explain the motives for action of a tragic hero who assumes the decision deliberated by a god, but "triple determination" to account for a heroic will which is always doubly determined, by the deity and by destiny.[12]

Minos' reaction to Theseus' intervention can be considered the second part of the initial phase of Manipulation. By his challenge to the Athenian hero, the hero of Crete imposes the narrative contract, which takes the form of a provocation. In his retort to Theseus, Minos also bases himself on his ancestry, which he compares with his adversary's genealogy; in both cases, he also insists more on his own relationship and his adversary's with the young mother, rather than on them both being descended from divine fathers. But first, Minos speaks directly to Zeus: if it is true that the god fathered him with the white-armed Phoenician maiden, let him send from the heavens a recognizable sign (*sâm' arígnōton*, line 57)! As for Theseus, son of the woman of Troizen and of Poseidon who shakes the earth, let him bring back the ring which Minos will throw in the depths of the sea! And so the terms of the (semio-narrative) contract which consecrates the Manipulation phase are drawn up; in this particular case, they are imposed by the Anti-subject become the subject, in the name of the power incarnate in Zeus, one of the main Senders in the narrative.

Particularly well-developed because of the presentation of the two narrative Subjects of the action along with their respective Senders, and the imposed narrative contract which sets the logical bases of the narrative action, the Manipulation phase thus sets off the sequence of three successive phases that the canonic schema leads us to expect. In Bacchylides' poetic narrative, the narrative development of these three other phases is much more succinct. Indeed, while introducing the two heroes and concluding the narrative contract occupies the entire first part of the poem, the rhythm of narration picks up speed in the second part in such a way that the three remaining phases (along with the brief enunciative conclusion) form a second unit of composition. This articulation into two narrative parts corresponds to the metrical form of the poem, and thus also to its choreographic form. The poem

---

[12] Sophocles *Oedipus Tyrannus* 1300–1311 and 1329–1332. The theory of double motivation was taken up and commented notably by Vernant 1972: 63–73.

is composed of two triads, sung and danced in a cretic rhythm, with several paeonic resolutions.[13] Reflected in its metrical and rhythmic structure, the diptych narrative structure of Bacchylides' poem seems to make this composition ideal for a reader inspired by structural analysis!

In this structural and semio-narrative perspective, the Competence phase thus coincides with the beginning of the second part of the dithyrambic composition. Responding immediately to Minos' call, Zeus not only occupies the role of Sender in the narrative action, but also associates his son with that position, at his side. Intending to grant his "dear son" (*phílōi paidí*, line 69) an exceptional honor, the god throws down a dazzling lightning bolt. This wonder (*téras*, line 72) causes an imbalance in the symmetry expected between the two Subjects confronting one another. Through the support granted by his father Zeus, Minos becomes the competent hero who apparently will have to take up conducting the narrative action regarding Theseus. For a while, in any case ...

As a result, we go immediately from the Competence phase to the narrative Performance proper. Given that at the end of the brief preceding phase Minos had appropriated the semio-narrative Competence, Theseus immediately obeys the challenge of the Cretan hero: he plunges into the depths of the sea without even invoking the name of his divine father Poseidon, who is nonetheless the Sender of his action. Minos recalls it once again in his final address to the young Athenian: "your father Poseidon will achieve for you the highest glory" (*kléos*, line 80). This means that the symmetric terms of the narrative contract imposed by Minos in the Manipulation phase are not respected. In fact, the development of the Performance shows a decided reorientation from that moment on. Neither Minos' ring nor Poseidon himself (except indirectly in lines 99 and 109 as Theseus' father) will be mentioned again. The narrative consequence is that Minos continues his voyage toward Crete (implicitly abandoning the confrontation and the ordeal); the explicit logical and moral consequence: Moira (*Moîra*, line 89) was preparing "another course" (different from the one laid out in the narrative contract)! It is the narrator who makes this declaration, an omniscient narrator here since he shows the superior force which presides over the destiny of mortals. One of the rare indirect enunciative interventions included in the narrative, this declaration echoes Theseus' claim that he is respecting the all-powerful destiny (*Moîra pagkratḗs*, line 24) pointed out by the gods. From the beginning of the narrative, the hero does indeed show his will to realize the ineluctable

---

[13] On the thematic and metrical structure of the poem, cf. Maehler 1997:171–174; cf. also Käppel 1992:169–173.

portion allotted to him (*peprōménan aîsan*, lines 26–27) "when it comes" (*hótan élthēi*, lines 27–28; once again the image of progressing!).

It all happens as if the narrative action were now following a divergent program, different from the contract imposed by Minos.[14] With the help of Moira, who in Greek epic narrative represents a force that the gods themselves cannot alter, Theseus now becomes the real Subject of the heroic action.[15] From this point on, he fulfills destiny's plan, and not the one invented by the Cretan sovereign, who is once again in the position of Anti-subject. The Athenian hero confronts the narrative Performance alone.

> ... but the whole group of young Athenians had trembled when the hero sprang into the sea, and they shed tears from their lily-bright eyes, expecting a woeful doom. But sea-dwelling dolphins were swiftly carrying great Theseus to the house of his father, god of horses, and they reached the hall of the gods. There he was awe-struck at the glorious daughters of blessed Nereus, for from their splendid limbs shone a gleam as of fire, and round their hair were twirled gold-braided ribbons; and they were delighting their hearts by dancing with liquid feet. And he saw his father's dear wife, august ox-eyed Amphitrite, in the lovely house ...

> Bacchylides *Dithyramb* 17.93–111 (trans. Campbell 1992:223–225)

The heroic test thus no longer involves bringing back the ring Minos flung into the depths of the sea, but being received in the "benevolent sanctuary of the sea" (line 85). The test is accomplished against Minos' plan, first thanks to the help of dolphins (dear to Apollo), then by the benevolence of the daughters of Nereus engaged in a choral dance (*khorôi*, line 107), and finally thanks to the protection of Amphitrite, wife of Poseidon.[16] The narrative Performance thus consists of a victory over necessity (*anágkē*, line 96). It develops in contrast to the waiting of Theseus' young companions, who are obliged to follow Minos toward Crete for a while longer, separated from the

---

[14] Ieranò, 1989:174–176, described this plot reorientation particularly well: "La moira *pagkratés* (v. 24), *Dika* (v. 25), *aîsa* (v. 27) e il *daímōn* (v. 47) sono richiamati da Teseo come gli unici e veri arbitri della contesa." Remember that this divergence has been interpreted as incoherent; cf. n7 above.

[15] On the purpose of the Homeric *moîra*, see the parallels given by Maehler 1997:189; on Bacchylides' poem, cf. Scodel 1984:140–143.

[16] Daughter of Nereus and of an Oceanid, Amphitrite is already Poseidon's spouse in Hesiod *Theogony* 930 (cf. 240–243); in both legend and religion Apollo maintains a special relationship with dolphins: cf. Calame 1996b:319–322.

itinerary (and the narrative program) of which Theseus is the protagonist (and the Subject)!

Corresponding from the point of view of meter to the epode of the second of the two triads which constitute Bacchylides' poem, the phase of the narrative Sanction is not delayed. Its unfolding is enhanced by a series of visual and aural figures.

> ... (Amphitrite) put a purple cloak about him and set on his thick hair the faultless garland which once at her marriage guileful Aphrodite had given her, dark with roses. Nothing that the gods wish is beyond the belief of sane morals: he appeared beside the slender-sterned ship. Whew, in what thoughts did he check the Cnossian commander when he came unwet from the sea, a miracle for all, and the gods gifts shone on his limbs; and the splendid-throned maidens cried out with new-found joy, and the sea rang out; and nearby the youths raised a paean with lovely voice.

> Bacchylides *Dithyramb* 17.112–129 (trans. Campbell 1992:225–227)

The glorifying conclusion of the plot is thus first marked by the two gifts of Amphitrite to Theseus: a purple garment (*aïóna porphuréan*, line 112) and a crown given by Aphrodite to Poseidon's spouse at her own marriage. Brought back from the depths of the sea, the red garment and crown of roses in some ways take the place of the ring that Theseus was supposed to bring back according to the narrative contract established by Minos. Seen from the narrative's logic, this first element of Sanction confirms the reorientation of the plot and its focus on Theseus, subject of the narrative action. The crown evokes the matrimonial union of the divine father of Theseus with Amphitrite, the young daughter of Nereus, while the purple garment echoes the *kálumma* given by the Nereids to the very young mother of Theseus at her union with the god (lines 35–38).[17]

The semio-narrative Sanction is extended by the sudden reappearance of Theseus, leaping from the sea to rejoin the Cretan ship. This exploit, presented as a cause for astonishment to everyone (*thaûma pántessin*, line 123) and confronting the defeated Minos, is a response to the thunderbolt thrown down by Zeus to confirm his son's legitimacy (lines 56–57); to the wonder (*téras*, line

---

[17] The meaning of *aïón* (hapax) has been debated as much as the meaning of *kálumma*: cf. Maehler 1997:191–192 and 203–204. Perhaps it means the scarf which Theseus wears on the famous red-figure crater at Harvard (Side A) on pp. 142–143; cf. Gentili 1954, and Maehler 1997:179–180, with the bibliographic references given here in n31.

72) produced by Minos' father, there is now a corresponding visual miracle, the return of Theseus from his father's home in the sea. The identical metrical position taken by the two expressions involved confirms this correspondence formally.[18] In recalling the brightness "visible to all" (*panderkéa*, line 70) of the sign sent by Minos' divine father, the gifts of the gods are conspicuous through their light which shines on the limbs of the young Athenian hero. Finally, the Sanction phase concludes with the ritual cries of the maidens (*koûrai*, line 125), accompanied by the echo of the sea itself and by the paean sung by the young men accompanying Theseus (*eítheoi ... néoi*, lines 128–129). This song of victory and thanks adds auditory impressions to the different visual facets of a luminous Sanction.

The forms *ōlóluxan* (line 127) and *paiánixan* (line 129) in the aorist, designating ritual cries and the paean, mark the end of the narrative: time of narration and recounted time come together. The Sanction of this heroic action recounted at length by Bacchylides proves finally to be a song of thanks.

2.2. From ordeal to tribal initiation ritual

Since the time of narration in Bacchylides' *Dithyramb* 17 follows a development which practically coincides with time recounted, independently from the time of the uttered enunciation, its very linear rhythm has fueled modern critics in their accusations concerning the poet's imagination. This narrative and temporal unfolding, which does indeed conform to the logic of the plot, nonetheless offers spatial devices which should arouse curiosity.

Certainly the space in which the narrative action takes place shows some blurring within its very unity. The protagonists of the plot are on a vessel propelled by Boreas on the "sea of Crete" (line 4), which is to say—for us—on a boat sailing south on the Aegean sea, somewhere between Athens and Knossos. But along with this horizontal movement on the sea, a vertical dimension is also developed. As regards Minos, the relationship of the Cretan hero with his father Zeus implies not only the lofty ether (line 73) from where Zeus sends the heavenly bolt of lightning (*ap' ouranoû*, line 55), but also the heights of Ida (line 30) where the hero of Crete was born (line 30). From this perspective, as we have mentioned, Minos pictures for Theseus glory which will spread throughout the "wooded earth" (*khthóna kat' eúdendron*, line 80). For Minos, Poseidon is the god who "shakes the earth" (*seisíkhthōn*, line 58), even if his palace is to be found at the bottom of the sea (line 63)! In contrast

---

[18] As pointed out so well by Burnett 1985:25–26.

to these celestial and terrestrial spatial images, Theseus' relationship with the depths of the sea is illustrated from the very beginning, and by Minos himself. Theseus is introduced as the son of Poseidon of the sea (*Póntios*, line 36), his birth under the protection of the Nereids (line 38). It is also the Nereids who receive the young Athenian hero in the undersea palace of their sister Amphitrite (lines 110–111). And the entire second part of the poem is dedicated to the Athenian's dive into the depths of the sea.

This structure, which we can reconstruct as the basis of the spatial configuration sketched in Bacchylides' poem, thus has three poles: the heavens (dominated by Zeus), the depths of the sea (the kingdom of Poseidon and his spouse Amphitrite), and the surface of the earth and sea on which mortals progress (with the help of Aphrodite and Athena, auxiliary Senders, but finally victims of their own *moîra*).

The structure of this tri-polar configuration and spatial representation apparently depends heavily on the temporal and logical development of the narration. After the long Manipulation phase, marked by a verbal exchange between the surface of the sea and the heavens, the moment of Competence is distinguished, in poem 17 of Bacchylides, by the vertical and punctual movement of the lightning bolt which descends from the ether toward the surface where mortals (heroes) progress. From a spatial point of view, the Performance phase is also characterized by a vertical movement, in this particular case from the surface toward the depths of the sea. But because of the divergence in reorienting the narrative program (already mentioned), this downward movement is accompanied by the horizontal movement of the vessel which stays on course toward Crete. Finally, the Sanction phase takes place partly in the depths of the sea (as regards the divine consecration which it represents), and partly on the deck of the ship (as regards the recognition by men). Multidimensional, the narrative episode put into poetry by Bacchylides ends up linking together the principal elements of the cosmos, as Greeks of the classical period imagined it. It takes on a cosmological depth which is essential to its pragmatic function, especially as it relates to the position of the island of Delos at the geographic center of what will become the Aegean sea.[19]

Modern readers, not particularly sensitive to the cosmological dimension of Bacchylides' narrative, have mostly focused their attention on the second part of the poem: Theseus' plunge into the sea, his welcome into the divine residence of Amphitrite, and his return celebrated by the choral victory ode performed by the young men and women accompanying the Athenian hero.

---

[19] For the cosmogonic and cosmologic position of Delos, see Calame 1996a:84–85.

Focusing on the dive, Theseus' marine itinerary has often been interpreted in initiatory terms, referring to three different types of rite of passage:

- tribal initiation rite securing the transition from adolescence to adulthood, like the version of the "myth" which tells of young Eumolpos, thrown into the sea, picked up by his father Poseidon, raised by a daughter of Poseidon and Amphitrite, as an adult befriending the people of Eleusis and participating in the founding of the mystery rites;

- rite of immortalization, like Glaukos, a young fisherman from Anthedon in Boeotia, who jumps into the sea to become a *daímōn*, and hence a seer for men;

- "ordeal" as a test of innocence with its purifying effect, like Aerope, the granddaughter of Minos who was accused of allowing herself to be seduced by a slave and was thrown into the sea, and later married Pleisthenes to whom she bore Agamemnon and Menelaus.[20]

Anne Pippin Burnett, summarizing the different interpretations given to Theseus' dive, concludes: "Theseus left the ship a boy but returns a man, prepared for a form of marriage with Ariadne, and prepared also to assume his father's duties when he gets back to Athens."[21]

But if we take into account the status of the protagonists both for the dive and for the entire narrative, along with the types of objects exchanged during that dive, the "initiatory" nature of the transition and the transformation undergone by Theseus is far from obvious.

2.3. Erotic images

First of all, as regards the figurative qualities of the principal protagonists of the plot, both Minos and Theseus are introduced from the start as heroes—war heroes, and consequently epic heroes. Minos is first explicitly described as a

---

[20] Biography of Eumolpos: Apollodorus *Library* 3.15.4 (cf. Euripides *TrGF* 349 Kannicht[2]); Glaukos: Pausanias 9.22.6–7, summarizing the plot of *Glaukos Pontios* by Aeschylus (*TrGF* 142–148 Radt); Aerope: Apollodorus *Library* 3.2.1–2. Organized somewhat differently, the various interpretive possibilities and more or less pertinent examples are touched on by Burnett 1985:29–32; associated with them are notably the names of Gustave Glotz, Louis Gernet, Henri Jeanmaire, Angelo Brelich, Pierre Vidal-Naquet, etc.; see also Ieranó 1987:168–172, for a comparison with the propitiatory rite performed by Jason before facing the test of the golden fleece (Apollonius Rhodius 3.1201–1224).

[21] Burnett 1985:32.

"hero" (*hérōs*, line 23), then as "warlord of the Knossians" (*polémarkhe Knōsíōn*, line 39) by Theseus, while the speaker-narrator describes him as "staunch in battle: (*meneptólemos hérōs*, line 73) and as "general of Knossos" (*Knósion stratagétan*, lines 120–121). The poet calls Theseus himself first "steadfast in battle" (*menéktu[pon*, line 1), "bronze-corsleted" (*khalkothóra[ka*, lines 14–15), "spear-valiant hero" (*arétaikhmos hérōs*, line 47), then, in turn, just at the moment when he dives, in front of the young people on the deck of the boat, simply "hero" (*hérōs*, line 94)! Minos' only advantage over Theseus is the wartime superiority granted him by his status as general, but he is never described as king (of Knossos).

As for the Athenian hero, he is never presented as an adolescent or as a young man, either before or after his visit to the home of Poseidon and Amphitrite. Theseus reappears perfectly dry (*adíantos*, line 122) after his dive into the sea. This miraculous fact no doubt relates to the visual wonder (*thaûma*, line 123) of the hero's appearance, in the light which shines on his body from the flash of the divine gifts he wears. It is also in this context that the reference to his curly hair (*kómai oûlai*, line 113) must be understood. This is undoubtedly not so much an allusion to the long hair of an adolescent as a reference to the curls "like hyacinth flowers" that Athena gives to Odysseus, when she intends to make the hero appear a god to Nausicaa; "truly, he looks a god," declares the girl, stricken by the graceful beauty of the adult metamophosed by Athena.[22] In this scene, the curls evoke both erotic light and divine appearance. Divine light emanating from Theseus himself, when he reappears from the bottom of the sea in a kind of epiphany, is substituted for the light of Zeus' lightning bolt brought on by Minos.

These, then, are the values implied in several of the images taken by the Sanction phase of Bacchylides' long poetic narrative. Much the same could be said of the gifts which Amphitrite gives to the Athenian hero. In itself an entirely polysemic ritual object, the crown that Theseus wears when he reappears on the deck of the ship sailing toward Crete is explicitly introduced as a wedding present given originally by the guileful Aphrodite. In this context, the purple garment (*aïóna porphuréan*, line 112), with the probable erotic connotation of its color, can be referred to the cloak which, in both love poetry and iconography, represents the union (matrimonial or not) between two adults, under the sign of Aphrodite and her familiar Eros. Associated with the erotic bond of marriage, the divine gifts (line 124; see also line 116) echo the "sacred gifts of Kypris" (*Kúpridos hagnà dôra*, line 10), the goddess with the headband

---

[22] *Odyssey* 6.224–243; on the meaning of *adíantos*, cf. Maehler 1997:207.

who inspires the desire of love; it is she who, just like the "bitter-sweet" Eros of Sappho, touches the heart of Minos; it is she who thus brings about the situation of narrative Lack which begins the story told in Bacchylides' poem.[23]

2.4. Aphrodite and marriage

Before granting any sort of initiatory interpretation to the transformation of Theseus after the test represented by his plunge into the sea and his welcome in the home of Amphitrite, we must turn to the semantic contrast which brings into relation the beginning of the narrative and its conclusion, and which carries the entire plot: the attempt at sexual violence by a hero and warlord on a girl (*parthenikâs*, line 11) contrasts with the reception of a warrior hero by the adult spouse of a sea god. The young spouse Amphitrite takes the place of the girl Athena as an additional Sender of Theseus. On the other hand, the initial narrative action and the final action are both placed under the sign of erotic gifts from Aphrodite, who, to accomplish the initial action, wears "a headband that inspires loving desire" (*himerámpukos*, line 9), and who, for the final action, is designated by the traditional description of "guileful" (*dólios*, line 116): Kypris attached by her name to an insular territory at the start of the poem, Aphrodite associated by legend with the sea at its conclusion—this may not be coincidental. However that may be, the "(aphrodisiac) gifts of the gods" (*theôn dôra*, line 124) given to Theseus when he reappears from the waves correspond to the "sacred gifts" of Kypris which strike Minos at the beginning of the poem (*hagnà dôra*, line 10), as we have just shown.[24]

What is striking in the miraculous reappearance of Theseus from the sea after his brief stay in the home of the divine Amphitrite, much more than any initiatory passage from adolescence to adulthood, is the deification of the epic hero, in a sort of epiphany. The process of deification is matched with a passage from the relationship of son to a nearly matrimonial relationship. After being

---

[23] Eros *glukúpikros*: Sappho fr. 130.1–2 Voigt; descending from the sky, this same Eros wears a purple mantle: fr. 54 Voigt; see also frr. 44.9 and 92.8 Voigt as well as Simonides fr. 543.16–17 Page. On the iconographic and textual meaning of erotic union under the mantle, see the references I gave in 1996a:134–138. The aphrodisiac connotations of the roses and the crown are described by Burnett 1985:165n16.

[24] This semantic echo which reinforces the erotic isotopy running through the poem is well explained by Brown 1991. On the two qualifiers used to describe Aphrodite, see the relevant parallels given by Maehler 1997:186–187 and 204. The probable contrast between the insular Kypris and the marine Aphrodite (see on this Walker 1995:92–94) was suggested to me by one of the participants in the EHESS seminar where this reading of the Bacchylides' poem was first presented.

recognized by the wife of his father, Theseus himself is treated like a young bridegroom; rather than a son-in-law, he in some ways acquires the status of Amphitrite's fiancé, while she herself seems to assume the status of young bride implied in having no child! Because the presents Amphitrite gives to the young Athenian hero all bear Aphrodite's values, it is as if the adult woman were seducing and attaching the young man to herself in an erotic relationship, in contrast to the beginning of the narrative where it is the adult male, Minos, who lays hands on the young girl Eriboia. If a comparative parallel is needed to confirm the plausibility of this reading of Theseus' deifying plunge into the waves, one could cite the narrative of the young Phoebus Apollo leaping like a dolphin onto the vessel of Cretan sailors (from Knossos!) to guide them to Krisa, then to commit them to found the sanctuary at Delphi, which could confirm the etiological and founding role of Bacchylides' narrative. We shall return to this. And as for a ritual parallel, it could be found in the wish of "Anacreon," as a poet "drunk with Eros,"[25] to leap into the sea from the famous promontory of Leukas.

From a semantic point of view, an erotic isotopy under the sign of Aphrodite and her symbols, runs throughout all of Bacchylides' *Dithyramb* 17. We witness the transition from the erotic relationship of an adult hero with an adolescent girl to the ambiguous relationship of an adult divinity with a young hero; in a sort of passage from war to love, this transfer by its reorientation leads us to witness a sort of "feminization" of the main protagonist of the plot. Theseus finally reappears among the young Athenian men and women being carried toward Crete, wearing the symbolic garment and crown that mark him as a young bride! From that, it is probably not a simple coincidence that the young Athenian hero bears a strange resemblance to the young Nereids he has just left. If the Nereids are said to be bathed in a bright light emanating from their limbs as they rejoice their hearts in a choral dance (*khorôi d' éterpon*, line 107–108), we learn that Theseus is also miraculously flooded with light coming from the gifts of the gods. His appearance prompts the choral song that has been mentioned, sung in a voice which inspires erotic desire (*eratâi opí*, line 129), in the expression which closes the entire narrative.

The Athenian hero thus attains a new status as a quasi-bride. His accession to this highly ambiguous status by his legitimization in the watery

---

[25] *Homeric Hymn to Apollo* 388–501: Anacreon fr. 376 Page, with the interpretation proposed by Nagy 1990a:228–234 (cf. also Ieranò 1989:182n42); other, less pertinent parallels are given by Burnett 1985:33–35. I owe to David Bouvier the remark on the status of *númphē* assumed by Amphitrite (in contrast to Athena *parthénos*).

divine palace is accompanied by a substitution of his stepmother Amphitrite for his father Poseidon, but also by a narrative substitution of a quasi-matrimonial relationship for one of sexual violence. Recognition and legitimization through the conferring of gifts, preparations reminiscent of a marriage ceremony, deification in epiphany: Theseus' destiny as it is redrawn by Bacchylides is nevertheless very different from that of the hero of marriage itself, Hymenaeus, who dies an adolescent before the transition takes place. And from this point of view it contrasts with the destiny reserved for the son of the Athenian hero, Hippolytus.

Starting from a debatable initiatory interpretation, we thus come to a spatial-temporal configuration that implies gender relationships so paradoxical and so ambiguous that only comparison with the workings of a contemporary exotic culture seems capable of supplying a hermeneutic expedient which could be relevant. We thus come to the third point of the proposed comparative triangle: from the contemporary idea of gender, to classical Greek poetics, and finally to the initiatory rites practiced along the banks of the Sepik.

3. From the Aegean Sea to the banks of the Sepik: Comparisons

And so we issue an invitation to a brief comparative incursion into Papua New Guinea, to the banks of the river Sepik. The author of these lines once visited the curved banks of this meandering and languid river, occupied by the lake-dwelling Iatmul in the central part, and by the land-dwelling Abelam a bit farther north. The occasion was to spend several weeks there in order to give a comparative aspect to a research project on political and "initiatory" reorientations of the legend of Theseus in classical Athens. But the brief and again comparative visit I offer here is based less on my own experience in the field than on reports and interpretations offered by my colleagues of the *Ethnologisches Seminar* in Basel. The glimpse which I shall try to provide of two communities and two cultures of the Sepik will thus be even more asymmetric, since the very quick spatial-temporal configuration I would like to display here is based on my own prefigurations and on some of the discursive and textual configurative elaborations supplied by those who visited the Iatmul and the Abelam before I did.[26] This double asymmetry is somewhat analogous

---

[26] On this constituent asymmetry of the anthropological view and on the subject of aspects of prefiguration and schematization found in the "documents" and "accounts," cf. chapter I, n46 and n57.

to the general position of the Hellenist, whose discursive configurations not only are marked by his own cultural preconstructions, but also depend on the orientation and representations which belong to the indigenous "documents" which make up his "field." Because of the essentially mediate nature of an "observation" which can be based only on the *enárgeia* produced by discourses, I shall demonstrate here several analogies which are at a rather abstract and functional level, leaving behind the contrasts praised at the end of the preceding chapter.

3.1. Masculine tribal initiation: The Iatmul

Despite the integration of both boys and girls into a European-type school system generally run by Christian missionaries, the various village communities of the Middle Sepik Iatmul continue to impose on their male adolescents a tribal initiation ritual, in the strict sense of that term in modern anthropology. After a period of several weeks of separation and seclusion, not in the forest but in the upper part of *haus tambaran*, the house of the men and the ancestors, young adolescents all of about the same age undergo a long and painful scarifying operation; the ritualized sequence takes place inside a ritual enclosure built on the ceremonial square in the middle of the village. Through practices easily interpreted in terms of a symbolic death, the initiates receive marks which leave folds in the skin on their backs, making them resemble the crocodiles of the Sepik. They leave the enclosure through a narrow opening, a ritual symbol of a new birth, following the same interpretive line. The public reappearance of the new initiates is marked by various ritual dances of welcome, in particular by their biological mothers. These choreographic movements are accompanied by the musical beating of drums made from hollowed-out tree trunks, whose sound is supposed to imitate the sounds of the crocodile. From this day forward, the young initiates will bear, inscribed on their bodies, the marks of a metaphoric identity which makes the Iatmul the sons of the Sepik.[27]

The etiological explanation of the initiatory tattooing summarized here was given to a researcher from Basel by a native of Yensan, the "mother village" of Palimbei where I once stayed as a brief ethnological preparation for my reading of Athenian narratives on Theseus.[28]

---

[27] Various ethnographic descriptions of the Iatmul tribal initiation ritual are reported by Roscoe and Scaglion 1990:415; see also Stanek 1983:292–296.

[28] Text in pidgin and in German translation in Schmid and Kocher-Schmid 1992:237–239 and 179–180. They report another etiological version (175–178) where the women undergo scarification, as well.

In the time of the ancestors (the Greeks would speak of *próteroi*), only one man carried the scars on his back, a man named Korubangi. The other men, who also wanted to have such marks, decided to catch as many crocodiles as there were men and male children. They enclosed the animals in a strong pen from which they could not escape, built just for this and called *ndimba*. When released inside the enclosure, the crocodiles attacked the ancestors and ate their sons. The men killed the crocodiles, and buried only the heads of their children, to let the skin and flesh rot away. The fathers kept the secret of their sons' deaths, and let their wives bring food for the children up to the moment when their wounds had scarred over and when they decided to leave the crocodile pen. The dancing women wept when they received the heads of their children, then buried them once again in the enclosure, and organized a large feast to mourn the deaths of their sons. Then, taking the initiative after the dramatic failure of their husbands, the women decided to take action on a symbolic level. They devised knives of bamboo, and inside a new enclosure they gashed their children's skin, then treated the wounds with salve made from a tree. When the scarring was complete, they took wood from another tree and made sound boxes whose vibrations, produced by a piece of rope, imitated the sound of crocodiles. When their children's scars were completely formed, the women and their relatives organized a celebratory dance in costumes around the house of the men, to welcome their sons who, healed, had left the enclosure.

More than with the narrative of Theseus' plunge into the Sea of Crete, this etiological narrative of the Sepik offers some strange analogies with the episode of the heroic biography of Theseus which immediately follows it: the test of the Labyrinth at Knossos. Superficial resemblances include not only the (symbolic and perhaps initiatory) death which the young Athenian men and women are subjected to when they are sent to be devoured by the Minotaur, but the various functions attributed to women as well. In both the Greek *mûthos* and in the Melanesian *sagi,* women take on the role of nursing mother (*deipnophóroi*) as regards their sons, but Ariadne's intelligent skill in mastering the Labyrinth and in inspiring the dance which celebrates it calls to mind the art of practical metaphor implemented by the women of Yensan![29] However,

---

[29] On various aspects of the episode of the Labyrinth at Knossos, see Calame 1996b:145–146 and 239–242.

these surface images offer nothing but figurative analogies which are not necessarily functional. The comparison cannot be confined to this very superficial level.

Nonetheless, the prose narrative from the Yensan "informant" offers several more pertinent semantic and pragmatic kernels to aid in understanding what is at stake narratively and functionally in the version of Theseus' dive poetically formulated by Bacchylides. On the one hand, we note the role played by women with regard to a series of symbolic objects and practices, in an etiological narrative meant to account for a tribal ritual initiation sequence intended for a group of adolescents. This narrative is part of an anthropology (understood as a representation of the human being and his creation) where one believes that the flesh is fed by the mother's blood, while growth of the bones depends on the male sperm. This representation of the differentiated development of the human organism must be understood within the context of an anthropopoiesis (understood as a representation of man's fabrication); according to this anthropopoietic conception realized in the ritual, at adolescence the mother's blood must be eliminated from the body of the young man and future adult.[30] We must also note the semantic position and profile assumed by an animal which, in various versions of the Iatmul cosmogonic narrative, represents the foundation of the world: a Yensan version, for example, puts forth a primordial crocodile reduced to feeding on air, in the process of creating the cosmos. His lower jaw becomes the earth, his upper jaw the sky, his eyes become the sun and the moon, while from his tongue are born the first two human brothers.[31]

3.2. Puberty rites for girls: The Abelam

The comparatist incursion into the Iatmul region of rivers and lakes showed us a version of a basic legend meant to explain the creation of a tribal initial rite for adolescent boys. If we are to glance at speculations brought about by social roles and reciprocal representations of both genders within ritual practice itself and involving adolescents, we must leave the banks of the Sepik to move on to the nearby hill country inhabited by the Abelam.

The very rapid geographic and intellectual tour offered here is conditioned by historic development, as well as by my own personal stay, which the

---

[30] A detailed description of such an anthropology and its initiatory and anthropopoietic use by men of the Sambia tribe is given by Herdt 1994:217–254 (for the feminine counterpart, see 172–202).

[31] Cf. Schmid and Kocher-Schmid 1992:10–12, 115–116, and 189 for Yensan; Stanek 1983:200–204, in Palimbei, for an entirely different cosmogonic version.

flooding of the Sepik turned away from Palimbei and its crocodile-haunted banks toward Kimbangawa in the area where yams are cultivated. The Iatmul, once headhunters, stopped organizing tribal initiation rites for groups of girls from prominent families and clans toward the end of the nineteenth century. And though the entire initiatory program for adolescent girls has been eliminated, an individual rite of passage for adolescent girls is still practiced today in the nearby villages occupied by the Abelam. In terms of categories accepted by anthropologists, this is not a tribal initiation rite, but rather a puberty rite, celebrated individually in that it is attached to the highly individual first menses of the girl.[32]

The Abelam puberty rite culminates in a public ceremony called *wambusuge*, from *wambe*, the name of the cane whose juice is used to wash the girl when she leaves the menstruation hut at the very edge of the forest; she is confined there at the first appearance of menstrual blood. While the adolescent girl is still confined in the ritual hut, her mother, helped by her relatives and also by her husband, collects various vegetarian foods, among them the yams called *wapi*. Exceptionally and for this occasion, women are allowed to handle these oblong ceremonial potatoes which are grown and cultivated by men and which are displayed before the painted facade of the ceremonial house. Cut up by the brothers and the father, these yams are then distributed, along with other foods, among the mainly female guests at the ceremony, in a large exchange involving only women. It is only the following day that the girl can leave the menstruation house, after having been washed with the juice of the cane called *wambe*. Her head is shaved, and during the several days which mark her return to the community she wears shell necklaces, as well as new textile made by her mother. About fifty years ago, the chest, stomach, and arms of the young Abelam girl initiate were scarified by a specialist, who used the same stone knife used to draw blood from the penis of the young bridegroom; through this practice equivalent to feminine scarification, the body of the young man was supposed to be freed from the blood accumulated during the first period of intense sexual relations with his young spouse.

Certainly the way of conducting puberty rites for young Abelam girls shows no surface similarities either to Bacchylides' narrative inspired by initiation or to what we know generally of initiatory rites of passage for adolescent girls in the cities of ancient Greece. But in order to understand the

---

[32] Cf. Hauser-Schäublin 1995:35–41, who refers to his own work related to this ritual. The occasional submission of girls to the tribal initiation ritual intended for boys among the Iatmul is reported by Schmid and Kocher-Schmid 1992:171–173.

implications both for spatio-temporality and for the gender relationships, it is essential to have some understanding of the meaning conferred by the natives on the ritual yams cultivated by the men of Abelam villages. Western anthropologists of course attributed to these ceremonial tubers the phallic meaning which their oblong shape evokes, along with their relationship to a typically masculine *ethos*, but the Abelam consider the *wapi* as human beings. In the metaphoric interpretation of the ritual potatoes, the different parts of the yam take the names of different limbs of the human body, while all signs of growth are associated with female childbearing organs; reciprocally, a ceremonial dancer is viewed as a yam. From that, the production of these long tubers represents for men their way of engendering and educating children, through an impressive series of metaphors referring to birth and nursing. Conversely, the young adolescent girl experiencing her first menstruation is compared to the secret stone kept in the ceremonial house; in comparison to the vulva or to a menstruating woman, this stone (despite its phallic shape!) is supposed to contribute to the growth of the *wapi* yams.[33] While a ritual for girls and women is involved, the technical practices and metaphorical anthropopoietic games are taken on by the men.

Consequently, practices of anthropopoiesis—or more precisely of andropoiesis and gynecopoiesis—of a native community depend heavily on an overall concept of human beings, of their organic and sexual identity. These relationships between ritual practices and anthropopoietic representations are so strong that their "translation" for a Western public precludes any projection of metaphors that support our own representations and relationships between the sexes, so strong that their specific nature forbids any direct transfer from an initiatory schema to the etiological legends which explain them and which justify their being carried out. The brief trip into Iatmul territory showed that in the etiological narrative, the central role played by women in a symbolic temporality and spatiality contrasts with the minor practical duties they assume in the time and space of the tribal initiation ritual for young men. By way of contrast, among the Abelam, the entire series of ritual gestures and manipulations brought about by a young girl's first menstrual blood is marked by interaction and complementarity between the organic and procreational duties specific to women, and the technical and metaphorical production role assumed by men. Through a concept of the nature of human

---

[33] The different metaphorical effects stemming from the ceremonial tubers are touched on by Hauser-Schäublin 1995:41–47, who gives references to different phallic interpretations proposed by modern anthropologists (41).

beings and of anthropopoiesis in which metaphor plays an essential role, the symbolic practices of ritual in some ways redress the "natural" and biological imbalance between the gender roles, where engendering is concerned. All in all, it is a compensation through symbolic means for the physiological and organic asymmetry between the sexes.

4. The practices of enunciative poetry

From this overly brief and too rapid comparative approach, we can draw at least two more general semantic conclusions. First of all, it seems that from the point of view of narration, the etiological explanation given for instituting a tribal ritual initiation practice can be founded in the narrative of the creation of the cosmos. And in moving from the (cosmogonic) "myth" to "ritual," we notice that ritual practice is composed of such a dense fabric of symbolic procedures and relevant concepts related to the practical metaphor that this interplay of symbolic creation and metaphoric translation can, both in social institutions and through the work of culture, rebalance the organic contribution and the "biological" status of each sex.

Through the metaphoric and symbolic rebalancing discussed, the question of syntactic and semantic logic which fits the sequence of ritual practices into the development of a narrative for memory for a polical identity thus brings us back to Bacchylides' *Dithyramb* 17 and its spatial-temporal logic.[34]

4.1. Time and space recounted in the spatial-temporal frame of enunciation

In Bacchylides' composition, the expected narrative movement from recounted time and space to the time and space of the (uttered) enunciation takes place only at the very end of the poem, in the last three lines.

> God of Delos, rejoice in your heart at the choirs of the Keans and grant a heaven-sent fortune of blessings.
>
> *Dithyramb* 17.130–132 (trans. Campbell 1992:227)

From a spatial point of view, the address to Apollo as the god of Delos relates the time of the poem's "performance" to that sacred island: the god is invited to rejoice in the choral dances of the people of Keos (*khoroîsi Kēíōn,*

---

[34] I tried to envisage this etiological relationship between "myth" and "rite" in semio-narrative terms in my work 1996b:162–177.

lines 130–131). In the same way, Apollo is involved in the interplay of *do ut des* which concludes, for instance, many *Homeric Hymns*. This poem itself, both in its long narrative of the great deeds of Theseus and in its choral performance, is thus presented to the god of Delos as an offering in exchange for the benefits which the gods may send to the performers of the composition.[35]

From this enunciative perspective, which poses the question of spatial relationship between the uttered enunciation and the historical circumstances of the poem's communication, one might well wonder why Apollo, as god of the lyre and of choral dance, is neither evoked nor invoked at the beginning of the poem, as the gods concerned are addressed in a *Homeric Hymn*, or as the Muses are at the beginning of an epic narrative poem, or even of a melic poem. As we have already mentioned, the beginning of the composition of *Dithyramb* 17 coincides atypically with the *incipit* of the narrative. In this beginning, which is narrative from the very start, the introduction of Theseus (line 2) in some ways substitutes for the expected address to the divine authority who inspires the poem. This may simply be one possibility offered by the rules of the dithyramb genre. Not content with an especially developed narration, the lyric form may also permit a "dramatic" staging, to take up the concept Plato develops concerning narrative and mimetic poetry.[36] Devoted to an exchange between king Aegeus and a choral group narrating the young Theseus' arrival in Athens, Bacchylides' *Dithyramb* 18, for example, shows the affinities of certain of these compositions labeled *Dithyrambs* with contemporary tragedy: and in this there is no place for a prelude or an invocation of the Muse. Unless Theseus, introduced narratively in the very first part of the poem and destined to reappear in an epiphany at the end of the narrative, takes the place of inspirational authority ...

There is also the question of the practical relationship between the fictional space shaped in the poem and the real space of its performance. This passage between two narrative utterances, the utterance of the enunciation and the situation of communication, leads us back to the spatial and temporal profile shaped by these three internal and external levels of discourse; it brings us back to the spatial-temporal regime formed by their interweaving and coinciding. But this question of temporal putting-into-discourse and pragmatics

---

[35] The movement of reciprocity in the offering is pointed out by Maehler 1997:209–210; it is explained for various forms of hymns by Vamvouri-Ruffy 2004b.

[36] Plato *Republic* 392c–395b, along with several remarks on this subject I made in 2000b:22–23; Plato himself (394c), places the dithyramb with the narration assumed by the poet (*di' appag-gelías autoû toû poiētoû*, 394c); see also Schröder 2000:137–149 or Ieranò 1989.

also immerses us in the controversy concerning the genre of Bacchylides' poem 17: a dithyramb as it is termed in the Alexandrian edition of the work of the poet of Keos, or a paean, as a series of intra-discursive allusions indicate?

The conclusion of Bacchylides' melic composition is particularly significant both for the space and time configured in the poem and for the question of poetic genre to which it belongs. During the concluding Sanction phase of the narrative, the luminous return of Theseus to the deck of the Cretan ship, like a god in epiphany, is celebrated with ritual cries (*ōlóluxan*, line 127; again in the aorist) of the young women (*koûrai*, line 125), while beside them the young men (*ēítheoi d' eggúthen néoi*, lines 128–129) sing the paean of victory (*paiánixan*, line 129; also in the aorist); they sing with a voice which arouses erotic desire (*eratâi opí*, line 129). Here we can recognize the complementarity established between *ololugé* and *paîan* in the religious tradition. In Bacchylides' poem 17, this ritual song is danced and sung by a mixed choral group; this group corresponds to the "twice seven youths and maidens" (*dìs heptà koúrous*, lines 2–3) mentioned along with Theseus in the initial part of the poem, by way of prelude to the poem. It is probably not a simple coincidence that the ring structure, which refers the end of recounted time and the time of narration back to their common beginning, places prominently this group, henceforth choral, of Athenian youths and maidens. It is certainly the mention of this choral group, from recounted space and time, that introduces the final evocation of choral groups which, in the time and space of the (uttered) enunciation, are likely to sing Bacchylides' poem.

In concluding the *Dithyramb*, choral groups of the Keans are thus called upon to rejoice the heart of Delian Apollo, who is invoked directly. But the mention of "choirs," in the plural, leaves unresolved several ambiguities concerning the precise relationship between this reference to the uttered enunciation and the cultural and historical reality of the "performance" of Bacchylides' poem.

For the moment, and quite separately from the question of the genre (paean or dithyramb?) to which Bacchylides' narrative composition belongs, we must turn from time toward space, to try to grasp the delicate passage that these final lines bring about, from the (uttered) enunciation to the situation of communication. Indeed, the epithet *Délios* (*Dálie*, line 130) used to invoke Apollo, relates back not only to the island of Delos—as we have already mentioned—but also to the festival of Delia, celebrated in honor of the god protecting the island. Everyone knows that even the bard of the *Homeric Hymn to Apollo* sang of the festive and religious gathering of the Ionians on Delos to celebrate and rejoice in the god of the lyre through their songs and dances.

Thucydides himself, speaking of the purification of the island after the first five years of the Peloponnesian War, mentions the choral groups traditionally sent by Ionian cities to Delos for this event. Later, the Athenians themselves joined in a quadrennial celebration which included musical competitions, notably in the famous naval procession which, according to Plato, postponed the time set for Socrates' execution.[37]

We should also mention the famous etiological legend of the crane dance, a ritual dance probably included in the celebration of the Delia. The legend tells that it was instituted and performed for the first time at Delos by the youths and maidens who had escaped from the Labyrinth in Crete, led by their choregos Theseus, along with honors given to both Apollo and Aphrodite at the same time. The crane dance refers metaphorically not only to the alternating flights of this bird, but, by imitation, to the comings and goings of the young Athenian men and women in the dwelling of the Minotaur. By staging after the Knossos episode the same young Athenian males and females that Bacchylides describes before their experience in the Labyrinth, this legend could help confirm the supposition that some of the adolescent choirs singing and dancing for the Delia were mixed groups. And including in the great festival of Delos a celebration related to Aphrodite seems to offer for the Delia the strong semantic correspondence which Bacchylides' narrative maintains with the seductions of Eros and with the transition to adult love.[38]

In summary, the last three lines of Bacchylides' poem offer not only a very clever temporal transition from the temporality of narration (Theseus sailing toward Crete) and recounted time (the era of Theseus) to the time of the uttered enunciation (choral performance by the "Keans"), to lead finally to the historical time of the extra-discursive communication of the poem, in Delos itself for the celebration of Apollo in the context of the Delia. But through their musical activity, these three lines also provide a geographical passage from recounted space (the depths of the sea) marked by the choral song of the Nereids to the equally narrative space of Minos' ship, with its choral "performance" of the paean by the fourteen young men and women accompanying Theseus, finally leading to the space enunciated in the poem (the choral area where the choral groups of "Keans" perform), which corre-

---

[37] *Homeric Hymn to Apollo* 146–175; Thucydides 3.104.1–6; Plato *Phaedo* 58a–b (cf. n43 below); cf. Burnett 1985:22 and 35–37; Ieranò 1989:151–161; Käppel 1992:173–178; and Maehler 1997:167–170, with the additional bibliographic information I gave in 1996b:159–161.

[38] Delia and Aphrodisia, as related to the etiological use of the Cretan episode of the Theseus legend, was the subject of a detailed study which I presented in 1996b:116–121, 159–162, and 251–254. On the crane dance, cf. n42 below.

sponds to the religious space of Delos devoted to Apollo.[39] Defining the twice seven young Athenian women and men as Ionians at the beginning of the poem is probably only a poetic way of indicating both their heroic quality and their Athenian origins, to make of them finally and etiologically the choral group paradigmatic of the one called upon to perform Bacchylides' dithyramb, in the *hic et nunc* of the celebration of the Delia.[40]

4.2. Signature, *aition*, and poetic genre

From an enunciative point of view, three conclusions may be drawn from this spatial-temporal movement which is narrative, enunciative, and pragmatic.

First of all, while probably echoing the description of the mixed group of young Athenian women and men as Ionians at the beginning of the poem, the concluding mention of the Kean choruses who are called upon to delight Apollo is doubly significant. Not only does this evocation represent a sort of synecdoche, recalling all the choral groups—from Ionia, from the islands of the Aegean sea, from Athens—who dance at the Delia in honor of the god of Delos, but because of the civic identity of these young men and women chorally celebrating Theseus' return to the Cretan ship, there is little doubt that this synecdoche also offers a form of *sphragís* at the end of the composition.

This signature in the form of a seal is double, in that it applies both to the choral quality and to the Kean origin of the groups mentioned. Indeed, both the voice of the probably mixed choral groups who perform the poem at Delos, and the voice of the poet Bacchylides of Keos who composed it, converge in the choral voice which realizes the interaction between the different spatial-temporal levels. Very probably, and contrary to what is generally believed, this chorus is Athenian rather than Kean, modeled on the legendary choral group celebrating Theseus' return to the ship. Such coincidence between the voice of the poet and the voice of the chorus singing the poem, despite a divergent civic identity, can be detected in a number of Pindar's compositions, whether in the *Epicinian Odes*, the *Partheneia* (sung by a chorus of girls), or the *Paeans*; through a subtle game of "choral delegation," the forms of *I/we* assuming the

---

[39] The chorus formed on Minos' ship by the seven Athenian youths being taken to Crete, accompanied by the ritual cries of their female companions, must not be confused with the chorus of the Nereids (*sic* Ieranò 1989:173–174): cf. Calame 1996b:206–209 and Maehler 1997:208–209, who points out that inserting the gnomic remark in lines 117–118 corresponds to the passage from the divine world to the mortal world.

[40] In the same way, in Bacchylides *Dithyramb* 18.2, Aegeus the king of Athens is called "Lord of the Ionians"; on this, see commentary by Maehler 1997:220–221.

position of the speaker, either alternately or simultaneously recall both the choral group singing the poem and the poet who composed it.[41]

Secondly, as I have tried to show elsewhere, the place of the aforementioned dance (without song?), organized and directed by Theseus under the watchful eye of Ariadne, following the victory over the Minotaur, was moved from Knossos to Delos. The move from the choral area laid out by Daedalus on Crete to Apollo's sanctuary on Delos no doubt relates to the etiological role given to this episode in the saga of the young Athenian hero, very probably in the first half of the fifth century. By moving from Knossos to Delos, this heroic scene became the foundation legend for the choral and ritual dance of the crane which we just discussed and which Theseus first led around the celebrated Altar to the Horns; as Callimachus' *Hymn to Delos* in particular reminds us in its etiological perspective, the twists and turns of its choreography evoked the wanderings of the young companions, male and female, of Theseus in the Labyrinth.[42]

It is as if in the enunciative movement as I have described it, this episode of the Athenian hero's dive and his visit to the home of Amphitrite, with its celebration by the seven Athenian youths and the seven Athenian maidens, assumes, in connection with the Delia ritual (a part of which is the "performance" of Bacchylides' poem 17), the same kind of etiological purpose as the episode of the first performance of the crane dance, also led by Theseus, assumes, in connection with the Aphrodisia. In such a way, a ritual poem, probably sung and danced by an Athenian mixed chorus, to celebrate Theseus in a first victory over Minos is added to the crane dance led by an actual choregos who identifies himself with Theseus in the legend, leading a mixed choral dance to celebrate victory over the Minotaur. The Athenian choral group singing Bacchylides' poem takes as its etiological and legendary model the chorus improvised on the Cretan ship by the seven Athenian youths and seven maidens sailing toward the Labyrinth. From the same etiological point of view, everything then points toward relating Theseus' legendary and victorious crossing, as well as the paean which celebrates it, to the repeated performance of Bacchylides' composition at the Delia, but also to the ritual commission of

---

[41] For an overview of the controversy that has lasted over ten years on the individual or collective aspect of the "lyric *I*", see the study by Lefkowitz 1995, who quotes most contributions to the philological dispute; cf. also n3 above. On the procedure of the *sphragís*, see Calame 2000b:70–72.

[42] Callimachus *Hymn to Delos* 307–315; see also Plutarch *Life of Theseus* 21.1–3; other accounts, information on iconography, and comments on the crane dance in Calame 1996b:118–120, 198–209, 239–242, and 424–429.

the Athenians' envoys to this great festival; before the celebration of Delian Apollo at the center of the Aegean sea, this maritime procession (which we have already mentioned) was believed to be led by a ship equipped with sailing tackle said to be that of Theseus himself![43]

Finally, hypothesizing the etiological function of a poetic narrative which places before us the performance of a paean confronts us with the controversial question of which poetic label we should apply to Bacchylides' poem 17. While its etiological dimension and the fact that it is destined for Apollo designate it as a paean, its narrative character, as well as the absence of any refrain, leads us to believe that the Alexandrian editors are correct in seeing in this highly original poem a dithyramb. We know, for example, that dithyrambs were sung in honor of Apollo at the Thargelia in Athens; we know also that the religious poem of Philodamos found at Delphi gives an example of a paean devoted to Dionysus, with a refrain which calls on the presence of Bacchus, while also invoking the god Paean.[44]

Through the narration of an original maritime episode in the heroic biography of Theseus prior to the test of the Labyrinth of Knossos, Bacchylides' *Dithyramb* 17 thus represents a religious offering to Delian Apollo; modeled on the legendary paean but also following the formal rules of the dithyramb, this musical offering is sung by a mixed choral group, probably Athenian; it is related to the maritime mission sent by the city of Athens beginning in the fifth century for the celebration of the Delia, at Delos.

---

[43] Pseudo-Xenophon *Constitution of the Athenians* 3.4, and Antiphon 6.11; Philodemos *Paean* 39 Käppel; cf. especially Käppel 1992:156–158 and 178–183, who goes too far in thinking that Bacchylides' poem could have been performed as a crane dance, and Maehler 1997:167–168. The chorus performing the dithyramb by Bacchylides would be Kean according to Fearn 2000:242–247. On the *theōrís*, see also Callimachus *Hymn to Delos* 314–315, Plato *Phaedo* 58a-b; cf. Calame 1996b:159–161, with additional references.

[44] So there is no need to suppose a Delian dithyramb contest, nor a classification of Bacchylides' poem as a hyporchema, as hypothesized by Hose 1995:304–307 and 311–312, as well as by Schröder 2000:128–144; see also Calame 1996b:366–369, with additional information given in n144, as well as Suárez de la Torre 2000:74–76 and 84, for other arguments justifying the placing of the ode in the category of dithyrambs and for other bibliographic information (n19); this in a study paired with the reflections of L. Käppel, who attributes the classification of poem 17 as a dithyramb to a performance by a *kúklios khorós*, those of F. García Romero who introduces the narrative character of *Dithyramb* 17 and the dramatic dimension of *Dithyramb* 18 as a new feature announcing the "new dithyramb," and those of J. M. Bremer, who follows Maehler in briefly defining the poem as a paean! For Schröder 2000:157–159, it would be for him a paean from which Bacchylides dropped the formal features (especially the refrain). On the *Paean* of Philodamos sung for Apollo and Dionysus, see Vamvouri-Ruffy, 2004:187–200.

4.3. The poetic legitimization of a maritime "empire"

Coming as it does between language rules and ritual and social rules, the question of poetic genre thus invites us to return to the circumstances of enunciation marked in space and time. In other words, it sends us back to the space and time of history, but also to the representation of it formed by contemporaries and practitioners, with the discursive configurations that they make of it. Related to calendar time in the space of its realization, and in the twofold linear and cyclical dimension of the calendar as defined in the introduction, this geographic and historical aspect of the ritual poetic "performance" finally brings up the double question of the date of its composition and of its ideological context, in a particular political and historical situation.

In the absence of any encoded data in the poem itself, three different dates have been proposed for the composition and performance of Bacchylides' *Dithyramb* 17. While comparison with iconography of Theseus' visit to the undersea home of Poseidon and Amphitrite directs us toward the first decades of the fifth century, and while the hypothesis of a linguistic influence by the *Persians* of Aeschylus would take the first "performance" of the poem to 472, the *communis opinio* places the poem immediately after the Persian Wars, which is to say between the founding of the Attic Delian League in 478/7 and the defeat of Naxos in 470/69.[45]

But we should repeat that history is not simply a matter of dates and chronology, either in its prefigurations or configurations of social time. The point of view adopted here is that of community representations, which select the most memorable events and configure them by transforming them into collective memory, thus inscribing them within a tradition. From this perspective, no historian from Thucydides on could deny that the major consequence of the Persian Wars was the decisive turning point that territorial, economic, and ideological expansion in the Aegean Sea imprinted on the politics of the city of Athens. This "imperialist" movement became a reality from 478/7 on with the progressive creation of the Delian League, which bore the name of what was its religious center and for a time its economic center. Tribute paid by the allies of Athens was collected on Delos, and their meetings took place in Apollo's sanctuary.[46] Among the practical consequences of this ideologically

---

[45] The various arguments leading to these three dates are summarized by Hose 1995:307–312, and by Maehler 1997:169–184.

[46] Thucydides 1.95.7–1.97.1; Pseudo-Aristotle *Constitution of Athens* 23.5.

essential alliance was the religious and political appropriation by Athens of the celebration of the Delia honoring Apollo, along with the probable institution of the ritual maritime mission.

In this context of representation of historical and social time and the concomitant reconfiguration of its space, it is surely not by chance that in the eyes of this same Thucydides, and despite accounts recognized as belonging to an oral tradition, Minos appears as a completely historical person, as does Polykrates, the tyrant of Samos, later on. The Athenian historian introduces Minos as the most ancient (*palaítatos*) of the pre-Hellenics who was able to control (*êrxe*) a large part of the "Greek Sea" (*hellenikề thalássē*), thus colonizing most of the Cyclades. As for Polykrates, the "archaeology" which opens Thucydides' treatise tells us that the tyrant of Samos subdued some of the islands of the Aegean Sea by relying on his fleet, and that he dedicated the island of Rheneia, neighboring Delos, to a god who was none other than Delian Apollo. Along with the Ionians who dominated these islands during a certain period in the time of Cyrus, Minos and Polykrates in some ways represent precursors to the political turn Athens took at the end of the Persian Wars: this turning point is marked by new aspirations to "thalassocracy."[47]

Following Themistocles and with Kimon, the Athenians launched a new policy of expansion no longer directed toward land, but toward the sea; legitimizing that policy pushed them to rethink the origins of their own community and consequently to reconfigure the past. In this symbolic speculation on the birth of a "nation" with its own political system, the paradigm of autochthony chosen by Athens and by other Greek cities as well to justify their territorial claims, is not completely pertinent; a few decades later, the city of Athens would be obliged to allow the devastation of its traditional territory—Attica— in order to plan for the sea defense of its maritime "empire."[48]

4.4. Symbolic births from the sea and iconography

In this historical and ideological context, the narrative of Theseus' dive and the "rebirth" of the hero when he reappears from the depths of the sea,

---

[47] Thucydides 1.4, 1.8.2, and 1.13.6; see also Herodotus 3.122.1; as related to Bacchylides' poem 17, see Segal 1979/1998:307 and Kowalzig 2007:88–94; also Fearn 2007:242–256.

[48] This is exactly what Pericles' speech, reformulated by Thucydides (2.62.2–2.63.3 ; cf. also 1.81.2 and 2.41.4), tries to commit the Athenians to at the beginning of the Peloponnesian War, after the second invasion of Attica by the Spartans and their allies. On the Attic stage, see also the pleas by Sophocles *Oedipus at Colonus* 707–719 (through the voice of the chorus) and Aristophanes *Wasps* 1091–1101 (also through the chorus).

shining like a god in epiphany, may be read as a legend of "autothalassy," or "autopelagia." It is less a parallel to the more ancient narrative of the autochthonous appearance of Kekrops, the first half-serpent king of Attica, than it is to the birth of little Erichthonios from the bowels of the earth.[49]

In the classical legend of the founding of Athens, Erichthonios is born from the soil of Attica made fertile by the sperm of Hephaestus, in his attempted rape of Athena. As Erechtheus, he becomes the conquering king of Eleusis and civilizes Attica. Similarly, Theseus the founding king of Athens and the inventor of democracy, reappears in a symbolic rebirth from the depths of the sea and consequently from the domain protected by the other tutelary deity of Athens: not Athena, but Poseidon![50] We should also remember that just as Erechtheus himself is struck down and buried by Poseidon in the very earth which he helped to civilize, so also Aegeus, the mortal father of Theseus, kills himself by plunging into the waves of the sea which henceforth will bear his name: upon Theseus' triumphant return to Athens, the Sea of Crete becomes the Aegean Sea. In addition, in the description of the fresco of Mikon in the new Theseion, which is contemporary with Bacchylides' poem and which depicts the young Athenian hero's dive into the waves, Pausanias speaks of the "reascendence" (*aneltheîn*) of Theseus from the depths of the sea; the reappearance of the hero is thus interpreted as a marine *anodos*. And similarly, when he describes the homologous fresco of the Stoa Poikilē showing the hero appearing from the earth of Marathon under the eyes of Athena and Herakles in an autochthonous rebirth, the geographer sees Theseus "issuing from the earth" (*ek gês aníesin*) ... And in the contemporary iconography where Apollo himself appears as the main protagonist in many scenes, Theseus in his poetic epiphany seems to undergo a sort of "apollonization" which transforms him not into a neo-initiate, but into a young god with feminine features.[51]

Just as in the episode of Erichthonios' autochthonous birth, the contribution of women proves indispensable in the "autothalassic" birth of the young

---

[49] The different versions of these two autochthonous births are very well described by Parker 1987:193–204 ; other sources and studies on this in Calame 2000b:133–135 (together with the numerous bibliographic references given in n40).

[50] Theseus appears as king and as champion of democracy in several classical tragedies: see Walker 1995:143–169, as well as Mills 1997:58–86 and 87–128, with the additional references I gave in 1996b:406–408 and 415–419.

[51] Pausanias 1.17.3 (cf. n54 below) and 1.15.3; I commented on this "autothalassy," which bears the marks of a symbolic death and an initiatory rebirth, in 1996c:438–441. It is to Moret's perceptiveness in 1982:121–136, that we owe the acknowledgement of Apollo's predominant role, often alongside Athena, in Attic iconography following the Persian Wars. On the feminization of Athenian ephebes, cf. Vidal-Naquet 1983:152–164.

Athenian. While for the young Theseus the sea essentially plays the role which Gaia, the Earth, plays in the legend of little Erichthonios, Theseus' stepmother Amphitrite, occupies a position analogous to Athena's role as regards the future Erechtheus. This quite appealing set of analogies could be represented in the following schema:

Birth	Rebirth
Earth-mother: Athena : :	Sea-mother: Amphitrite
Erichthonios/Erechtheus	Theseus

In both cases, for Hephaestus as well as for Poseidon, the male contribution is (almost) negligible! In the legend of Theseus' poetic dive, we find a symbolic compensation procedure concerning gender roles which is analogous to those noted in the etiological legend and in the ritual practice of the initiatory process of the Iatmul and the Abelam of Papua-New Guinea.

In this way, it is possible to grasp the poetic and metaphorical use Bacchylides makes both of the possible schema at the base of any tribal initiation rite and of that other rite of passage, marriage, while he also exploits the frequent inversion of signs marking the social relationships of the sexes in these two rituals of transition.[52] If Theseus reappears from the waves of the sea not only as a god resembling Apollo, but also like a young fiancée, it is because for Poseidon's young wife, Amphitrite, he acquires a position and status homologous to those of the child Erichthonios-Erechtheus for Athena, the virgin goddess, probably through a metaphorical play on the sexual ambiguities of adolescence. We should also remember that in Bacchylides' poem, Amphitrite as *númphē* takes the place of Athena the *parthénos* as Sender of the young hero, in a kind of feminine ring structure! From the point of view of sex roles and their representations in classical Greece, the ambivalence conferred by Bacchylides' poem on the future king, hero of Athenian democracy, finds unexpected confirmation in contemporary iconography.

And again, it is certainly not by chance that among the eight images we have of Theseus being welcomed in the depths of the sea, the first dates from 490, most of the others from 480 to 470, and the last from 420![53] The high

---

[52] References to a number of studies devoted to practices and metaphoric actions which first confuse and then reaffirm the values of the two "genders" on these occasions in Calame 2002a:101–145. Walker 1995:84–92, rightly insists on the role played by women and particularly by the (step)mother in the narrative of Bacchylides' *Dithyramb* 17.

[53] This iconographic case is taken up exhaustively by Maehler 1997:174–181, who gives all the essential bibliographic references.

Figure 1a. Attic red-figure kylix, side A: Theseus in the palace of Aegeus. Attributed to the Briseis painter, ca. 480 BC.

point for iconographic representations of Theseus being received in the sea coincides with the restoration of the heroic sanctuary dedicated to the young Athenian king and to its painted ornamentation, begun in 475. In a description which replaces the represented scene with a mythographic sort of narrative which follows the plot that Bacchylides perhaps imagined, but which doesn't entirely conform to it, Pausanias says that the previously mentioned Mikon fresco showed Theseus springing from the sea with the golden crown given by Aphrodite, but also with the ring (*sphragís*) Minos threw into the sea.[54] And so both the temporal coincidence of this painting with the maritime reorientation of Athens' political expansion, and the location of the Theseion between the political space and the religious space of the city, show the correspondence between the symbolic creation of an entirely specific episode from the heroic biography of the hero of classical Athens, the time and space which are constructed in them, and the geographical-historical conjunction which is at the origin of its dissemination.

---

[54] Pausanias 1.17.3 and 1.17.6 (cf. n51 above), indicating that the restoration of the Theseion coincides with the return of the hero's bones from the island of Skyros by Kimon, the son of Miltiades. cf. also Hyginus *Astronomica* 2.5, who follows the same version, but substitutes Thetis for Amphitrite. The function, dating, and iconographic program of the Theseion are referred to in Calame 1996c:153–156, 262–266, 360–362, and 443–446.

Figure 1b. Side B: Poseidon, Triton, Theseus, Nereids.

The decoration of a very beautiful red-figure cup dated to around 480 sets out the represented meaning of the episode as if it were a comic strip.[55] A first scene (Figure 1a), very probably in the Athenian palace of Aegeus, shows the protection which armed Athena grants the young hero; he holds in his left hand a sword (unsheathed but at rest) while three of the four young girls

Figure 1c. Interior: Theseus and Amphitrite

(of Athens?) who surround him offer him ritual headbands. A second scene (Figure 1b) shows the arrival (or departure?) of Theseus in Amphitrite's home;

[55] Metropolitan Museum of Art, 53.11.4; *ARV*² 406.7, Add. 115 (*LIMC, Amphitrite* 76 and *Theseus* 219 and 309); see the analysis of iconographic decoration suggested by Sourvinou-Inwood 1990:416–422, who develops good arguments for seeing the first scene rather as a representation of Theseus' return to Athens.

141

Figure 2. Attic red-figure cup, interior: Theseus and Amphitrite, with Athena. Attributed to Onesimos, signed by Euphronios as potter, ca. 500–490 BC.

he is guided by Triton under the eye of a Poseidon gesturing protectively and of three Nereids, one of whom prepares a libation. Dressed in these two scenes in a short chiton, the young Athenian directs a gesture of adoration both to Athena and to Poseidon. But in the center of the cup (Figure 1c), it is Amphitrite alone who prepares to place a crown on the head of Theseus, shown here beardless, an ephebe wearing both a sword and a short chiton, but with the cloak which Poseidon's wife probably gave him. In a syntactic connection which is certainly debatable, the three scenes seem to bring together three of the Senders who guarantee the action of Theseus that is heroicized in the narrative episode as Bacchylides imagined it, first Athena, then Poseidon, and finally Amphitrite in the tondo of the cup. While the absence of any allusion to Delos may explain the absence of Apollo in an iconographic sequence which cannot hope to represent all the imagery of the poetic narrative, the predominance of feminine figures is striking, all facing a Theseus whose features here recall those that contemporary iconography attributes to Apollo.

Feminine presence also distinguishes the other classical representations of Theseus' reception by Amphitrite, including the central image of a famous cup by Euphronios, dating to the first decade of the fifth century, and displayed in the Louvre (Figure 2). The marine scene constitutes the high point of the cycle of the Athenian hero's great deeds, shown on the outside face of the cup in his combat against Skiron, Procrustes, Kerkyon, and the bull of Marathon. Seated and richly dressed, Amphitrite offers a crown to the young Theseus who wears a short chiton and a sword, and who is carried by a little Triton, while at the center of the image it is Athena, fully armed as a

Figure 3. Attic red-figure pelike: Theseus and Amphitrite, with Poseidon. Attributed to the Triptolemos Painter, ca. 480–470 BC.

Figure 4a. Attic red-figure column crater, side A: Theseus and Poseidon clasp hands. Nereus (or Aegeus?) and a Nereid at left, Amphitrite at right. Attributed to the Harrow Painter, ca. 475 BC.

warrior, who oversees the scene of welcome; this contrasts with several other analogous images where this role is more naturally taken by Poseidon, as on the red-figure pelike in Copenhagen (Figure 3), roughly contemporary with Bacchylides' *Dithyramb* 17.[56]

But for someone attempting to address a poetic and practical configuration of time and space from an anthropological gender perspective, the best surprise was a visit to the Fogg Art Museum at Harvard University, where these remarks were first presented. In the collection is the well-known and remarkable crater with colonettes dating from about 475, which presents the

---

[56] Musée du Louvre, G 104; *ARV*² 318, 1 (*LIMC, Amphitrite* 75 and *Theseus* 36); compare with the pelike in Copenhagen (Ny Carlsberg Glyptotek), IN 2695; *ARV*² 362, 19 (*LIMC, Amphitrite* 78a).

Figure 4b. Side B: bearded man with three youths, one playing the kithara.

young Theseus wearing a short chiton and a sword, between his divine father Poseidon and his stepmother Amphitrite (Figure 4a).[57] Turned toward the god whose hand he has taken, the young hero wears the shawl probably given by Amphitrite; the goddess herself is giving him the (matrimonial?) crown mentioned in Bacchylides' text; to the left of Poseidon, recognizable from his trident, is an old man (Nereus or Aegeus?) as well as a Nereid who consecrates the scene of welcome with a libation. Direct observation allows us to establish a strong relationship between the recognition of Theseus' divine and mari-

[57] Cambridge, MA, Arthur M. Sackler Museum, 1960.339; *ARV*² 274, 39 (*LIMC, Amphitrite* 78 and *Theseus* 220). The antiquities personnel at the Sackler Museum were kind enough to offer to this philologist and anthropologist the distinct pleasure of an active individual viewing of this exceptional piece.

145

time legitimacy and the double scene on the other side of the vase (Figure 4b) where, beside what is probably a scene of erotic courtship between an adult and an ephebe, another ephebe plays the kithara, facing a young trainer. And the same brief "field" work, without allowing us to identify the rounded object that Theseus holds in his hand, reveals that the young beardless man wears the same kind of chiton as the beautiful Amphitrite, leaving them both with bare shoulders. Facing the tutelary god of Athens, Theseus assumes the position of a young bride whose eyes are turned to her spouse, while perhaps also being associated with the young lyre player engaged in the Muses' art on the other side of the crater.

The iconography, like the poetic narrative devised or transfigured by Bacchylides, through the different versions it presents of an ideologically charged legendary episode, presents the effect of symbolic compensation necessary to reestablishing the complementarity and balance between the roles of sexes, just as do the cosmogonic and cosmological etiological legends and the tribal initiation and puberty rituals of the Iatmul and the Abelam. The transition (first narrative, then linear and enunciative) created by Bacchylides in his *Dithyramb* dedicated to Apollo, from the recounted time and space of the legend (with its foundational effect of *arkhé*, origin), to the truly cyclical time of ritual practice through the *hic et nunc* of the poetic performance, leads to three results, from the perspective adopted here: the passage from a feminized individual narrative identity to a mixed community and political ritual identity, but also the metaphoric collaboration of the genders in the cosmological legitimization of a territorial policy dependent on a particular historical situation, and finally the practical collaboration between the sexes in the ritual and religious fulfillment of this policy in the sanctuary of Apollo at Delos.

The musical and ritual performance of Bacchylides' *Dithyramb* and of Theseus' narrative at the Delia gives to the Athenian politics in the Aegean a new "historical" and practical meaning, inscribing it in a new common memory, a preferred memory. Is it going too far or is it too simplistic to state that there is also coincidence between temporal origin and spatial center? Be that as it may, from the *Homeric Hymn to Apollo* to the historiographer Thucydides, all discourses on the honors given to Apollo at Delos stress the participation of girls and women.[58] It looks as if the musical and religious performance of the narrative and poetic creation of Bacchylides would be a symbolic and memorial enactment of Athens' new politics.

---

[58] Cf. n37 above.

In the context of spatial-temporal passage from a singular identity to a collective identity, as well as in procedures for the political creation of the human, marked by gender, this is an opportunity for us to rethink the modes of social distribution of sex roles, in time and in space, in ancient Greece as well as in contemporary post-modernity. This anthropopoietic procedure, both symbolic and ritual, depends on a spatial-temporal configuration which fully displays its effect, narratively and historio-poetically, in a religious performance, presented as an offering to the very god of Athens' control over the maritime domain of the Aegean.

IV

REGIMES OF HISTORICITY
AND ORACULAR LOGIC

How to Re-Found a Colonial City

1. Cyclical and philosophical temporalities

IT IS A COMMON OPINION that Greek concepts of time are deeply marked by the image of the circle, that they refer to a fundamentally cyclical temporality. Historians of "Greek thought," while applying this traditional idea for themselves, also introduced a whole series of nuances concerning its development. The idea of cyclical time, it is said, is based on the deified function of Memory which permits mortal man to come into contact with the divine; its origins would be religious, attached to the belief that ritual funeral honors accorded to Lethe and to Mnemosyne allow one to escape the cycle of Becoming, even the cycle of (re-)birth. But in this train of thought the gradual abandonment of heroic values, in a "lyrical" consciousness more and more sharply aware of the vicissitudes of the life of the individual, would have had a twofold effect. On the one hand, it leads to a concept where the representation of linear time, subject to the unpredictable hazards of an existence which is by definition ephemeral, replaces human time modeled on cosmic time, in the succession of generations. And on the other hand, "sectarian" movements following Pythagoras and Orpheus tried to offer the soul, detached from the body, the mnemonic means necessary to leave the supposed cycle of births through *anamnesis*, and by this abandonment of human time to attain the immortality of the gods.[1]

---

[1] These ideas proposed by Vernant 1965:60–73, specifically in a reinterpretation of the etymologizing speculations of Onians 1951:249–251 and 442–445; see also Momigliano 1966/1982:72–74, who shows that attributing a cyclical concept of time to the Greeks goes back to Saint Augustine. This study, presented in part at the colloquium "Mites de fundació de les ciutats del món antic" held at the Architectural Technical School in Barcelona, June 8–10, 2000, and organized by Pedro Azara, was commented on by Marcel Detienne and Irad Malkin.

But to make followers of Pythagoras and Orpheus into the precursors of Plato in *Phaedrus* or *Timaeus* is to make philosophers of these simple advocates of a more balanced life style; it is to make metaphysicians of time from those who practiced a certain way of life with the hope of a more pleasant *post mortem* existence (to which we shall return in the next chapter). And it especially ignores that accounts attributing a cyclical concept of time to the first Greek "thinkers" are from much later, and that they are easily recognized as influenced by neo-Platonic, even Christian, readings of the classical texts.

Khrónos agéraos, then, ageless Time as a mythical figure, like the serpent curled on itself, or like the Ocean river whose circular currents wind around the inhabited earth? In the classical era, only Critias, the sophist and sometime author of tragedies, introduces the figure of a "tireless time" which progresses by generating itself in a continuous and eternal flux. But its progress is not circular, as the expression perì-phoitâi (a tmesis) might lead one to conclude; it follows the vault of the sky, which obviously is only semi-spherical! These lines, pronounced by the chorus of initiates into the Eleusinian Mysteries in a fragment of a tragedy which is also attributed to Euripides, may well have been intended as parody.[2] Empedokles cited as witness to the belief in a cycle of reincarnations and the expiatory journey of the soul? Only if one reads the famous poetic fragment on the restless wanderings of "demons," separated from the gods and through a series of mortal forms, in terms of a representation of the "cycle of ages;" there is actually nothing circular about this journey lasting three times ten thousand seasons, presented as taking place simply "through time" (dià khrónon).[3] The Iliadic reflections of Glaukos the Lycian, confronting Diomedes the Greek who has just learned at his own expense that a mortal should not attack a deity, then, as Homeric testimony recalling an ancient "cyclical" concept of the life of men, carried along in a "circular becoming?" Only if one interprets the comparison of the hazards of mortal lives with the deciduous nature of leaves, falling in autumn to be born again in spring, in terms of cycle, and not in terms of the simple alternation that

---

[2] Critias *TrGF* 43 F 3 Snell (formerly Euripides fr. 594 Nauck²); cited as parallels, the texts of Hesiod *Theogony* 789–792 and Aeschylus *Prometheus* 138–140, concern only the circular figure attributed to the Ocean river which surrounds the inhabited earth (at *Iliad* 14.200–201, Ocean, located at the ends of the earth, is simply considered the original father of the gods): as regards this circular representation of the inhabited world and its limits, see especially Herodotus 2.21! At Hesiod fr. 70.23 Merkelbach-West, it is the Kephisos which is said to move along "by winding" (which is to say displaying its meanders) through Orchomenos (and not around the city!) like a serpent.

[3] Empedokles fr. 31 B 115.4–8 Diels-Kranz; cf. Gallavotti 1975:276, who understands very well that the number given simply refers to a very long time, as well as Trépanier 2004:79–85.

occurs, for example, in Herodotus' famous beginning reflections on the destinies of man's cities: "those which formerly (*pálai*) were great have become small, most of them, and those which in my time (*ep' eméo*) were great, once were small." In a less well-known passage, Herodotus does indeed use the term *kúklos* to describe the alternations of good fortune, but the remark is placed in the mouth of Croesus confronting Cyrus, imperialist king of the Persians, and the circle image applies only to sudden reversals in human affairs.[4]

For that matter, even in those rare classical texts which seem to mention an eschatological perspective, neither the itinerary of the soul nor the space and time in which the journey takes place is circular.

Often cited is the promise made to Theron, the tyrant of Agrigentum, in Pindar *Olympian* 2: after a three-part stay divided between the world of mortals and the world below, the soul of the just man will accede to the final goal, represented by the Isles of the Blessed. In its alternation, this promise seems to recall the destiny assigned to Persephone, who divides her time between Hades and Olympus, near her mother Demeter; but the difference is that if the immortal residence of the goddess Kore is indeed organized according to the (cyclical) rhythm of the year, the journey of the soul detached from the mortal body ends, finally and not circularly, in a dwelling ruled by Kronos and his golden age.[5] Similarly, on one of the so-called "Orphic-Dionysiac" lamellae found on a skeleton in Magna Graecia and whose text will be introduced in the next chapter, the soul who pronounces the words written on the lamella sees the demise of his mortal shell as a passage toward an existence henceforth shared with the immortals, near Persephone. While a "circle" (*kúklos*) does indeed appear in the performative text written in this veritable passport for the great beyond, it designates the cycle of griefs and sorrows from which the soul has just been liberated, by death.[6]

This tension, even this contradiction, between the feeling of the irreversible fluidity of mortal time on the one hand and the permanence attributed to the world of the gods in this polytheistic system on the other, is far from being the product of any new "lyric" consciousness: it marks the entire

---

[4] *Iliad* 6.145–149: the alternating movement is marked by the double use of the connecting device *mén ... dé*. See Herodotus 1.5.4 (as well as 9.27.4) and 1.207.1–2, but also *Iliad* 21.464–466, as well as Mimnermos fr. 8.1–8 Gentili-Prato or Aristophanes *Birds* 685–689, all in reference to the ephemeral nature of human existence as opposed to the immortality of the gods: cf. Fränkel 1960:23–29.

[5] Pindar *Olympian* 2.75–82, to be referred to the *Homeric Hymn to Demeter* 445–447; cf. chapter IV, section 2.3.1 below.

[6] Lamella from Thourioi A 1.5 Zuntz; cf. chapter IV, section 3.2 below.

development of Greek culture. In their discursive representations, as well as in their social and institutional practices, Greek efforts to escape the unpredictable inconstancy of both the individual temporality of men and the collective temporality of cities were both numerous and varied. Rather than clinging to the over-interpreted meaning of a few words and metaphors, one of the best ways to grasp these indigenous representations and configurations of time as it relates to the spaces put forward by them is simply to pay careful attention to the use of verb tenses. The Greek narrative text, readily conceived not only as a crafted artisanal object but much more specifically as a weaving, is articulated through a temporal-spatial fabric which obviously is constructed by verb tenses and the localization of the actions referred to. Just like the melic poem called *húmnos*, a name whose etymology recalls the verb *huphaínein*, "to weave," the epigraphic text can assume a narrative form fashioned and structured by the same sort of spatial-temporal texture.[7]

This interweaving of spatial-temporal references, often combined with enunciative indices, is all the more interesting to unravel when the temporal and discursive configuration is displayed in a narrative concerning the founding of the city which produced it. Through an epigraphic text officially consecrated in a shrine, the community of citizens tries to give itself a memorial representation of its past, while also affirming this past institutionally (even ritually) in the city's present, in order to orient its future. Through the dialectic of collective *idem* and *ipse*, it is thus a question of reformulating and reaffirming a temporal (but also spatial) community identity. Even a cultural identity based on a memory, if one allows that "culture is not something defined once and for all, nor is it a "real" practico-symbolic entity which develops based on its own "laws," but rather something which results from interaction and agreement among communicating subjects."[8] The temporal (and spatial) architecture constructed by means of discourse undoubtedly offers an identity-related political and social antidote to any possible feeling of the irremediable flight of human time with all its hazards, far better than could any supposed circular and cyclical image.

---

[7] "With the Graces, your guest has woven the song he sends to your glorious city," sings Bacchylides 5.9–10, who also takes up the same play on words, relating to the collaboration of the Muses and the Graces, in 19.1–10. On Greek representations of text as fabric, cf. Scheid and Svenbro 1994:119–138.

[8] As defined by Fabietti 1998:55.

2. A doubly-founding document

The inscription called the *Stele dei Fondatori* or *Oath of the Founders* was consecrated at the beginning of the fourth century in the great shrine of Apollo which the inscription itself calls *Pythian* (line 8), and was discovered in the 1920s on the site of Cyrene, the flourishing Greek colony in Libya. The stele had been re-used during the imperial era for constructing terraces for the southern basin of the *frigidarium* of the Lesser Baths, or Baths of Trajan.[9] This epigraphic text engraved on marble presents three main points of interest to anyone interested in Greek concepts of time and space. In a first section, the inscription presents the text of a popular decree on rights of citizenship. These provisions, sanctioned by a decision of the assembly of citizens in the fourth century and consecrated in the shrine of Apollo Pythios, refer to the founding decree of the city of Cyrene, in a narrative version which recalls that of Herodotus a century earlier. In a second section, the epigraphic text relates and describes the circumstances which long ago led the inhabitants of Thera-Santorini to send a colonizing expedition to the coast of Libya. Finally, at the end of this narrative and descriptive section, the text evokes the ritual which consecrated the solemn oath taken at the colonists' departure. Alongside the modes of narration of a founding event and the tension established in the two sections between the legendary past and the political present, there is also the combining of the performative temporality of the oath that was sworn and the constituent time of the ritual act which accompanied it.

In this respect, the more specifically linguistic perspective adopted here, in a reading once again inspired by discourse analysis (as regards the enunciative aspect), requires a brief reminder of the distinctions made in the introductory chapter. From the point of view of the spatial-temporal putting-into-discourse of a basically narrative text, we must remember that the empirical time and space of the text's enunciation, that is to say the extra-discursive spatial-temporal circumstances of its production, must be distinguished from the intra-discursive time and space of the enunciation as it often manifests itself in the text.

In the particular case of the Cyrene inscription, the effective time and space of the ritual (the political and religious consecration of the epigraphic text in a shrine) are indeed different from the time and space of the enuncia-

---

[9] Physical description and dating of the document in the *editio princeps* by Ferri 1925:19–20, and in Oliviero 1928:222–223. Commentary in Graham 1960, with French translation in Chamoux 1952:106–112 and in Dobias-Lalou 1994:246–252.

tion as they may appear in the text, especially through the enunciative indices of the *hic et nunc* (in the description of the popular decision in the assembly); they are also different from the time and space of the narrative (long ago, between Delphi, Thera, and Cyrene). And from the intra-discursive point of view of the utterance of the narrative, the tempo of the narration (*Erzählzeit*) with its accelerations, its flashbacks, its projections into the future, and the spatial shifting which flows from that obviously does not accord with the linear time (*erzählte Zeit*) that may be reconstructed by reconstituting the chronology and thus the sequencing of the argumentation or of the narration. That means that the rhythm of the *Erzählzeit* of the inscription with the astonishing alteration of verb tenses in a narration which goes back from the present to the past is very different from the enunciated and narrated time, leading from preparations for the colonial expedition under the aegis of the oracle at Delphi to the consecration of the stele in the sanctuary of Apollo Pythios in Cyrene.[10]

Reading of the temporal framework of the epigraphic document and its putting-into-discourse will thus follow two divergent lines. First, from the internal point of view of the intra-discursive, the reading of indices of temporality and spatiality given especially by the use of verb tenses will lead from the time and space of the "uttered enunciation" ("*énonciation énoncée*"), to that of the narration itself, and then lead to a reconstruction of narrated time in its more or less linear chronology of succession. Then, in terms of pragmatics, it will be possible to pose the question of the relationship between, on the one hand, the temporality and spatiality of the enunciation inscribed in the text, and on the other, the (extra-discursive) exterior time and space of the document's production and its circumstances. In the confrontation with other versions of this same narrative and religious relationship of the community with its founding past and its civic memory, a comparison which is not external, but rather internal to Greek culture, will allow us to grasp some of the identity-related issues of a very polymorphic poietics of history.

From the point of view of empirical history which always goes hand-in-hand with archaeology, we should point out that scholars have tried to make the date of production of the *Founder's Oath* text coincide with the historical moment of the Greek colony's founding in Libya. Indeed, archeologists and historians have agreed to take seriously the latest date of foundation proposed by ancient chronographers; by reference to our own system of historic chronology, the colonization of Cyrene dates to 632 before the supposed moment of that other founding event, the birth of Christ, which contributed to giving

---

[10] Cf. Chapter I, section 2 above.

Western chronology its strange and irrational double orientation. As for whether the text of the oath goes back to that date, the modern question of authenticity seems not to have much worried the ancients.[11] This difference in perspective constitutes one of the points of this reading.

From a concrete point of view, we note that the text presented by the marble stele is engraved in carefully traced letters; they are underlined in the famous scarlet paint which allowed the Greeks, in one of the etymological games they liked so well, to relate the origin of "scribe" (*phoinikastás*) and that of purple letters (*phoinikḗïa grámmata*) to Phoenicia and its alphabet![12] In addition, the arrangement of the text graphically distinguishes the two sections of which it is composed. Introduced by a separate line bearing the title "Gods. To good Fortune," the text of the fourth-century decree is cleanly separated from the somewhat longer text related to the founding act. This second section is also introduced and distinguished by a heading which labels it as the "Oath of the Founders": from that comes the modern (and misleading ...) name for the inscription.

3. Temporal and enunciative architecture

Here is the translation of the epigraphic text, both of its sections marked by a specific heading:

> God. Good Fortune. | Damis son of Bathykles made the motion. As to what is said by the Therans, | Kleudamas son of Euthykles, in order that the city may prosper and the Pe|ople of Cyrene enjoy good fortune, the Therans shall be given t||he citizenship according to that ancestral custom which our forefathers establish|ed, both those who founded Cyrene from Thera and those at Thera who re|mained—just as Apollo granted Battos and the Thera|ns who founded Cyrene good fortune if they abided by the | sworn agreement which our ancestors concluded with them when || they sent out the colony according to the command of Apol|lo Archagetes. With good fortune. It has been resolved by the People | that the

---

[11] On the question of the historical date of the founding of Cyrene, see Calame 1996a:57–60. The question of the exact date of the Oath itself in terms of "authenticity" is broached by Graham 1960:95–97; see also Meiggs and Lewis 1969:7–9 and Dušanić 1978.

[12] See Herodotus 5.58.2 and the Cretan inscription *SEG* XXVII (1977), 631, A5 and A11 (where the verb *poinikázein* is found alongside *mnamoneúein*, in an activity attributed to the engraving specialist, the *poinikastás*); cf. Detienne 1988:47–80.

Therans shall continue to enjoy equal citizenship in Cyrene in the sa|me way (as of old). There shall be sworn by all Therans who are domicil|ed in Cyrene the same oath which the others onc||e swore, and they shall be written on a stele | of marble and placed in the ancestral shrine of | Apollo Pythios; and that sworn agreement also shall be written down on the stele | which was made by the colonists when they sailed to Libya wit||h Battos from Thera to Cyrene. As to the expenditure necessary for the s|tone or for the engraving, let the Superintendents of the Accounts pr|ovide it from Apollo's revenues.

vv | The sworn agreement of the settlers. | Resolved by the Assembly. Since Apollo spontaneously told B[at]||tos and the Therans to colonize Cyrene, it has been decided by the Ther|ans to send Battos off to Libya, as Archagetes | and as King, with the Therans to sail as his Companions. On equal a|nd fair terms shall they sail according to family (?), with one son to be consc|ripted adults and from the [ot||her] Therans those who are free-born shall sail. If they (the colonists) establi|sh the settlement, kinsmen who sail | later to Libya shall be entitled to citizenship and offices | and shall be allotted portions of the land which have no owner. But if they do not successfully estab||lish the settlement and the Therans are incapable of giving it assistan||ce, and they are pressed by hardship for five years, from that land shall they depart, | without fear, to Thera, to their own property, and they shall be citiz|ens. Any man who, if the city sends him, refuses to sail, will be liable to the death-|penalty and his property shall be confiscated. The man ha|rboring him or concealing him, whether he be a father (aiding his) son or a brother his brot||her, is to suffer the same penalty as the man who refuses to sail. On these conditions a sworn agreement was ma|de by those who stayed there and by those who sailed to foun|d the colony, and they involved curses against those transgressors who would not ab|ide by it—whether they were those settling in Libya or those who re|mained. They made waxen images and burnt them, calling down (the following) c||urse, everyone having assembled together, men, wom|en, boys, girls: "The person who does not abide by this | sworn agreement but transgresses it shall melt away and di|ssolve like the images—himself, his descendants and his prope|rty; but those who abide by the sworn agreement—those || sailing to Libya and [those] staying in Thera—shall have an abundanc|e of good things, both themselves [and] their descendants."

trans. C.W. Fornara (1977), with Jeffery (1961) and Graham (1964)

3.1. The first section: "Gods. To Good Fortune."

The decree whose text is consecrated on the stele displayed in the shrine of Apollo Pythios in Cyrene concerns a decision for isopolity; that is to say it foresees giving to inhabitants coming from Thera, the city of the semi-legendary founders of the Greek colony in Libya, the citizenship that their ancestors enjoyed.[13] The wording of the decree approved by the people's assembly is situated exactly in the center of the text (on line 11 of the 22 lines of this first part!). *Dedókhthai tôi dámōi*: the "popular" decision is presented in the traditional wording, but in a form of the perfect which definitively establishes its validity in the present.

3.1.1. The narrative of the act of foundation

The reader is led to this temporal core of the decree, which marks its content with the seal of permanence, through two embedded (and oral!) voices: the voice of Damis son of Bathykles, probably the *próxenos* who intervened before the assembly to formulate the adopted isopolitical proposal; and the voice of Kleudamas, the son of Euthykles, probably the spokesman for the Therans claiming the right of citizenship in Cyrene. The first voice, that of the intermediary, is situated by a form of the aorist (*êipe*, line 1) at the moment of the assembly; the second, collective voice manifests itself in a present (*légonti*, line 1) expressing in its duration the demands of the Therans, taken up before the assembly by the voice of Damis. Expressed in two oral speeches, one past and the other present, the demand itself is formulated in the infinitive, one of those infinitives with an imperative value which we shall also find in the wording of the decree itself; citizenship must be restored (*apodómen*, line 4) to the Therans. Under this infinitive form which makes of it both a requirement and a speech reported in indirect discourse, the "actual" proposal of the Theran people is situated temporally in tension between future and past. First the future: through the intermediary of a final proposal, the granting of citizenship aims to insure the prosperity of the *pólis* and the happiness of the

---

[13] The question of isopolity is taken up in other studies: cf. Gawantka 1975:57–62.

Cyrenean people (*dâmos*, line 2);[14] then by reference to the past: they claim the tradition of the fathers (*katà tà pátria*, line 5), a memorial tradition which goes back to the very moment of the colonial city's founding. With verbs in the aorist, the reference to the act of foundation of Cyrene takes a narrative phrasing: this is the tradition established by those who founded Cyrene from Thera and by those who remained in Santorini—in accordance with the privilege given by Apollo to Battos and to "the Therans who founded (*toîs katoikíxasi*, line 8) Cyrene," the text reiterates.

We shall of course come back to the celebrated figure of the founding hero of Cyrene and to the oracles who directed the process of foundation from Delphi. For the moment, we will limit ourselves to three remarks, all intra-discursive. First of all, from the point of view of the enunciative modalization of the utterance, we notice that the aorist participle used to designate the act of foundation as a completed act places it either in the perspective of the decree's speaker, or that of the utterance, and not in that of a subsequent intervention by Apollo continuing to protect the founders. Also, the good fortune (*eutukhén*, line 8) promised by Apollo merely anticipates the prosperity (*eutukhêi*, line 4) which should result from the Cyreneans giving citizenship to people coming from Thera. This relationship, woven by the promise of a prosperous life between future and past, echoes both the decision made by the assembly and the title of the text which publishes its content: the utterance of the decision and the title of the stele are both placed under the sign of Good Fortune—*Túkha agathá* (line 1) taken up again by *agathâi túkhai* (in the dative, line 11), in a chiasmus! Finally, the double use of the technical verb *katoikízein* to designate the act of foundation reinforces the historical character conferred on it by the final reference to the order (*epítaxin*, line 10; and not the oracle!) given by Apollo concerning the sending of the colonial expedition (*apoikían*, line 10), in the repetition of the spatial relationship between Thera and Cyrene.[15]

Through the regressive temporality of the uttered enunciation, we thus go back to the founding event: the order given by Apollo *Archēgétēs*. The word

---

[14] The respective semantic values of the perfect and of the infinitive are explained by Humbert 1960:148–149 and 125. This form of double vocal subordination of the text of the people's decision is found in other inscriptions of the same era: see for example the wording of Athenian rules relative to the cult of Asclepius (11 Sokolowski *Suppl.*), as well as commentary given on this by Seibert 1963:13–17. He also refers "the city" to Thera and "the people" to Cyrene (16).

[15] The meaning of the technical terms *katoikízein* (in the sense of settlement or resettlement of a community) and *apoikía* (in the sense of establishing a colony by immigration) is explored by Casevitz 1985:165–173 and 114–135. On the role played by Tyche in the stele's title, see n25 below.

of the "chief founder" is thus situated at the beginning of the chronology of the recounted or enunciated time. Despite an epinician by Pindar (to which we shall return), and if we are to believe the text of the oath itself (line 27), this epiclesis is traditionally less that of the Apollo of Delphi and more that commonly attributed to Battos, venerated in Cyrene as founding hero![16]

3.1.2. The cultic consecration of the decree of Cyrene

Just after the narrative reference to the act of foundation come the clauses of the decree which finally resulted from the order issued by Apollo, the "beginning author". With one exception, they are formulated in the aorist infinitive as imperative, just as are the collective demands of the Therans. Not only do the Therans keep their citizenship once they are established in the colony, without any temporal limit, but all the Therans who emigrated to Cyrene also swear (in a present which could represent either reiteration or duration: (*poieîsthai*, line 13) "the same oath (*hórkon*, line 14) which the others once swore (*potè diórkósan*, line 14–15)." This return to the time of the narrative contributes both to providing a base for the identity of the terms of the oath by giving it historical legitimacy, and to situating its origins in an indeterminate "long ago" which we would call "the time of myth." The result of this is the integration of the citizens of Thera enjoying isopolity in the political structure of the city: being assigned to a tribe, a phratry, and one of the nine *hetaireîai*. This political and social organization, which may go back no farther than the speech of the legislator Demonax in the middle of the sixth century, recalls not only that of Thera, the former mother-city of Cyrene, but also that of classical Athens.[17] All this as regards the decision of isopolity whose utterance appears at the exact physical center of the first section.

---

[16] Pindar *Pythian* 5.60. On the description of Battos as *archēgétēs*, see also *SEG* IX. 72, 22 = 115, A 22 Sokolowski *Suppl.* and Jeffery 1961:143–147 (as compared with other heroes or founder kings), and the complementary references given by Calame 1996a:154–155. Despite the title which Detienne 1998:95–104 gives to one of the excellent chapters he devotes to Apollo the founder, the god of Delphi bears the epiclesis of *Archēgétēs* only in the Pindar passage cited, in Thucydides 6.3.1, on the "Founders' Stele," and in the inscription in Hierapolis (153 Judeich); cf. Malkin 1987:241–250, and 1994:153–157.

[17] The division of Cyrene citizens into tribes, phratries, and *hetaireîai* is commented on by Chamoux 1952:213–214, who presents documents attesting to a similar structure in Thera; for Athens, see for example Stockton 1990:28–41, and Jones 1999:151–173, 195–216, and 223–227. The reform introduced by the Arcadian legislator Demonax of Mantineia, called as arbiter under Battos III (Herodotus 4.161.2–3) to integrate the new arrivals into the three "Dorian" tribes, is discussed by Jeffery 1961:142–144.

Rather surprisingly, the remaining two-thirds of the text of the decree (and thus of the first section of the inscription) are devoted to arrangements related to the engraving of the *pséphisma* itself (line 16), to the consecration of the stele in the ancestral shrine of Apollo Pythios, and to related expenses, to be taken from the revenues of the god. The order to engrave the text of the oath is also placed in this sequence of prescriptions expressed by the aorist infinitive, paired with a final form in the imperative of the third person plural (*komisásthōn*, line 22): a pretext for a new incursion into the past time of the narrative with an allusion to the founders sailing (*hoi oikistêres*, line 19) with Battos to Thera in Libya. The pragmatic effect of this arrangement is twofold, since while it confirms the relationship already established between the past time of the founding act and a present to be carried out, it also furnishes the written consecration of the oral word of those who swore the oath; just as the inscription of the text of the decree itself sets in writing, on a stele of especially precious marble, the twofold oral speech mentioned at the beginning. There is a strong contrast between the initial forms *êipe* and *légonti* (line 1)—oral—and the triple repetition of *katagráphen* and *katagráphan* (line 14, 18, and 21)—writing down—at the end of this first section of the Cyrenean stele.

Oriented toward a future so near that it assumes the permanence of the present, the time of enunciation of the second sequence of utterances which radiate out from the center of the decree of isopolity thus also finds its foundation in the past of the founding act.

3.2. The second section: "Oath of the Founders"

After the decree of Cyrene comes the text of the "oath" of Thera, whose title is doubly misleading: under such a title, utterances related to the text make up barely more than half of this second section of the stele, and the text does not coincide with the *expressis verbis* swearing of a true oath. Indeed, we have gone from the oath (*hórkos*, line 14) mentioned in the first section to a *hórkion* (line 24; already in line 18), that is to a word, often in the plural, which can take on the wider meaning of contract, treaty, or convention. And it is precisely this word in the plural (*hórkia*, line 40; with the same use in lines 47 and 49, but already in line 9, in a wording which recalls that of the end of the stele) which we find again at the beginning of the second part of the second section; there it designates oath-related practices guaranteeing that the barely-mentioned convention will be honored. Indeed, the end of the stele's text is entirely devoted to those ritual gestures which confirmed the contract; all this in a narrative mode which is also used at the beginning of the second section, to recall the circumstances surrounding the drafting of the contract.[18]

3.2.1. The contractual decree of foundation

The text cited in the second section of the stele is thus not the expected text of the oath, but rather corresponds to a decision made in contractual form, by the assembly (*ekklēsía*, line 25) of Thera—for us, an institution whose existence cannot be attested before the fourth century.[19] In contrast to the decree of the "people" of Cyrene mentioned in the first section and phrased in a form of the perfect which ensures its permanency in the present, the decision of the Theran assembly is presented in the aorist, as a unique fact in the past (*édoxe*, line 25, in contrast with *dedókhthai*, line 11), which is to say as a historical fact; but the utterance of its content, referred to the Therans in general, is given in the present (*dokeî*, line 26). It is as if the specific temporal effect of the perfect were broken down into its two constituent moments: a decision in the past, whose validity extends into the present. This enunciative split allows giving to the popular decision the essentially narrative turn that the second part of the stele will take.

The text of the decree begins by narrating the origin of the decision to send an expedition of Therans designated as *hetaîroi* (line 27) to Libya, led by Battos, who is both *archēgétēs* (founder, leader) and king: the origin is the oracle given spontaneously (*automátixen*, line 25) by Apollo to this same Battos and to the Therans, enjoining them to colonize Cyrene. And so there is a reappearance of nearly all the terms which concluded the first part, used in the description of the engraving of the stele and in the consecration of the "oath" (*hórkion*, line 18) to Apollo Pythios: Thera, Libya, Cyrene, Battos, Apollo. In this reappearance of terms belonging to the fourth-century decree in the supposedly more ancient Theran text, we must of course wonder about the explicit and precise naming of Cyrene, which obviously did not yet exist at the moment of the decision to colonize it ... In other versions, the oracle simply indicates a direction, with no toponymic reference whatever!

---

[18] The absence of the text of the oath itself confirms for Chamoux 1952:109, that the document transcribed does not correspond to the original Theran decree (*contra* Seibert 1963:50–52 and 57–66, who attempts to reconstruct the text of the original decree, distinct from later additions). On the meaning of *hórkion* and of *hórkia* as "contract," see Graham 1960:104, as well as Seibert 1963:60–67.

[19] The possible existence of an *ekklēsía* in sixth-century Thera is mentioned by Graham 1960:104.

Be that as it may, the alleged Theran decree details the composition and the line of conduct imposed on the colonial expedition, using the forms of the infinitive as imperative also present in the Cyrenean decree. It will include, on equal terms, one son from every household, as well as those who have reached adulthood and those who want to sail with the Therans and who have the status of free men[20]—depending on the preferred interpretation of this incomplete text. If the colonists succeed in establishing the settlement, the Theran who joins them later will enjoy the citizenship attached to the land given him. If they do not succeed after five years, colonists may return to Thera where they will recover both their property and their citizenship. These arrangements also have a constraining character given them by a final rule expressed in the imperative and in the future: confiscation of property, forfeited to the people, and the death penalty for anyone who refuses to go, and thus disobeys the city, as well as for anyone who protects him, even inside his own family.

From a temporal point of view, the contractual decision of the *ekklēsía* of Thera, stated in the present (*dokeî*, line 26), is situated exactly between the oracle of Apollo and the two scenarios imagined for what may happen with the colony. Expressed twice in wording which uses the jussive infinitive with its future temporal value, the arrangements concerning citizenship retained (either by Therans joining the colony or by colonists obliged to return to the main island) take on an obvious argumentative purpose in the fourth century, when the Therans of Cyrene request that their citizenship be restored. The provisions of the Cyrene decree can thus appear as the realization, centuries later, of those provisions made by the assembly of Thera.

3.2.2. Contract, imprecation, and ritual gesture

As we have said, the text of the oath which sets out the convention agreed to by the citizens, announced in the title of this second section, and which one would expect to read just after the text of the popular decree of Thera, is conspicuous by its absence. In its place, and in the narrative aorist mode, is the simple mention of (language-related) gestures which marked the way it was carried out (*hórkia epoiḗsanto*, lines 40–41). These gestures were accepted by those "remaining here" (*auteî*, line 41) and by those preparing to depart to found the colony (*oikíxontes*, in the intentional future, says the speaker, who now places himself spatially in a Theran perspective ("here" is Thera!). As has been pointed out, the absence of performative expressions which should

---

[20] The composition of the expedition expressed in this incomplete text corresponds only partially to information given by Herodotus 4.153; cf. Jeffery 1961:139–140, and Oliver 1966.

compose the oath is in some ways compensated for by the imprecations which follow its simple mention.[21] In the same utterance, the oath itself and the curses hurled by those who participate against those who would transgress, both among those citizens leaving for Libya and among those staying "here" (*auteî*, line 43—in Thera; in the position of a chiasmus, in a Gorgias-like figure of speech!) are both related in the same narrative mode, in the past.

It is as if it were left to the ritual gesture described at the end of the text to confer a performative dimension to an oath and to gestures whose expression is simply narrated in a form of the aorist which follows and echoes the form used to introduce the original decision of the assembly. This means that from a spatial point of view the fulfillment of the agreement is indeed situated in Thera and from a Theran perspective, while from a temporal point of view the reference is to the time of the decree at Cyrene in the fourth century! And the curse described is accompanied by the burning of molded wax images; the entire community—men, women, boys, and girls—participate in this ritual.

It is not too surprising to find *kolossoí* in a ritual imprecatory gesture which foresees performatively, through the melting of wax figures, the fate of anyone who would break the oath; in a metaphoric liquefaction (*kataleíbesthai*, line 47), he will disappear without a trace, eliminating any possible memory. The guilty party, his descendants, and his property will all disappear. On the one hand, in the song of reproach brought on by Helen's betrayal, the chorus of Aeschylus' *Agamemnon* recreates the plaintive words of the prophets: the absent Helen in her home is only a *phásma*, a simple apparition; she appears to her spouse only in dreams, assuming the vain and elusive appearance (*dóxa*) of dream figures; and thus she is like one of those statues (*kolossoí*) whose grace ends up becoming an object of hatred, since Aphrodite's erotic flux cannot emanate from lifeless eyes; a clever and elusive figure who attracts the eye, only to fade like appearances in dreams. In its inconsistency, the *kolossós* in this case is a visual illusion, like, for example, the *eídōlon*, the image of the dead Patroclus which Achilles sees before him in a waking dream, but which he cannot grasp.[22] The *kolossós* thus represents the "person," and it can also fade away without leaving a trace.

---

[21] The absence of "explicit performatives" in the text of the "oath" was studied by Létoublon 1989:103–104. She sees in this narrative phrasing of one part of the corresponding utterance a form of indirect discourse; in the case of the decree of Thera, the fusion of the figurines seems to take the place of the sacrifice which one would expect to accompany the sequence "summary expression of commitment—invocation of a deity—imprecation against possible perjury": cf. Lonis 1980:267–278.

[22] Aeschylus *Agamemnon* 410–426, as well as *Iliad* 23.59–108; cf. Vernant 1965:251–264.

On the other hand, the famous "sacred law" of Cyrene itself, a set of rules governing purificatory practices found on another stele which dates from the fourth century, prescribes another use for *kolossoí*. When a suppliant is received within a host's house, and cannot name the person who sent him because of that person's death, he must invoke that nameless person as a human being, whether a man or a woman; after making male and female figurines of wood or earth, the suppliant's host must serve them a portion of everything, and then after completing these rites (*tà nomizómena*) he must deposit the figurines and the portions served to them in a forest that has not been cut.[23] Ephemeral substitutes for an individual without renown and thus without civic identity, or representatives of a suppliant considered demonic because he can provide no one to vouch for him, these *kolossoí* are condemned to disappear in a wild place, with no grave and no memorial rite.

In these nearly contemporary inscriptions from Cyrene, the *kolossós* appears not only as ritual substitute for someone who has passed on, or who is destined to disappear leaving no memory, but appears also (in comparison) as the double of the word which must act on him. Following the narration of those ritual gestures which accompanied the composing of the oath of Thera and the curses which accompanied it, the text of the second section (and thus of the entire text of the stele called the "Oath of the Founders") concludes with the utterance of the curses themselves. An ambiguous utterance if ever there was one, since its enunciation, while seeming to assume an indirect discourse form, takes up the imperative, expressed as an infinitive, of both the Cyrenean decree of isopolity and the Theran decree on founding the colony:[24] May he who breaks the terms of the oath dissolve and liquefy, assimilated to the wax figures, (*hôsper toùs kolossoús*), while those who honor it, along with their descendants, will know great good fortune; both "those who sail to Libya and those who remain in Thera," the document adds. This wording again uses that of the narrative part of the text; it refers the time and the "here" (*autêi*, lines 41 and 43) of the oath and the curse to the (present) moment preceding the departure, in Thera. Mentioned at the end of the imprecatory expression, and thus at the very end of the stele's text, the advantages (*agathá*, line 51)

---

[23] *SEG* IX (1938), 72.110–121 = 115. B 29–39 Sokolowski (*Suppl.*); Parker 1983:347–349. In his commentary on this strange procedure, he mentions the possibility that in this ritual the suppliant is considered a harmful demon; see also Johnston 1999:58–60. On the concrete aspects of establishing a contract, see also the parallels given by Bettini 1992:60–64.

[24] The indirect discourse form of these last utterances was recognized by Létoublon 1989:104, who tries to reconstitute the text of the imprecation in direct discourse, an effort obviously rendered unnecessary by the infinitive forms of the imperative.

promised to both the Therans and the future Cyreneans recalls the prosperity mentioned at the beginning of the inscription; the same prosperity expected from the decree of isopolity (*eutukhêi*, line 4 and line 8) is inscribed in the text's dedication to Good Fortune (*Túkha agathá*, line 1 and line 11).

The text plays on the hopes nourished by a divine being with well-defined responsibilities, quite independently of the epigraphic convention which leads to a number of decrees of this period being dedicated to the gods in general and the *Agathè Túkhē* in particular. Reigning over assemblies, this daughter of Ocean and Zeus himself, sister to Eunomia, distinguishes herself through abundance, which iconography from the fourth century on symbolizes with a horn of plenty; this symbol indicating prosperity is often accompanied by a rudder recalling the conduct of human affairs.[25]

3.3. Temporal-spatial networks

Thus the temporal-spatial reference centered on Cyrene is added to the semantic echo which rests on the founding oracular speech, to make the first part of the stele, which carries the Cyrenean isopolitical decree, accord with the second section which enunciates and sets out the Theran colonization decree. But those are not the only discursive elements which insure the coherence of the whole text consecrated in the shrine of Apollo Pythios.

Once again from a temporal point of view, the mention of ritual gestures ensures a strong relationship between the first and second parts of the stele. The procedure which consists of a comparison related both to gesture and to language, used both to affirm the conclusion of an oath and to show its consequences, has an astonishing parallel in the oath sworn in the *Iliad*, between Achaeans and Trojans, to end the war by a single combat between Menelaus and Paris.[26] Not only is the ritual oath sworn on that occasion designated by the same plural term *hórkia* found in the narration of the decree of Cyrene (line 40) (which also corresponds to a solemn agreement); and not only does the oath sworn in Agamemnon's address to Zeus foresee two possible situations based on the outcome of the duel, in the same terms the Theran decree uses in foreseeing two possible outcomes for the colonial expedition to Libya:

---

[25] Several references on epigraphic convention can be found in Henry 1977:51 and 82–83 (a work brought to my attention by Anne Bielman). Concerning the functions attributed to Tyche even in "archaic" poetry, see Villard 1997:115–117 (with numerous bibliographic references), especially concerning Pindar *Olympian* 12.1–5, and fr. 40 Maehler.

[26] *Iliad* 3.245–301, in an interesting parallel pointed out by Létoublon 1989:105; on this, see also Stengel 1920:136–138.

the *ei mén ken ... ei dé ke* of the *Iliad* is answered by the Theran decree's expression *ai mèn dé ka ... ai dé ka* (line 30 and line 33). But even more importantly the sacrifice of two lambs which consecrates Agamemnon's language act is followed by a double ritual of language and gesture which strikingly recalls the procedure outlined in the "Oath of the Founders." In a speech pronounced by each participant, both Achaeans and Trojans hurl an imprecation in which the libation of wine which accompanies the sacrifice is compared with the fate of anyone who would violate the contractual oath: may his brains be spilled on the earth like "this" wine (*hōs hóde oînos*, line 300), and may his family and children suffer the same fate. Through metaphor, the Iliadic ritual gesture thus gives a sort of material confirmation to the perjurer's future, assigned to him by the imprecation. In the same way, between the past (configured by recounted time and time of narration) of the oracle of Apollo, the present of the decree (with its indices of uttered enunciation), and the near future of the different scenarios that the official text (between intra- and extra-discursive) imagines, it thus belongs to the (extra-discursive) ritual gesture to establish a relationship of tension which confers a form of material realization on the enunciatively-imagined future.

The same is true of the first part of the text where (as we have said) the engraving of the decree on a stele and its consecration in the shrine of Apollo Pythios confirm the permanence of the anticipated result of the (present) recognition of isopoly between Cyrene and Thera, by concrete and ritual gesture. This recognition is guaranteed by the return to the past of the Theran decree concerning colonization, and by reference to the role played by Apollo of Delphi and his oracular commands. The time of the narrative of past actions presented as motivations, especially through its use of jussive infinitives, also leads to the present of the uttered enunciation, even before the description of ritual gestures ensures the relationship with an extra-discursive time which corresponds to future social realization. With its two references to the spoken word, the enunciative speech which introduces the decree of the Cyrenean people by reference to the past act of colonization follows the same movement: the past words of Damis (*êipe*, line 2) introducing in the present the demands of the Therans and Kleudamas for the future good fortune of the city and the people of Cyrene.

Certainly, from the point of view of narration and consequently of the narrative putting-into-discourse of recounted time, the text of the first section of the stele is organized in what we call a *Ringstruktur* or *ring structure*. Like the "hymnic" relative, the relative pronoun *tá* (line 5) returns to the tradition of the ancestors and introduces the narrative of the colonization following

Apollo's order, in the aorist. From this founding past, the repeated evocation of good fortune ensures transition to the permanence of the decree's present (*dedókhthai*), placed as we have said in the physical center of the text; from the near future of the decree and its engraving on the stele, the return through *tó* (line 19) of the allusion to the original oath refers us once again to the aorist of the colonial expedition. Similarly, the initial allusion to the past of Apollo's oracle to the Therans concerning the colonization of Cyrene finds a ring-structure echo in the second section, with the final mention of the oath sworn both by those citizens leaving for Libya and by those remaining in Thera.

But from the spatial-temporal point of view, this mention is expressed in the very near future (*êmen*, line 50) expected from the imprecation ritual conducted "here" in Thera. But rather than following a ring structure, the utterances which make up the second section follow the chronological order of actions given in the narrative mode, in the aorist: decree of the assembly (*édoxe*, line 25), "oath" (*hórkia epoiésanto*, line 41; succession stressed by *epì toútois*), imprecations (*aràs epoiésanto*, line 42), wax figures consumed by fire (*kolosòs ketékaion*, line 44; in the imperfect tense). While the *epoiésanto* forms evoke forms organized similarly in ring structure in the first section, particularly striking in the second section are the three repetitions, through a series of participial constructions, of two distinct groups: those who stay "here" in Thera, and those who sail to Libya. The repetition of language here takes on an incantorial aspect which seems to correspond to the phrases pronounced in performing the ritual. This coincidence between time of enunciation and time of the ritual draws us from the intra- to the extra-discursive, by evoking the real prosperity expected from honoring the oath and by perpetuating the memory of those who are not reduced to wax figures, because they honor the oath. This oath was already evoked in the first section, where the Therans who founded Cyrene are distinguished from those who stayed in Thera! The structural circularity is broken, and leads to pragmatic realization in the near future marked by permanence.

Insofar as it may be pertinent, the question of the text's "authenticity" (so often posed in terms of dialectal forms, lexical usage, and political institutions) may perhaps be made clearer through the semio-narrative, enunciative, and even anthropological views adopted here. Indeed, the coincidence between the narrative aspect of the exposition of ritual procedures accompanying an oath whose text is not mentioned in the second section, and the narrative forms through which old times are evoked in the first section, makes one think of a document, rewritten probably from a Theran perspective and designed to respond to the requirements of a political situation in fourth-century Cyrene.

167

In this, comparison with other accounts of the founding of Cyrene may prove relevant.

4. Time of the oracles and time of the citizen

The question of the relationship between the intra- and the extra-discursive in this strange document whose temporal and spatial architecture we have just studied has been generally posed in terms of authenticity. As regards the "oath" of Thera, it was approached in terms of the relationship between the stele and history; more specifically, the relationship the text is supposed to have with an original assumed to date from the moment of founding has been examined. After an exhaustive study devoted to the question concerning the existence of the historical "source," the historian comes to the conclusion that an allusion by Herodotus to the decree of Thera "is favorable to the hypothesis of a recorded decree at Thera and more favorable than not to the possibility that this is the decree produced with changes of wording at Cyrene."[27]

In this quest for the original historical document, oracles play an essential role, while they also draw us into this comparative internal approach. Not satisfied with simply sending us back to the point of origin of the brief narrative plot opening onto the future presented by both sections of the stele, the oracles given by Apollo recall both the Theran and the Cyrenean versions of the narrative of Cyrene's founding summarized by Herodotus. The spontaneous order (*automátixen*, line 25) given to Battos and to the Therans to colonize Cyrene, as claimed at the beginning of the Theran decree and as repeated in the Cyrenean decree as a simple injunction (*epítaxin*, line 10) from Apollo Archēgétēs, with its guarantee of prosperity for the Therans who founded Cyrene (line 8), must be compared to the repeated and connected orders mentioned by Herodotus' *lógos*, in an investigative narrative whose meaning and direction are often provided by oracular responses.

In brief, the Theran narrative of Cyrene's colonization as Herodotus presents it begins with two oracular answers. The first, given to the king of Thera who was consulting the Pythia on other matters, told the sovereign (and Battos who was accompanying him) to found a city in Libya; the second oracle is just a repetition of the first, after seven years of drought brought on by failure to honor the oracular injunction. The colonial expedition, chosen in the manner stated in the first part of the stele and led by Battos, named as commander and king, was organized only after a fruitless first attempt on the coastal island of

---

[27] Herodotus 4.153, commented on by Graham 1960:111; see also Chamoux 1952:108–114.

Plataea. The Cyrenean version, on the other hand, is punctuated with no fewer than three oracles: the first is given directly to Battos whose stuttering, at the beginning of his question to the Pythia of Delphi, is changed through a play on words into an order to assume sovereignty over a colony founded in Libya; the misfortunes resulting from failing to understand this first oracle lead to a second question and a second answer which apparently gives the precise destination of the colonial expedition—Cyrene (!); after an unfortunate attempt to return, then a fruitless attempt on the island of Plataea, a third consultation at Delphi indicates that the colony must take hold in Libya, "feeder of flocks," on the continent itself.[28]

Beyond the differences in the oracle's answers, what is important to note here is the existence of two versions of the narrative of Battos' colonization of Cyrene, even in the fifth century. Each offers a specific temporal and spatial perspective. One could point out that the Cyrenean version related by Herodotus and the text of the Cyrene decree in the first section of the stele are the only ones which name the exact destination of the expedition, contrary to the previously mentioned habit of the oracle at Delphi, which was to give only a direction, and even that often encoded.[29] Probably an indication that the *lógos* related by Herodotus and the text of the decree both refer to a document written *a posteriori*, whether an inscription or a narrative (depending on the oral tradition?). But it is very strange to find the explicit mention of Cyrene occurring also in the evocation of the first oracle in the decree of Thera (line 26); it appears in the second section of the epigraphic text, which is to say in the text of the "Oath of the Founders" itself, which is supposed to go back to the seventh century! One might find in this oracular mention of Cyrene an additional proof that, in spite of the Theran spatial perspective already mentioned, the decree of Thera is really a recreation by the fourth-century Cyreneans and Therans, possibly based on a more or less original Theran "document."

The question becomes even more complicated when we notice that the spontaneous aspect of the oracle given to Battos (*automátixen*, line 25) recalls the most poetic version among those dramatized by Pindar:

> O son of Polymnastos, blessed, by this decree
> the oracle steered your course
> in the voice unasked (*automátōi keládōi*) of the bee-priestess,

---

[28] Herodotus 4.150.1–4.159.1; in 1996a:128–156, I presented a semio-narrative analysis of these two versions, together with numerous bibliographic references to other studies on the subject; see also the additional comments by Bremmer 2001:155–157.

[29] References on this in Malkin 1987:29–88.

> who with threefold salutation revealed you
> destined king of Kyrene
> as you came to ask what release the gods might grant of your
> stammering voice.

Pindar *Pythian* 4.59–63 (trans. Lattimore)

So it is worded in *Pythian* 4, in contrast to the allusion mentioned in *Pythian* 5, also an epinician composed in praise of Arkesilas IV, the king of Cyrene whose four-horse chariot won at the Pythian Games of 462.[30]

Inscribed within the process of constant poetic recreation which characterizes the narrative we choose to call mythic, especially in Greece, these reformulations of the founding event of Cyrene during the fifth century make vain any attempt to reconstitute the original document. These different narratives must be taken for what they are: discursive and symbolic representations of time and space from a certain historical situation (past and present) on which they speculate. It is through these fictional spatial-temporal configurations that community memory and tradition are formed and evolve, along with their ideological function.

From this point of view, it is no accident that the oracle of Apollo contributes heavily to integrating the temporal fabric of the (second) Theran section of the "Stele of the Founders" into the fabric of the (first) Cyrenean section. On the one hand, as narrative origin, the Pythian oracle determines the ritual acts which come to confirm and realize the Theran decree, and consequently the act of founding; on the other hand, the "automatic" oracle given by the god of Delphi to Battos and to the people of Thera, in the form of the injunction by Apollo *Archēgétēs*, comes to guarantee the good fortune and prosperity promised to the people of Cyrene in the fourth century. Promises made in the first section thus follow the model of promises made to the colonists who honored the original founding contract. So there is a correspondence between the oracle pronounced by Apollo at Delphi which constitutes the axial point of time, and the reconfigured memory in the Cyrene decree with its central spatial position in the shrine in Cyrene itself, where the stele is consecrated to this same Apollo Pythios.

Narratively, it is essentially the Pythian oracle which ensures the transition between recounted time in the first section of the epigraphic text and the combination of recounted time and time of narration in the second

---

[30] Pindar *Pythian* 4.58–60. In addition to the two versions mentioned here, see the very different narrative offered in *Pythian* 9; on this, see study and references in my work 1996a:99–116.

section. Inscribed on the same stele, consecrated in Apollo's shrine at Delphi, the Cyrenean decree (*psáphisma*, line 16) becomes a sort of copy of commitments made "long ago" (*pote*, line 14), in a time whose date is simply that of the god's will. Granting isopolity to Therans who live in the city of Cyrene in the fourth century essentially comes down to refounding the colonial city, as concerns future prosperity and good fortune. In this, consecrating the stele (its permanence granted by being written within Apollo's shrine) seems to be a ritual equivalent to burning the wax figures. Through antiphrasis, the ritual is meant to ensure the continued effectiveness of the original contract, and the harmonious development of the colonial community that the convention proposes to organize. But in contrast to the versions of Cyrene's founding set forth by Herodotus and by Pindar in the fifth century, royalty no longer figures in the fourth-century text. Battos appears implicitly and paradoxically as the founder of a democratic regime! Between the two centuries, the Cyrenean dynasty of the Battiads had had to concede its power to the demos.[31] The political paradigm determining the memory of the civic community has changed!

5. Weaving space and time between Delphi and Cyrene

Apollo who points the way, Apollo the ram-horned leader, Apollo walking, Apollo the surveyor and measurer, Apollo the architect, Apollo the civilizer— many ancient and modern epicleseis were devised to name the god of the oracle in his function as founder and *archēgétēs*.[32] Pindar himself is not untouched by the spatial organization of the "well-built city," to refer to just one example of local representations of Cyrene's founding. Assuming the responsibilities of the *archēgétēs* god, Battos-Aristoteles not only opened up full access to the deep sea for the colonists' ships, but also traced out the paved street that would be taken by chariots and processions dedicated to Apollo, the protector of mortals; indeed, one of those teams of horses ensured the Panhellenic fame of the colonial city and of its sovereign, Arkesilas IV. In a poetic fiction which does not correspond exactly to what the archaeologists have been able to reconstruct, the straight line of this avenue leads directly to the agora on the stern of which the founding captain, now transformed into

---

[31] Arkesilas IV, a descendant of the founder Battos and last Battiad king of Cyrene, was forced to flee the city in 440; see to the historical reconstruction proposed by Chamoux 1952:25–38.

[32] See especially Malkin 1994:143–158, and Detienne 1998:85–111.

an *archēgétēs* hero honored by the people, will have his tomb (Figure 5). In the metaphor woven here, maritime progress is transformed into the wide street which organizes the political and religious space of the colonial city.[33]

But in Pindar's poem, the spatial progress of the founders develops in parallel with the extremely complex temporal development which leads from the act which founded its heroic origins, going back to the time of the Trojan War, up through ritual honors enjoyed by Battos and his successors. Its final stage is the celebration of the Pythian victory of the Battiad king Arkesilas IV, with performers singing and dancing (probably at the Karneia festival of Apollo) the epinician of a poet who claims to be related to the founding hero, through distant ancestors! The symbolic weaving which inserts the founding act into a narrative continuity placing the event in the perspective of the heroic age of the Trojan War thus undoubtedly shares affinities with the spatial line followed by the performers of Pindar's poem: perhaps in a real processional route through the city, from the place of religious celebration of the winner, very probably near the Garden of Aphrodite placed inside the great shrine of Apollo, patron god of Cyrene, toward the tomb of the founding hero, on a straight path which forms the main axis of the urban space surrounding the agora.

In the hymnic poem dedicated to him by Callimachus, it is Apollo himself who "weaves" the founding of cities, which he contributes to creating by furnishing a model of this territorial and architectural "weaving," the altar at Delos which the god "plaits" with the horns of goats sacred to his sister Artemis; this first act of founding is followed in the narrative logic of the Greek poem by the narrative of the founding of Cyrene and the establishment of the Karneia festival by Battos-Aristoteles.[34] The axial moment of the first founding by the god himself orients the entire chronological line which goes through Sparta and Thera to place Apollo and the Karneia in Cyrene and extends through successive celebrations of the festival; it is anchored in an architectural and etiological gesture conceived as a weaving.

As for the temporal interlacing woven in the "Stele of the Founders," attention is focused on the founding gesture ordered by the god, first by the misleading central title which divides the text into two sections, and then by

---

[33] Pindar *Pythian* 5.77–95; see also the commentary I gave on this specific passage in 1996a:57–60 and 119–128; on the architectural reality concealed by the poetic metaphor, see Gentili et al. 1995:535–536.

[34] Callimachus *Hymn to Apollo* 55–96; cf. Calame 1996a:109–113 and Detienne 1998:96–100.

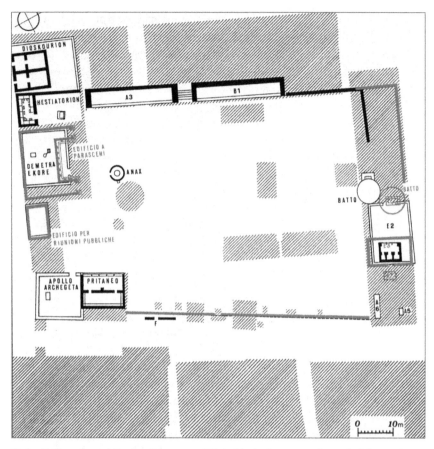

Figure 5. The agora of Cyrene, 5th century BC. In black, the area at the end of the regal period; in grey, the structures built in the second half of the century; shading indicates areas of subsequent occupation.

the reminder in each of the two parts of the oracle given by Apollo to Battos and the Therans, ordering colonization of a site specifically named Cyrene. Through the narrative and descriptive means discussed so far, and through the verbal expression of the twofold gesture of melting the wax figures and of religious consecration of a written document, displaying the stele in the shrine of Apollo Pythios constitutes a second gesture of founding the city; the fourth-century document takes over a contract originally made between colonizers and colonists, between the existing country and the future colonial city.

Like the founding act related by Pindar which opens with the sequence of kings descended from Battos and continues to the reign of the sovereign celebrated in the *hic et nunc* of the poem, like the narrative of founding taken up by Callimachus and which leads to the succession of annual celebrations of the Karneia, the act of establishing a colony represented by the stele and its decree reduplicates, through a written "performance," the founding act desired by Apollo, while it also projects into a very near future the good fortune expected from the decision on isopolity.

While it is able to provide a passage from narrated time and time of narration to a time of active enunciation in the present (thanks to the oracle), the text of the decree shows none of the forms of "I" usually interpreted as strong indicators of the utterance of the enunciation. Forms of the third person are substituted for the expected first-person utterances; these forms credit first the decision on the decree of isopolity, and then the decision on the colonial expedition, to the *dêmos* of the people of Cyrene (*dedókhthai tôi dámōi*, line 11) and to the Theran assembly (*édoxe tâi ekklēsíai*, line 25). In their third-person wording, and as regards the text inscribed on the stele of *sphragís*, these traditional utterances assume the role of "signature" taken on by the last lines of Bacchylides' *Dithyramb* 17, when it alludes to the choral groups of Keans.[35] And so the narrative identity which surfaces in the Cyrenean text consecrated in the shrine of Apollo merges with that of the community of citizens meeting in assembly.

By its response to the act of democratic foundation, and through decision and consecration procedures where the community claims the authority of the god of Delphi, the *ipse*-identity of the individual citizens of Cyrene with which the Therans hope to be associated must become stabilized in an *idem*-identity which is obviously community-related. This is less an ethnic identity than a political identity, religiously consecrated both in time, through reference to the founding oracle of Apollo, and in space, through the consecration of the text within the shrine of the god himself; an identity of a cultural and memorial sort which came out of an agreement made according to the rules of "democratic" debate, in a very Greek perspective.[36]

In the way in which a history (legendary in our eyes) is used, it is not the image of cycle, but rather the dynamic continuity established by the connection between the founding event and the performing of rituals which allows one to struggle against the feeling of the ephemeral nature both of the indi-

[35] On this process of the authorial seal, see details given above at chapter III, section 4.2 above.

[36] These two concepts of *ipséité* and of *mêmeté* developed by Ricoeur were discussed in references given in the introduction n55. On objects and places of ethnic and cultural identity, see thoughts of Fabietti 1998:145–153.

vidual and of the community of citizens; in the repetition of recounted time and space through the rhythm of narration, the spatial-temporal configuration constructed in this epigraphic discourse plays a determining role as intermediary. In this transforming of a regime of historicity into a spatial-temporal logic and a regime of politically and culturally active truth in the present and the immediate future, it is not the profane time of history which is based in the atemporal permanence of sacred myth, as one might expect if one adopts the Eliadian perspective. Rather Apollo and the heroic act intervene directly in the political present and in a central religious space (related to Delphi), in order to guarantee the validity and the permanence of a new founding act, thus establishing a determining pragmatic and memorial tension between the founding past and the near future. Community memory is mobile!

In our own eyes, a document is certified authentic if it has a date, location, and signature. For the community of citizens of the Cyrene of the fourth century, the authenticity of a document depends as much on its consecration in the temple of the city's founding and protecting god as it does on the discursive fabric which places its utterances in the temporal and spatial perspective of the first act of founding. Quite differently from the traditional philosophical perspective, and far from the idealizing interpretations it has fostered even among our contemporaries, the representation of time underlying temporal and spatial configurations set forth in the epigraphic text from Cyrene is essentially political, in the widest sense of the term, as the Greeks themselves would have understood it.

V

RITUAL AND INITIATORY ITINERARIES TOWARD THE AFTERLIFE

Time, Space, and Pragmatics in the Gold Lamellae

WESTERN POSTMODERNISM, moving now toward hyper- or meta-modernism, has been characterized both by the desire for imme-diate profit and by the development of means of communication and multi-media. These two phenomena are brought together by the omni-presence of advertising in all the new technical means of communication, an advertising designed to drive consumption and thus immediate gain in a productive society; they have brought about an acceleration of social and individual time, coupled with a explosion of knowledge. On television and on the internet, perhaps a bit more interactively on the internet, theoretical and practical knowledge are fragmented and constantly reassembled to respond to the needs of an individualism which must be constantly sought and revived.

From a spatial-temporal point of view, this accelerated production of a knowledge which is more and more diverse has brought about a fragmenting both of our history and of the space in which that history is broadcast. This vast space-time is focused on the immediate and on what is intended to shock and to provoke, throughout the entire world: an accelerated "presentism" with no thought for coherent continuity, for relating rationally, or even for long-term perspective.[1] This geographic explosion in an economic and ideo-logical "globalization" prohibits any construction of spatial-temporal configu-rations designed to serve social, reflexive, and critical observation.

The competitive market of hypermodernity and its spatial-temporal regime are very far from the preoccupations of Greek citizens, concerned with the spatial-temporal line ensured by destiny and guaranteed by the different

---

[1] The neologism is taken from Hartog 2003:28; cf also 119–127.

deities of the pantheon appropriate to each city. The memory of the community, with its heroic models often ritually active in the present, with its epic traditions and its local and pan-Hellenic genealogies, with its poetic and plastic creativity, with its specific places of religious celebration, nurtures the collective past of individual human itineraries—as has already been said often enough. The future of these women and men, deeply conscious of the ephemeral and finite nature of their destiny, was essentially driven by their desire for immortality. As a brief comparative study will demonstrate, there is a strong contrast between this representation of a linear mortality, the object of many points of reference in space and in time, and the spatial-temporal paradigm founded on the labile network of post-, hyper-, and metamodernism. The ideology of adolescence and concern for permanent youth in this world that were mentioned in the introduction have largely replaced the preoccupation with a generally collective form of survival, both in the community of mortal men and in the afterlife. Many fantasies of permanence are maintained by the illusory prospects of genetic "engineering," from purely technical manipulations of the human genome to the possibilities of identical reproduction offered by cloning![2]

1. Neo-mystical aspirations

It would be wrong to think that belonging to a present and to a space both constantly renewed, and thus largely fragmented, keeps the representatives of a neocapitalist, postindustrial mediated society from aspiring to another world. But these other worlds are syncretic and easily re-created by computerized virtual reality; they are worlds which root themselves in the past, fabricated as they are from heterogeneous historical materials: prehistoric men confronting monstrous Paleolithic animals, heroic characters with super-human powers drawn from Greco-Roman antiquity, feudal lords defending their stern and impregnable keeps, all taking off occasionally on unlikely interstellar shuttles. Worlds of science fiction feeding paradoxically on the great historic moments of a western civilization universally set up as human civilization—as globalization demands ...; syncretic worlds which owe more to the vaguely historical and vaguely mystical makeshift than they do to

---

[2] The old fantasies of immortality and reincarnation which have been fed by the magical reproductive perspectives of enucleation of the ovum and genomic transplant are discussed by Atlan 1999:30–37; these fantasies are maintained by such organizations as the American group Life Extension Foundation.

any historical cross-fertilization or thoughtful multicultural synthesis; worlds where the immutable moral qualities of heroes always young, strong, and triumphant can be displayed; worlds generally accessed in ways resembling the initiatory itinerary: "Myth is real. And like real life, you die every five minutes. In fact you probably won't die at all (...). Pay attention to detail and collect information, because those are the pieces of the puzzle you'll use to uncover the secrets of Myst," says the advertising for the electronic game *Myst*, in encouraging an initiatory "rational" trip into a true fictional world.[3]

But beyond the fictional games of a world-wide computerization, directed by a few powerful North American multi-media and technology companies allied with the major European press groups, technological hyper-modernism proves to be driven (paradoxically) by a vague mysticism. More than just creating "new religious movements" and filling our classrooms with students of the history and science of religion, as they do, these indistinct mystical aspirations seem designed to make up for the worries and pressures which spring from the necessities of a youth-oriented present, subject to the necessities of constant innovation.[4] This diffuse neo-mystical fascination is no doubt involved in the increase in the number of interpretive studies brought about by the recent publication of several new gold lamellae; these precious gold tablets are part of the (limited) corpus of funerary documents tradition-ally classed under the composite label "Orphico-Dionysiac," and are a godsend for advocates of an interpretation whose very name indicates its mystical tendencies.

Whether their text is a simple graffito or an effort at epigraphic callig-raphy, whether they were found near buried remains or on them, whether they were to accompany a man or a woman on the journey toward Hades, the funerary lamellae which have been unearthed by archaeologists in the most diverse sites throughout the Greek world show an interesting variety in their representations of time and space. These temporal configurations generally converge toward the same goal: a near future which coincides spatially with the afterlife. And so, after studying the depth of a heroic past touching on the time of the gods in order to base human mortality in civic justice, after

---

[3] Miller and Miller 1996:3.

[4] In this regard, two collections published by Moreau 1992 and by Padilla 1999, are significant, as they offer the entire gamut of uses and abuses of the semi-formal category of "initiation rite" as an interpretive key less for ritual practices than for narratives in the Greek tradition; on how this vague operative idea was formed and on its application to various manifestations of Greek culture, see remarks I proposed in each of these two collections: 1992 (II):103–118 and 1999:278–312.

studying the poetic transformation of sexual relationships in a legendary narrative to legitimize religious and territorial policy, and after studying the reconstitution of a founding oracular past for ritual reaffirmation of civic identity based on a communal memory, this fourth temporal model establishes forms of discourse where time and space overlap to ensure an individual future of a collective sort; this in relationship to the funerary ritual on which the lamellae offer a sort of commentary, but a performative commentary!

While representing the ritual which they enunciate, the generally poetic texts aim to integrate an individual identity into a community identity by means of a specific spatial-temporal configuration. Unlike all the texts addressed so far, the corpus of the so-called "Orphico-Dionysiac" lamellae covers a wide swath of time; the documents extend from the beginning of the fourth century BC to the middle of the third century of our era. And the publication of the lamellae, which started in 1836, extends down to our own days, depending as it does on chance archaeological discovery;[5] the commentaries and revisions brought on by each new epiphany of a gold lamella sketch and punctuate a time in research marked by the epistemological paradigms of the moment, a time which the vicissitudes of discovery and publication also open to the hopes of the future.

The generally poetic nature of these texts which consecrate a funeral ritual suggests an approach based on discourse analysis, and sensitive to their pragmatic elements; but the plurality of voices which can express the utterances once again requires attention to enunciative phenomena. While we remain sensitive to the pragmatic (not to say performative) dimension of the words written on the lamellae, the discursive coherence of these texts makes us contest any too-rapid application of convenient labels. This widely-practiced attribution is nothing more than a classification, based on *ad hoc* ideas and composite categories such as "Orphico-Dionysiac"; but it also leads to the projection of mystico-metaphysical concepts of time and space, especially as it relates to the transmigration of souls and reincarnation. Finally, on a compara-

---

[5] Found in Petelia, near Croton, and dating from the first half of the fourth century BC, the first gold lamella (B 1 Zuntz = 476 F Bernabé) was reported in 1834; see Pugliese Carratelli 2001:67–71, bibliography in Bernabé 1999:61n14. The various texts have just been catalogued and collected in the provisional edition by Riedweg 1998:389–398. Here I follow the numbering proposed by my colleague from Zurich, adding the order number which has been adopted by A. Bernabé in his edition of the *Poetae epici Graeci. Testimonia et fragmenta, Pars II. Orphicorum et Orphicis similium testimonia et fragmenta*, Munich (K. G. Saur) 2004 and 2005, vol. 2; for now, see also the edition of these different texts given by Bernabé and Jiménez San Cristóbal 2001:257–281 (for an exhaustive bibliography, see 343–371 and the new editions by Graf and Johnston 2007 and Tortorelli Ghidini 2006 [for both these volumes, see my review in *Kernos* 21, 2008]).

tive level, comparison to the contemporary iconography geographically near to the most numerous lamellae will help us to trace the outlines of these spatial-temporal representations, of a discursive sort and with a ritual purpose.

2. The spatial-temporal itinerary of a dead woman at Hipponion

Choosing the oldest text as the introductory and privileged example obviously runs the double risk of making the *arkhḗ*, the beginning of one's own research, coincide with a model given as both prototype and stereotype: a first diachronic model in a coincidence between the chronology of poetic production of the anonymous texts and the time of research, but also an abstract synchronous model serving as normative reference for all other texts of the same type. Found in a tomb dating from the end of the fifth century or the beginning of the fourth century, the gold lamella from the necropolis of Hipponion, in the Gulf of Sant'Eufemia in Calabria, nonetheless has the advantage of a particularly well-developed text. Quite apart from any historical quest for the Ur- and thus for a textual "archetype" which would constitute the point of origin of a very philological *stemma codicorum*, quite apart as well from any reconstruction of an *Idealtyp* on the synchronic level, the Hipponion text must be placed in a series of versions linked together by a narrative plot of the same sort.[6]

This plot does not seem to be organized along the lines of the semio-narrative scheme offered by the "canonic schema" in the reading grid used in Chapter III, to help understand the narrative development of the Theseus legend offered by Bacchylides in his *Dithyramb* 17; on the other hand, its formal organization does show some similarities to the no less canonic tripartite schema proposed in analyzing rites of passage. This is probably not surprising in a text whose act of narration is to be understood not as a narrative, but rather as fulfillment of a ritual.[7] From a figurative point of view, this textual plot will thus propose a spatial-temporal itinerary of a ritual sort.

---

[6] Efforts to organize the various reconstructed texts of the so-called Orphic lamellae into a stemma going back to an archetype were presented by West 1975:229–230 and 235–236, as well as by Janko 1984:98–100; most recently, Riedweg 2002:468–477, proposed a reconstitution of the *Hieròs Lógos* allegedly at the origin of the most narrative texts. From the point of view of historical time, the *arkhḗ* for us would be the Hipponion lamella which will serve as the foundation for the analysis proposed here: B 10 Graf = 474 F Bernabé; bibliography in Bernabé 1999:60n13 and commentary in Pugliese Carratelli 2001:39–68, with an updated bibliography in the French translation of 2003:33–58.

[7] See chapter III, section 2.1 above, with n9.

2.1. Narration and enunciation

> Of Mnemosyne is this tomb; on the point of death
> you will go into the well-built dwelling of Hades: to the right
>   there is a spring,
> alongside it stands a glowing cypress;
> it is there that the souls of the dead descend and there they
>   refresh themselves.
> To this spring you must not draw near.
> But farther on, you will find cold water which flows
> from the lake of Mnemosyne; above it stand guards.
> They will ask you, in certain judgment,
> why you explore the shadows of dark Hades.
> Say: "I am a son of the Earth and the starry Heavens.
> I burn with thirst and my strength fails me; give me quickly
> a drink of the cold water which comes from the lake of
>   Mnemosyne."
> And they will question you, as the king of the Underworld
>   wishes.
> And they will give you a drink of the water from the cave of
>   Mnemosyne.
> And you, when you have drunk, you will travel the sacred
>   way
> on which the other *mustai* and *bakhkhoi* also advance in glory.

> > English version from the French translation by A.-Ph.
> > Segonds and C. Lunda, slightly modified by C. Calame

The text carefully incised on the Hipponion lamella is thus expressed in the future. To the extent that the corresponding verbs assume various forms not in the first person, but rather in the second, the text does not show the enunciative auto-referentiality that one often finds in a melic poem. Which is to say that the discursive subject does not describe the (verbal) action in which he is engaged. So the future forms presented in the Hipponion text have none of the "performative" value (in the strict sense of the term) that they assume in a metrical poem, when the poem becomes a religious act.[8] In the absence of any allusion to a sung "performance," as was the case indirectly

---

[8] On this "performative" aspect of the expression of the lyric *I*, see references given in chapter III, nn3 and 41.

at the end of Bacchylides' *Dithyramb* 17, the series of actions which makes up the narrative fabric of the Hipponion text is presented as a sequence of injunctions. These are addressed by an anonymous speaker and narrator to an interlocutor (Benveniste would say an "*allocuté*" or an "*allocutaire*") who is equally anonymous; he becomes the grammatical "you" as subject of the actions recommended. One might propose "The Underworld: A User's Guide," if asked to give a title to these injunctive texts.

So the temporal line which organizes the sequence of suggested actions can be followed, along with the spatial itinerary sketched by it. This series of spatial-temporal directions is intended for interlocutor-*you*, no doubt corresponding to the deceased person carrying the lamella. But to speak of narrative development of an itinerary is also to speak of constructing a space-time with obvious practical aims. The coherence of stages in the discursive and enunciative development of the space-time in the Hipponion text will require comparison with the two texts from somewhat later, found in tombs located in Petelia (a colony of Croton in Calabria) and in Pharsalus (in Thessaly) respectively; comparison will then continue with the incomplete text (published provisionally for now) which probably comes from Entella in western Sicily.[9]

2.1.1. An incipit in the form of a sphragís

The poetic text of the Hipponion lamella opens initially with a *sphragís*, which more closely resembles the signature opening the text of Herodotus *Histories*, for example, than it resembles the indirect procedure concluding Bacchylides' poem. As in Herodotus, and by its mode of internal reference, the inaugural deictic *tóde* (line 1) designates the text which follows. But in its general content it names the text not as a Herodotean "demonstration" (*apódeixis*) but as a "tomb" by the addition of the Homeric term *ếríon*. From the intradiscursive reference of the deictic *tóde*, we thus pass on to its possibility of external reference. Through the play of the deixis, it is the lamella itself which becomes a metaphoric tumulus whose author seems to be Mnemosyne, mother of the Muses and incarnation of Memory. Indeed, in its syntactic structure, the expression "here is the tomb of Memory" is based on a genitive which is

---

[9] B 1 Zuntz = 476 F Bernabé (see n5 above); B 2 Zuntz = 477 F Bernabé (bibliography: Bernabé 1999:61n15); B 11 Riedweg = 475 F Bernabé; texts and references in Riedweg 1998:394–397, as well as Bernabé 1999:54–55, for B 11; see also the synthesis table developed by Graf 1993:257–258.

not objective, but subjective.[10] And so, from the concrete situation in which the deceased bearer of the lamella finds himself, the metaphoric usage of the term *ēríon* returns us to the memorial aspect assumed by the tomb in ancient Greece: an equivalent in this particular case to *mnêma* rather than *sêma*.[11]

Thus signed, the text is placed under the authority of Mnemosyne. From the very start, it integrates the *you*-addressee to whom it speaks at a precise moment in time: the moment of death. This instant is modalized both by a verb which situates it in the very near future and the syntactic indicator of eventuality (*epeì ám mélleisi thaneîsthai*, "since you are / when you will be at the point of death"). From the point of view of the time of the uttered enunciation, the text is supposed to be pronounced just before the death of the deceased addressee. This temporal situation is itself coupled with a spatial indication: "you will go into the well-built dwelling of Hades."[12] At least, this is the way the form *eîs*, which introduces the second period, should be understood, in a first form of the injunctive future which corresponds to the performative futures of the first person: *eîs* from the verb *eîmi*, "to go" (with a future meaning!) which takes a simple accusative, and not the preposition *eis*.[13] Because of the enunciative modalities of this "narrative," the time of the uttered enunciation coincides from the start with the time of narration (and with the beginning of recounted time).

---

[10] Herodotus, *Proem: Herodótou (...) historíēs apódeixis hḗde*; on the process of *sphragís*, see chapter III, n41 above, and on *deixis*, chapter I, n33 above. It is Achilles who imagines for Patroclus (and for himself) a "high burial mound" (*Iliad* 23.126). The document allows no reading other than ERION. A number of ways have been tried to correct this expression, among them the *thríon* correction proposed by West 1975:231, which could make sense by reference to the physical form of the lamella, which is indeed that of a leaf, though not necessarily a fig leaf. One should read commentary proposed by Pugliese Carratelli 1976:458–459 on these various corrections, but without necessarily following it in its suggestion that *ēríon* be understood as a bad interpretation of an original *sêma* (sign and not tomb), which would make of the lamella a *sphragís*, a "signature" (Pugliese Carratelli 1975: 228–229); returning to the reading, the Italian scholar proposed in 1993:23–24, the correction *tóde <h>ierón*. By referring to the thread of Memory, the reading *e(í)rion* conceived by Musti 1984:79–83, goes along with the meaning proposed here, on which see also Baumgarten 1998:92 with n94. Philological and metrical analysis of the text in Tessier 1987.

[11] To good effect, Sourvinou-Inwood 1995:127–128 bases her argument on a passage from the *Constitution of the Athenians* (55.2–3) attributed to Aristotle, to show that *ēríon* takes on the meaning of "grave" as memorial. Arguments in favor of reading *érgon* (see Guarducci 1985:387–389) seem weaker to me, a correction which hardly represents a *lectio facilior*.

[12] In line 2, I retain the reading *euéreas*, and do not go along with the correction to *heuréseis* proposed, for example, by West 1975:232.

[13] For the construction of *eîmi* without a preposition, see *Odyssey* 1.176, 188, and 194; and for the form *eîs*, see Hesiod *Works and Days* 208; see Pugliese Carratelli 1974:11 and 2001a:47 (2003:41).

2.1.2. The two springs

The mention of the dwelling of Hades introduces a distinctly descriptive passage. Syntactically, this insertion is added to a procedure of asyndeton; such an absence of any connector is no doubt expected in a observational utterance, and purely assertoric, it begins with the verbal form of existence *ésti* "there is" (line 2)—and not "there once was." The very usage of the present with a third person indicates that we have passed from the "discourse," not to the "narrative" (or to the "story," as Benveniste would have said, in a distinction already mentioned and still disputed[14]), but rather to a descriptive procedure. Not time, but rather space enunciated or recounted; space marked by a spring situated on the right, from the perspective of the narrator-speaker and of his interlocutor.

This implicit enunciative intervention related to the speaker's point of view, in a sequence of seemingly assertoric utterances, has tested readers of this text. Indeed, two lamellae from a bit later insert the same information directly into the itinerary prepared for the *you* of the addressee, but one of them places the spring to the left "of the dwelling of Hades."[15] This divergent location of the spring in a generally negative position could be attributed to the fact that the expression used is referenced from the outside of the Underworld, and not from the internal perspective which determines the spatial orientation of the utterance in the other texts.

Whatever the location of the spring, the different versions of the text agree that the site is marked by the presence of a "white" cypress. This whiteness has given rise to the most fantastic interpretations, some going as far as making the cypress thus described into a tree of life comparable to that mentioned in Genesis, or even the symbol of the cyclical rebirth of the soul. The cypress is actually often associated with death and with Hades in Greek representations of funerals.[16] In this funerary context, it is most likely the first

---

[14] See chapter I, n21 above.

[15] B 1, 1 Zuntz = 476 F, 1 Bernabé in contrast with B 2, 1 Zuntz = 477 F, 1 Bernabé, but also B 3–8, 2 Zuntz = 478–483 F, 2 Bernabé, B 9, 2 Graf = 484 F, 2 Bernabé, and B 11, 4 Riedweg = 475 F, 4 Bernabé (text conjectural). On the favorable values attributed to the right, see the numerous references given by Pugliese Carratelli 2001a:56–57 (2003:49–51), following the distinction pointed out by Aristotle fr. 200 Rose, and attributed to the Pythagoreans; see also *Metaphysics* 986a22–30 where the Pythagorean right is associated with light, while the left has characteristics of darkness.

[16] Interpretations mentioned by Bernabé and Jiménez San Cristóbal 2001:44–49; see especially Guarducci 1974:18–21. See also Edmonds 2004:46–52. In several Indo-European cultures, paradise is illuminated by eternal light: cf. Lincoln 1991:24–29.

meaning of *leukós* which is realized. The adjective designates the luminous brightness of a tree which serves as a point of reference in a place filled with darkness. This reference point could be one indication of an itinerary leading the deceased toward the eternal light of an Elysian dwelling which we have yet to describe.

In one of those word plays which the Greeks liked so well, and which is explicitly repeated in that collection of ontologizing etymologies which is Plato's *Cratylus*, the next descriptive utterance attributes a function to the spring: it is there so that the souls of the dead, souls traveling downward, may refresh themselves (*psukhaì ... psúkhontai*, line 4). For Plato, the double meaning of *psúkhō* ("to breathe" and "to refresh") allows us to associate the soul with the breath of life which animates the body through (humid?) coolness.[17] Water from the spring in Hades, marked by the glowing cypress, thus seems to hold the power to resuscitate the souls of the dead entering the kingdom below.

How surprising it is, then, to read the following recommendation, relayed by assertive description through discourse! "To the spring you must not draw near"—the return of direct address to the anonymous *you* turns the interlocutor away from this spring, and in a new future injunctive (*heuréseis*) directs him instead toward the cold water flowing from the marshes of Mnemosyne: from the speaker's perspective, this lake of Memory is located farther into Hades; and above the water stand guards.

Of all the parallels mentioned in various interpretations of this passage, and intended to account for the contrast between the spring with its glowing cypress and the marshes of Mnemosyne, none is really pertinent. It is true that in the description Pausanias gives of a consultation of the oracle of Trophonios in Boeotia, the purified supplicant is led to two neighboring springs; at the first he drinks the waters "of Forgetfulness" to be liberated from his former thoughts while at the second the "waters of Memory" will allow him to remember what he has seen in his oracular descent.[18] But the first spring described in the Hipponion text is not related to forgetfulness in any way, and the person consulting the oracle of Trophonios is invited to drink from both springs, not to avoid the first one!

---

[17] Plato *Cratylus* 399de; on this, see study by Jouanna 1987, along with additional information given by Pugliese Carratelli 2001a:58–61 (2003:51–54), and for Homeric poetry, Clarke 1999:140–148. In the Egyptian *Book of the Dead*, it falls to Osiris, whom Herodotus already likens to Dionysus, to give to the deceased the cool water which will revive them: cf. Merkelbach 1999:2–7.

[18] Pausanias 9.39.5–9; also the parody of a consultation given in Aristophanes *Clouds* 483–508 in an oracular *katábasis* already mentioned by Herodotus 8.134.1; cf. Bonnechère 1998:445–447 and 457–459, along with a series of bibliographic references on the oracle of Trophonios.

Similarly, in the famous narrative of Er which concludes Plato's *Republic*, souls follow the path crossing the arid plains of Forgetfulness, seeing no trees at all, and drink from the river of Unmindfulness, following an itinerary which is the exact opposite of the one proposed in the gold lamella.[19] After the choice of a new mortal life, with a new destiny woven by the Moirai and marked with the seal of Necessity, Plato's souls forget the past and return toward the surface of the earth! Which leaves only the parallel which might be furnished by comparison with the Semitic Middle East, through the cosmo-theogony of the *Enuma Eliš*. But while the Assyrian texts repeatedly mention the gods of the Underworld, six hundred Anunnaki who were banished to Hell by the will of Anu, the spring which they guard is nothing more than the effect of an interpretive reading of the cosmo-theogonic poem.[20]

Comparison with Semitic texts is not particularly informative in specifically defining the guardians of the lake of Mnemosyne, except in very general terms. On the other hand, from Hesiod to Heraclitus and to Plato, many poets and philosophers in Greece took up the native belief in the existence of anonymous divinities, *daímones* who assume roles as guardians, especially in the Underworld. In Hesiod's narrative of the succession of human species studied in the second chapter, the blessed mortals who came from the silver species seem to take on in the Underworld the same role of *phúlakes* assumed on earth by their fellow creatures, the demons of the gold family. As for Heraclitus, he mentions in his enigmatic way the awakening of guardians assigned to the living as well as to the dead. Elsewhere, Socrates calls on popular tradition (*légetai*) in the *Phaedo* to explain the process which allows the soul of the deceased to purify itself of its earthly past, assigning to each individual a *daímōn* charged with guiding him in Hades and with helping him make his way in a place of numerous paths, forks, and crossroads.[21]

So there is really no surprise in finding that the domain of Hades created by the poetic Hipponion text is peopled with generically named guardians; they take on the role of guides and ferrymen in a nebulous space where points of reference are rare and difficult to interpret.

---

[19] Plato *Republic* 620d–621b (see also Aristophanes *Frogs* 185–187); the differences between the itinerary which Plato imagines and the one proposed in the Hipponion lamella are well defined by Bernabé 1991:226–231.

[20] See especially the cosmogonic poem *VAT 8917/KAR 307*, re-edited by Livingstone 1989:99–102. The parallel was proposed by Pugliese Carratelli, 2001a:59 (2003:52).

[21] Hesiod *Works* 122–126 and 140–142; Heraclitus fr. 22 B 63 Diels-Kranz; Plato *Phaedo* 107d–108c; see also Plutarch fr. 178 Sandbach; see above chapter II, n19 above, and West 1978:186–187.

2.1.3. Declaration of identity

In a new form of the future destined to happen, the interlocutor-*you* is
forewarned of the question which the guardians of the Underworld will ask
him: "These (i.e., the guardians) will ask you in their prudent spirit what you
could possibly be seeking in the darkness of Hades" (lines 8–9). A question
to the one who arrives in the dark domain of Hades, about the object of his
quest; a question introduced in "free" indirect discourse in a patchwork of
Homeric expressions and of formulae which are also found in other lamellae.
While the "prudent spirit" of the demons of the Underworld recalls the form
of intelligence which Athena attributes to herself in the *Iliad*, the phrasing of
the question asked, along with the verb which introduces it, calls to mind both
the parallel text from Pharsalus and the reconstructed text from Entella.[22] For
anyone who must describe those responsible for giving information about
the itinerary, there is nothing surprising in attributing to the guardians
below, serving as guides and interpreters, the prudent wisdom of the gods of
technical intelligence, by means of Homeric formulae. Finally, the exercise
in formulaic composition leads to the injunction which constitutes the very
center of the text: "speak," "say" (*eîpon*, line 10).[23]

The invitation to the bearer of the lamella to express himself leads to a
true declaration of identity. In this central act of discourse; as in Petelia and
in Pharsalus, the deceased speaks directly and declares himself, here and now,
a "son of the Earth and the starry Heavens." This has been rightly interpreted
both as a "password" and as a "passport." In specifying the current identity
of the deceased by attributing to him an Ouranian ancestry, the Petelia text
does not simply link his identity to a divine origin: the declaration of identity
evokes the divine couple who engender all things in Hesiod's *Theogony*, among
them gods such as Kronos, the father of Zeus. So it is not surprising that the
Pharsalus lamella establishes this original ancestry in the proper name of
Asterios, a name which recalls an epiclesis of Zeus as well as the name of the
human father of Minos.[24] Like all the other deceased who enter the realm of

[22] *Iliad* 8.366 (see also 14.165 for Zeus, or 20.35 for Hermes); B 2, 6 Zuntz = 477 F, 2 Bernabé and B 11, 10–11 Riedweg = 475 F, 10–11 Bernabé.

[23] *Eîpon*, as an imperative form of aorist *éeipa* (see Pindar *Olympian* 6.92) compared to the infinitive as imperative *eipeîn* which initiates the same declaration in B 1, 6 Zuntz = 476 F, 6 Bernabé as well as B 2, 8 Zuntz = 477 F, 2 Bernabé (see also B 11, 12 Riedweg = 475 F, 12 Bernabé).

[24] Hesiod *Theogony* 126–128 and 132–138 (cf. 685 and *Works* 548), who describes Ouranos as *asteróeis*; on Asterios or Asterion, see Hesiod fr. 140 Merkelbach-West and Pseudo-Apollodorus *Library* 3.1.1–3, along with remarks by Calame 1996b:194–195, 210–211, and 220; see also Morand 2001:222–223.

Hades, this son of Gaia and Ouranos is parched with thirst. As if threatened by a second death (*apóllumai*, line 11), he asks the guardians to give him access to the cool water which flows from the lake of Mnemosyne.

2.1.4. The four elements

Were it not for fear of the overused systematization to which badly understood structural analysis has often led, one might see in the deceased's password the presence of all four elements that make up the cosmos. In the *Theogony*, Hesiod seems to reprise a representation of Tartarus at whose exit were the "roots" of the earth and the sea, then of both the springs and the ends of the earth, of Tartarus itself, and of the sea and the sky. Since Tartarus itself is described with the adjective *ēeróeis*, which brings to mind opaque humidity of the air, and since the sky is described as *asteróeis*, referring to the light of the stars, some have seen in this image of the origins and ends of the cosmos the presence of the four elements: earth, air, water, and fire.[25]

The same could be said of the famous Empedokles fragment, where the descriptions of the four divinities who represent the four "roots" of all things also make the gods correspond to the four elements: Zeus the resplendent for fire, Hera who holds the *bíos* and gives life for earth, Nestis the tearful for water, and Aidoneus-Hades (by inference) for air—such, at least, is the interpretation of the passage given by Diogenes Laertius. And the *Iliad* could also show an echo of this four-part concept, especially in the formulation of oaths; in the famous scene where the pact is concluded in *Iliad* 3, Agamemnon invokes not only Zeus, but also the Sun (fire?), the Rivers (water), Gaia (the earth), and the gods below (air?).[26] And so in his speech act, which takes the form of a declaration of identity when confronting the guardians of the Underworld, the bearer of the lamella lays claim through his ancestry to the earth and to the fire of the sky, before speaking of his thirst (which is perhaps brought on by the dark air of Hades as it was on the arid plain of the Er narrative) which he wishes to quench with the water of the lake of Memory.

---

[25] Hesiod *Theogony* 726–728 and 736–739 = 807–810: the structure of this passage on the imprisonment of the Titans in Tartarus is explained by West 1966:356–359, who considers lines 807–810 authentic and in their proper place (see also West 1966:363–364). In Hippocrates' treatise on the environment (*On Airs* 6.2–3 and 15.1–2), the term *ēér* designates air saturated with humidity and which light from the sun can illuminate.

[26] Empedokles fr. 31 B 6 Diels-Kranz; cf. Diogenes Laertius 8.76; *Iliad* 3.275–280; on this, see the study by Cerri 1998 (though I do not necessarily support all his equations, sometimes made too quickly); see also Rudhardt 1971:39–44.

In this context, we would like to be able to read at the end of the line preceding the utterance of the declaration of identity the qualifier *ēeróentos*, "misty", "dark" (or *euróentos*, "humid", "moldy"); but at the end of line 9 the legible traces on the lamella only allow us to guess the form *o[ro]eentos* ("mountainous?"), which makes no sense for a description of Hades in the genitive. Once again, in the *Iliad* it is the first qualifier used for Tartarus, as well as for the shades of the deceased whose lot is Hades, probably a reference to the dark (or misty) density of the air.[27] Also, in the text of the lamella itself, *ēeróentos* appears at the end of the period in the same metrical position as the form *asteróentos* in the following line. This coincidence would seem to underline the strong contrast between the shadowy darkness of Hades and the luminous filiation from Sky, which the deceased claims for himself in his "password." The case is even stronger, since in Iliadic poetry the term *skótos*, describing the shadows of Hades, refers metaphorically to death itself, and since Hesiod in his *Theogony* contrasts dark Tartarus to the starry sky three times.[28]

2.1.5. Access to the realm of the blessed

The reaction of the guardians of Hades to the deceased's declaration of identity is given in a description which returns to the forms of the near future used in earlier statements: they will address the one for whom the lamella is meant, and will allow him to quench his thirst in the lake of Mnemosyne. In the Hipponion text (as well as the one from Petelia), the reappearance in the form *dósousi* ("they will give," line 14) of the request made by the deceased, *dóte* ("give," line 11), underscores the perlocutionary and pragmatic nature of the declaration of identity: it has an immediate effect. In this context, there is no reason to correct to *eleoûsin* ("they will take pity") the reading *ereoûsin* ("they will speak," line 13), given in the text and attested in Homeric poetry, from the future *erô*.[29] Similarly, at the end of this period, we must keep the

---

[27] *Iliad* 8.13 (see also *Theogony* 119, 721, 736 = 807, etc.) and *Iliad* 15.191 (see also 23.51); see also *Homeric Hymn to Demeter* 482, with the variant *euróeis* "moldy": see Richardson 1974:315. On the possible correction mentioned here, cf. Cassio 1987; other proposed inclusions and corrections are given in the *apparatus criticus* by Riedweg 1998:396–7; in the incomplete text of B 11, 11 Riedweg = 475 F, 11 Bernabé, he suggests reading *orph[o]éento<s>*, with a meaning similar to that of *ēeróentos*.

[28] See *Iliad* 4.461 and 4.503, 6.11, etc., in reference to B 1, 14 Zuntz = 476 F, 14 Bernabé; cf. Guarducci 1985:391–393; *Theogony* 682, 736, and 807.

[29] *Iliad* 22.108, *Odyssey* 6.285, etc.; cf. Plato *Cratylus* 398d. Unattested in the future, the form *eleoûsin* would also imply a construction *eleéō* with the dative *toi* understood as the pronoun form in the second person, while in correspondence with *autoí* in B 1, 10 Zuntz= 476 F, 10 Bernabé, the form of the pronoun is in the third person.

reading given in the text, *basilei*, which should be read as *basilêi* (in the dative) by reference not to Persephone, queen of the Underworld, but to its king Hades, already mentioned in line 9. The guardians will address the deceased, under the influence (*hupó*, line 13) of a sovereign who is called *khthónios*, like many other underworld deities in archaic and classical poetry.[30]

This new geographic indication moves the text, as well as the one for whom it is meant and who carries it, toward its temporal and spatial conclusion. Time and space merge when the interlocutor-*you* of the gold text is led to the present through yet another Homeric from of a verb of movement (*érkheai an*, line 15). Having drunk the waters of Memory, the *you* can continue, in the present, on the same sacred path followed by other "initiates and bacchants filled with glory." Widely diffused throughout Greek literature, the image of the path appears especially in funerary contexts, used to designate the journey which leads the chosen deceased toward the realm of immortality, the Elysian Fields or Isles of the Blessed—as we shall see.[31]

Assuming in its verbal form the Homeric idea of immortalizing heroization through glory represented by *kléos*, the qualifier *kleinoí* confers the status of hero on those privileged to follow this itinerary. Placed between gods and men, heroes can attain the happiness experienced by immortals through the brilliance of *kléos*. Such is the case for Io, the spouse of Zeus in Aeschylus, of Herakles the son of Zeus in Sophocles, and of the heroic founder of the city of Etna in Pindar; and such especially is the case for the interlocutor and addressee of the Petelia lamella, brought to reign "among the heroes" in a world vastly different from the Homeric Hades where souls wander like shadows.[32]

---

[30] Zeus Chthonios as early as *Works* 463 (see *Theogony* 767, for Hades); see later Aeschylus *Persians* 628 and 632, Sophocles *Oedipus at Colonus* 1606, Euripides *Alcestis* 237 (for Hades itself), etc. In strong contrast, *hupokhthónios* is attested only once at this time, in *Works* 141, to describe the "blessed" below; cf. Pugliese Carratelli 1974:112–113, and 1976:461–462. The iota preceding the expression *hupò khthoníōi* in the text remains unexplained, especially given the dactylic meter, which obliges us to read the adjective in the dative.

[31] See especially *Odyssey* 4.561–565, and Pindar *Olympian* 2.68–75 (cf. n51 and n53 below) or Plato *Gorgias* 524a; parallels to the image of the path: Feyerabend 1984:1–10, who would replace *kleeinoí* with the form *kleitán te* (to refer to a path), and Bernabé and Jiménez San Cristóbal 2001:78–80. On the verb form *érkheai*, see *Iliad* 10.385; in this same line 15, the reading *sù pión* is far from certain (see the apparatus of these texts presented by Riedweg and Bernabé).

[32] Aeschylus *Prometheus* 834; Sophocles *Trachiniae* 19; Pindar *Pythian* 1.31; B 1, 11 Zuntz = 476 F, 11 Bernabé; see also B 11, 2 Riedweg = 475 F, 2 Bernabé. Whatever the status of souls revived by Persephone in fr. 133 Maehler of Pindar (cf. n53 below), reinterpreted in terms of palingenesis by Plato *Meno* 81a–c, they are honored by men, for all eternity, as "respectable heroes" (*hérōes hagnoí*): cf. n54 below.

But even more significant is the association of the interlocutor-*you* found in the Hipponion text with other "initiates and bacchants" (*mústai kaì bákhkhoi*, line 16); after tasting the waters of Memory, they are called upon to follow the spatial-temporal itinerary shown to them: it leads toward what appears an eternal dwelling. A godsend for those who love initiatory interpretations and who see, in an epigraphic document from the end of the fifth century, the occurrence of technical terms capable of sustaining any number of mystical fantasies. So what about this?

2.2. Enunciative pragmatics: The funerary context

Following the purely intra-discursive reading of the text in its spatial-temporal aspect, we must move on to the extra-discursive. Considering what we know of conditions surrounding the putting-into-discourse and the communication of the Hipponion text is all the more important since it provides us a major surprise, from the enunciative point of view.

2.2.1. The poetic workings of gender

While the indices of enunciated utterance given in the text refer us to an interlocutor (and a speaker in the declaration of identity) of the male sex (*huòs gâs*, probably in line 10; *aûos*, certainly in line 11, *pión*, probably in line 15—all masculine forms), the body that carried the lamella in the Hipponion tomb was that of a young woman. The burial objects dating from the end of the fifth century and found in this relatively modest tomb probably mean the deceased young woman was an average citizen in the context of a small colonial city founded by another colony, Epizephyrian Locris. Folded four times vertically and once horizontally, the lamella had either been placed in the mouth of the deceased, like the passport that the obol for Charon represents, or more probably (as in Pelinna, for example) on the sternum of the body. In her left hand had been placed a small terra-cotta lamp, no doubt intended to help guide the young woman during her travels in the darkness of Hades described in the text itself.[33]

This correspondence between the ritual funeral arrangements made for the corpse and the spatial indications given by the text of the lamella makes

---

[33] Description of the situation of the dig and of funeral items in Foti 1974 (with corresponding plates); cf. also Pugliese Carratelli 2001a:44–45 (2003:39–40). On the social status of deceased men and women who carried lamellae, see Graf 1993:255–256.

that enunciative discrepancy even more surprising. In this regard, parallels offered by other lamellae are unfortunately of no use. While it is true that the Pharsalus text of the declaration of identity is also enunciated in the masculine, the lamella corresponds to was placed on an urn, and the incinerated remains give no clue about the sex of the deceased. As for the Petelia text, while it does present one promising feminine form (*aúē*, line 8), the archaeological circumstances of its exhumation, and thus its ritual placement, are unknown to us![34] Faced with this double aporia, one might cite the Thourioi lamellae, which present the opposite scenario from Hipponion: enunciative forms in the feminine, but pronounced by deceased individuals whose buried remains prove them to be of the male sex. It is true that the feminine form *kathará* given in these texts could refer to the soul of the deceased. There remain only the Pelinna lamellae, placed on the chest of the corpse of a woman when a gold coin was also placed in her mouth, to furnish a possible parallel to the enunciative situation of the poetic text from Hipponion, but that text compares the interlocutor to masculine animals, the bull and the ram![35]

But any specialist in archaic and classical Greek poetry knows that funerary lamellae are not the only texts to pose the problem of a surprising enunciative "gender" discrepancy. Alcman and Pindar, masculine poets, composed poems to be sung and danced by choral groups of girls, who take up the singing of the poem in the first person; and through the intermediary of the mask to which the Dionysiac ritual gave authority, actors of classical tragedy acted feminine roles in plots which gave rise to the poetic expression of the most passionate feelings.[36] As for a dead woman assuming a voice which expresses itself in the masculine, we must take into account the traditional and poetic character of a language which distinguishes itself for us through the lexical, dialectical, and rhythmic color appropriate to the diction of epic poetry: we have merely pointed out a few of its elements in passing. From a militant feminist point of view, Greek poetry has the disadvantage of not bending to the requirements of a linguistic usage which should appear "politically correct ..."

---

[34] B 2, 9 Zuntz = 477 F, 2 Bernabé and B 1, 8 Zuntz = 476 F, 8 Bernabé; see also B 11, 2 Riedweg = 475 F, 2 Bernabé where the word *hérōs* in the masculine is found: cf. Bernabé 1999:57.

[35] P 1–2, 3 and 5 = 485 F–486 F Bernabé: cf. Tsantsanoglou and Parassoglou 1987:3–4.

[36] Consult remarks and bibliographic information I gave on this subject in 2000b:34–45; see also 1998a:100–107.

2.2.2. A few intertextual echoes

Again from an enunciative point of view, the six lamellae found at Eleutherna in Crete and dating from the end of the third century, as well as the fourth-century lamella probably from Thessaly, bear only the text of the declaration of identity, enunciated in the first person; with a significant modification, however, since, independently of variations in details, the state of thirst and the desire to drink expressed by the speaker's voice come before the declaration of identity, which is enunciated in terms practically identical to those of the poetic text from Hipponion.[37]

> I am burning with thirst and I am dying:
> give me water to drink from the spring which flows
>   constantly
> there where the cypress is.
> "Who are you? Where do you come from?"
> "I am a son of the Earth and the starry Heavens."
>
> English version from the French translation
> by A.-Ph. Segonds and C. Luna

In this text from Crete, anticipation of the declaration of identity is caused by the absence of the other instructions which surround the password itself in the Hipponion document: thus it is caused by the disappearance of the scenario which presents the first-person declaration as an address to the guardians of the Underworld. Substituted for it are, first, the priority given to the thirst of the speaking subject, which constitutes the expected state of narrative "Lack" and begins the micro-plot assumed and spoken by the speaker-*I*; and, second, the insertion of a question in direct discourse on his own identity, which rather than being auto-referential could be assumed by the guardians of Hades: "who are you? where are you?" (*tís d' essí; pô d' essí*; line 3). A similar procedure calling for a declaration of identity can be found in the famous Egyptian pharaonic *Book of the Dead*.[38]

Just as in the texts from Hipponion and Petelia (and probably in the one from Entella), the state of dehydration suffered by the speaker-*I* is associated

---

[37] B 3–8 Zuntz = 478–483 F Bernabé, and B 9 Graf = 484 F Bernabé (here B 6 Zuntz = 481 F Bernabé); note that one of these texts, unfortunately one whose archaeological situation is unknown, could show one mark of gender: <th>u<g>*átēr* instead of the masculine *huiós*: cf. Pugliese Carratelli 1993:43.

[38] See references and careful commentary by Zuntz 1971:370–376, and by Pugliese Carratelli 1993:45.

with his death (*kaì appóllumai*, line 1): it is as if the state of death continued into Hades. But in contrast to the more developed texts, the speaker himself uses an infinitive with an optative value (*piém moi*, line 1) to express his wish to drink from the spring "of eternal flowing," on the right and indicated by the cypress, the very same spring that the longer texts recommend avoiding![39] This paradox must be understood within the framework of reversed enunciative order, in the text from Crete. The declaration of identity here is assumed directly by the voice of the one carrying the lamella, while the question to which it responds is assumed indirectly, probably by the guardians of Hades. We add that, just as in the Petelia text and probably in the one from Entella, the lamella from Thessaly specifies maternal ancestry of the Earth and paternal ancestry of Heaven by indicating the celestial origins of the deceased (*autàr emoì génos ōránion*, line 5); while it evokes the same meaning, this indication substitutes for the proper name *Asterios* which recalls this celestial identity in the Pharsalus lamella.[40]

While any possible reference to the four elements is less obvious in the briefer texts, where there is only implicit allusion to Hades and the darkness of the humid, saturated air, the double ancestry claimed by the speaker (and thus by the deceased) is echoed in a funerary inscription from Pherae in Thessaly. The deceased who pronounces the text inscribed on that funerary stele gives his civic identity, but says that he was born seemingly of the "root" of great Zeus, but really of immortal fire. Through an identity-related utterance phrased as a chiasmus, he associates this identity, divided between appearance and truth, to a double ancestry: the Earth on the mother's side, the stars of the sky on the father's side. The (mortal: *sõma*) body is attached to the mother-earth, while actual life (*zõ*, in the present), which is to say eternity, is attached to the light of paternal fire. This igneous element recalls the fire in the *Homeric Hymn to Demeter* through which Demeter plans to immortalize little Demophoon, offspring of the legendary sovereigns of Eleusis; and according to Euripides, fire consumed the mortal shell of Herakles before transforming the deified hero and his spouse Hebe into bright stars.[41]

---

[39] On the exclamatory infinitive with optative sense, see Humbert 1960:125–126, and on the dialectical form *piém*, see Cassio 1994:184–192. On the description *aeíroos*, cf. n50 below.

[40] B 9, 5 Graf = 484 F, 4 Bernabé, compare to B 1, 7 Zuntz = 476 F, 7 Bernabé and B 11, 15 Riedweg = 475 F, 15 Bernabé; cf. B 2, 9 Zuntz = 477 F, 9 Bernabé; cf. n22 above.

[41] *SEG* XXVIII (1978), 528 = 466 T Bernabé; the immortalizing uses of the brightness of fire are analyzed by Scarpi 1987:211–213; see *Homeric Hymn to Demeter* 235–255 and Euripides *Heraclidae* 853–858 and 910–918.

With the Thessalian inscription, the double ancestry of the deceased is no longer confined just to the folds of a gold lamella buried along with human remains in the infernal darkness of the sepulcher. This terrestrial and celestial identity reminds us of the destiny Sophocles gives to Oedipus in the Athenian market town of Colonus, when he places the Theban hero both on Olympus, in an assumption announced by a thunderbolt from Zeus, and in the bowels of the earth of Attica.[42] But beyond these common traits, the widespread representations of double identity among Greek heroic figures, divided between terrestrial and mortal nature on the one hand and celestial immortality on the other, offer no reference to the deceased's thirst, nor any reference to water during the funerary journey in the darkness of Hades.

2.3. Initiatory itinerary under the aegis of Dionysus

In the end, the spatial and temporal configurations suggested by the gold lamella from Hipponion are addressed to the group with which the interlocutor and addressee of the text is associated, the group composed of "initiates and bacchants" (*mústai kaì bákhkhoi*, line 16). The usual and generic translation of *initiate* is well suited to the meaning of *mústēs* in that, from the fifth century on, this term means any person participating or having participated in an initiatory rite. Especially in classical Athens, a *mústēs* is anyone initiated into the official Eleusinian Mysteries, and in a well-known passage Heraclitus anathematizes initiates whom he associates, by an etymologizing reference to mysteries and to *mueîsthai* ("to be initiated") with charlatans of the night, with magi, with maenads, and with bacchants![43] Three funerary lamellae from the Hellenistic period, all found in a necropolis at Aigion in Achaia, describe the deceased (identified with his own name) as *mústēs*, while in Pella in Macedonia a gold lamella shaped like a laurel or myrtle leaf, probably dating from the end of the fourth century, describes a man named Poseidippos (the Alexandrian author of epigrams?) as a devoted *mústēs* (*eusebés*), and addressed by the text to Persephone.[44]

---

[42] Sophocles *Oedipus at Colonus* 1650–1662; cf. Calame 1998c:345–354. On the various (generally Orphic!) interpretations given to this dual descendence, see Betz 1998:404–411.

[43] Heraclitus fr. 22 B 14 Diels-Kranz = Orphica 587 T Bernabé. On initiates into the Mysteries of Eleusis, see Euripides *Herakles* 613 (*tà mustôn órgia*) as well as Herodotus 8.65.4 and Aristophanes *Frogs* 370 (*mústai khoroí*, a complement to the *teletaí* celebrated for Dionysus): cf. Burkert 1987:7–10, and n46 below.

[44] *SEG* XXXIV (1984), 338 and XLI (1991), 401 A and B; on the lamellae from Pella, see references given by Riedweg 1998:391, and by Dickie 1995:82–83, who sees in the form *Persephónēi* not a

But while the dead woman who carried the gold lamella of Hipponion was associated with a group of mystai, directing us essentially toward Eleusinian mysteries, the parallel designation of initiates as "bacchants" sends us back toward initiatory rites dedicated to Dionysus: Dionysus Bacchus himself, known within the cult as *Lúsios,* the "Liberator," and under this double identity venerated on the Mount Kithairon frequented by Theban women, as well as near the theater in the city of Sikyon.[45]

In a more decidedly funerary context, an inscription from Cumae and dating from the fifth century warns the passerby: "It is not permitted that anyone lie here who has not been seized by Bacchus (*bebakhkheuménon*)."[46] Even if Euripides speaks of an Apollo Bacchus, and even if, in the second drama that the tragic poet devoted to Hippolytus, Theseus waxes ironic on the exclusive love that the young man expressed for Artemis, accusing the likely initiate of the Eleusinian Mysteries of also being a bacchant under Orpheus' direction, the term *bákkhos* and its derivatives recall Dionysiac possession, whether metaphoric or not.[47]

2.3.1. Initiates' shortcuts in Hades

And so the relationship seems inevitable between the integration of the addressee of the poetic text of Hipponion with a group of initiates, and the two possible itineraries offered at the beginning of the text. It is as an initiate, no doubt, that the young deceased woman is led to avoid the spring on the right, marked by the glowing cypress, and goes instead toward the Lake of Memory.

We must remember that not only is the Hipponion discourse-tomb placed from the beginning under the authority of Mnemosyne, but in its metrical correspondence to a paroemiac, the formula mentioning the pres-

---

dative dedication, but an address to the deity, similar to the one mentioned in the Pelinna lamellae; see also the Pherai document cited in n55 below.

[45] Pausanias 2.2.6–7 and 2.7.5–6; see references given on this by Burkert 1987:21–22, who a bit too quickly presents the Dionysiac mysteries of Magna Graecia as equivalent to the rites of Eleusis; and see also commentaries I cited in my study of 1996:24–26.

[46] *DGE* 792 Schwyzer = *LSCGS* 120 Sokolowski, along with references I gave in 1996d:25n21. We must remember that the members of the chorus in Euripides *Cretans* (fr. 472.9–15 Kannicht) are defined as *místai* and bacchants for Zeus on Ida, Zagreus, the Mountain Mother, and the Curetai!

[47] Euripides fr. 477 Kannicht and *Hippolytus* 24–28 and 952–955, compare for example with Aeschylus *Seven Against Thebes* 497–499 (a metaphoric use relating to the madness of warriors) or with Herodotus 4.79.5 (thiasus of Dionysus). See reply on this given by Pugliese Carratelli 1976:462–464 to West 1975:234–236, who refuses to automatically associate bacchants with Dionysus.

ence of the water of memory punctuates the text three times (lines 6, 12, and 14). In this regard, it seems proper to wonder if the short texts of the lamellae of Eleutherna from Crete are not addressed to common mortals; their souls are destined to drink from the eternally-flowing spring on the right, the one that the addressees of the longer texts are advised to avoid! By contrast, the male or female initiates of Hipponion, Petelia, Pharsalus, and probably Entella are invited to drink water with specific qualities; this cool water is capable (through an intervening play on words, *psukhaí—psúkhontai—psukhrón* in Hipponion and Entella) of giving a vital force to their parched souls, but is also capable of reviving the (initiatory?) memory, which will allow them to take the path which will lead them among the "glorious" in Hipponion, among the "heroes" in Petelia.[48]

If the short texts seem to be addressed to mortals in general while the long texts are meant for initiates, the identity shared by their respective addressees is what brings the two groups together. They are associated into the movement of *communitas* which anthropologists find characteristic of any group of initiands: all are sons of the Earth and the starry Heavens.[49] This identity, integrated into the password, comes before being faced with the Underworld. It is threatened by thirst, which may destroy the deceased. In all of the texts (with the exception of Pharsalus) this feeling of thirst is accompanied by the "performative" declaration *apóllumai,* "I am dying." But only the short texts attribute to the spring on the right a flow whose eternity (*aieiróō*, line 2) seems able to supply a palliative to the threat of death which weighs on the soul there.[50] The water on the right thus seems to fulfill the same purpose for the addressees of the short texts that the water of Mnemosyne fulfills for the addressees of the long texts. But whether one is advised to avoid it or to drink from it, the right-hand spring is never associated with Lethe, antiphrastic (in forgetfulness) to Mnemosyne!

So it is as if the bearers of the long texts had additional information allowing them to follow an itinerary reserved for them alone, beyond the source on the right at which the general run of souls are called to drink. We

---

[48] B 3–8 Zuntz = 478 F–483 F Bernabé and B 9 Graf = 484 F Bernabé. West 1975:235–236, could not resist the temptation to reconstruct an archetype!

[49] References to this distinctive trait of the initiation ritual in my study from 1999:285–288.

[50] Marked also by a glowing cypress, the right-hand spring mentioned in the short texts is described either as *aiénaos,* or as *aieíroos:* cf. *Works* 478, for the first, and Sophocles *Oedipus at Colonus* 469–470, for an adjective similar to the second. Especially Bernabé 1991:226–227, makes the unwarranted connection with the spring of Lethe mentioned by Plato *Republic* 621a–b (but also cf. 230–231): see n19 above.

mentioned above that the *Odyssey* gives a double image of the afterlife, related to two different realms. On the one hand, "the wide-doored house of Hades," where the souls and shades of heroines and heroes stay, answering the sacrificial call of Odysseus, he himself stands at the mouth of Erebos, on the edge of the Ocean River, in the country of Kimmerians wrapped in mist and fog (*ēéri kaì nephélēi*); among the heroic figures reduced to this state of *eídōla* are Epikaste, Leda, Phaedra, Agamemnon, Achilles, and even Minos the son of Zeus, who "renders justice to the dead." On the other hand, the Old Man of the Sea when consulted by Menelaus in Egypt predicted that the king of Sparta, "raised by Zeus" and his son-in-law, would escape death; he will be sent by the immortal gods to the Elysian Fields, at the ends of the earth, where he will meet Rhadamanthys, the brother of Minos, to enjoy life in a golden age, without seasons but soothed by the breezes of the Zephyr which "refreshes (*anapsúkhein*) men."[51]

Remember that in the narrative of the five generations told in his *Works*, Hesiod situates this funerary realm at the ends of the earth, in the "Isles of the Blessed"; the climate of this far-off region is so favorable that it ensures frequent harvests enjoyed not only by Menelaus, but also by some of the blessed heroes (*ólbioi hḗrōes*) who fell before the gates of Thebes fighting for Oedipus' inheritance or on the plains of Troy in Helen's name. We saw that Hesiod's poem stresses that this life of carefree abundance is granted those "set apart from men" by Zeus.[52] Despite the difficulties presented by literal translation of the text, Pindar in his second *Olympian Ode* offers a representation of the afterlife with the same underlying dichotomy. In this epinician composed and performed for Theron of Agrigentum, the realm where men "with nothing" are judged for their crimes is clearly set off from the Isle of the Blessed, whose favorable breezes guarantee constant blossoms. Following the "way of Zeus," those who have kept their souls from unjust acts through several lives can enter this realm; there they share the company of Rhadamanthys, under the control of Kronos, master of the golden age. Among those blessed who have joined the gods, Peleus and Kadmos, but also Achilles, the hero par excellence, are examples given to the tyrant of Agrigentum, to

---

[51] *Odyssey* 11.14–50 and 568–571 especially, contrasting for Menelaus with 4.561–569 (cf. n31 above); see also *Odyssey* 24.1–23, where Hermes leads the souls of the candidates beyond the Ocean River to the "asphodel meadow" (cf. 11.539 and 573) where *eídōla* such as Achilles, Patroclus, Agamemnon, and others await them ...; see especially Sourvinou-Inwood 1995:17–92; see also Brown 1994:397–401. The study proposed hereupon by Griffith (1997:226–230) is clever.

[52] *Works* 156–173: cf. chapter II, section 2.1.4 above.

whom the ode is addressed, and who for his generosity is promised the same immortal destiny.[53]

The common trait among these different representations seems clear: unlike the souls of mortals (like those of certain protagonists of the *Iliad*) wandering unhappily in Hades, the heroes of legend, and humans of the present day distinguished by their ancestry and by their exceptional values, may attain a special place and status. This final and privileged state is secured in a sort of return to the golden age, by association with the Blessed in their Isles or in the Elysian Fields. It is well known that *mákar* designates the status of eternal happiness enjoyed by the gods, set apart from any productive labor.

2.3.2 Mústēs *and bacchant: A preliminary status*

In two (perhaps even three) of the long texts studied thus far, and in sharp contrast to the short texts, this privileged status at the end of the itinerary is described meaningfully: "hero" in Petelia and perhaps in Entella; "glorious" (with all that the *kléos* implies about sharing in immortality) in Hipponion.[54] Attached to the power exercised by the gods (*anáxeis*, "you will reign," line 11 of the Petelia text), this group status comes after the status designated by being descended from Earth and Heaven, which is also stated in the short texts. We must remember that this latter status is associated with the state of dehydration and mortality experienced by the soul before it can taste the waters of Mnemosyne and continue with the other *mústai* and bacchants on its way toward the place ruled by the immortalized heroes. This coincidence between space traversed and time traversed is well marked in the Petelia text which ends, "and it is then later, among the other heroes, that you will reign" (line 1). Through the intermediary of the poetic discourse, Memory relates the past of the initiate with the future of a quasi-divine identity.

The nearly-divine collective identity acquired by drinking the waters of Memory thus seems reserved for those *mústai* who will know to turn away from the spring on the right, reserved for more common sons of Gaia and

---

[53] Pindar *Olympian* 2.57–80 (cf. n31 above); see commentary by Lloyd-Jones 1985:249–279, who connects the representation of the afterlife found in this epinician with the images of it given by the gold lamellae texts (especially Hipponion); these are not necessarily "Orphically" inspired, as Bernabé and Jiménez San Cristóbal 2001:229–242, tend to reaffirm. A similar representation of the afterlife is also presupposed by frr. 129–130, as well as by fr. 133 Maehler (cf. n32 above), also of Pindar.

[54] B 1, 11 Zuntz = 476 F, 11 Bernabé and B 11, 2 Riedweg = 475 F, 2 Bernabé: B 10, 16 Graf = 474 F, 16 Bernabé. On the heroic status promised by the text, see especially information given haphazardly by Scarpi 1989:207–216, as well as n32 above.

Ouranos, in order to reach the specific and exclusive realm of godlike heroes. In this context, it is easy to understand why the speaker in the Petelia text places himself in the perspective of a future hero, situating the spring marked by the white cypress negatively, on the left.

We can, then, grasp the meaning of the term *súmbola* which appears at the end of the incomplete Entella text. Generally designating recognition signs, the term *súmbola* serves as a title for a gold lamella from the end of the fourth century, found near Pherai in Thessaly: *Súmbola. Andrikēpaidóthurson — Andrikēpaidóthurson. Brímō — Brímō. Eísithi hieròn leimôna. Ápoinos gàr ho místēs.* †*ápedont*.[55] The lamella's text begins by dramatizing, in a way, the meaning of its title. The exact repetition of the first two expressions in the vocative correspond to a putting-into-discourse and a textualization of both the practice and the literal meaning of "symbol": a gesture of identification and recognition by means of two matching elements.

The Pherai text is introduced by a double call to an addressee, described as an "adult adolescent," who corresponds either to the one carrying the lamella or to Dionysus himself, to take up his thyrsos. It is followed by a repeated and symmetrical invocation to Brimo, an avatar of Hecate, sometimes assimilated to Demeter in an Eleusinian context, or to Persephone in an Orphic context.[56] Following these two repeated calls, the receiver, whom we can now identify with the addressee and bearer of the lamella of Pherai, is invited to enter a "sacred meadow" easily identified with the *leimôn* of the Isles of the Blessed.[57] Before the brief conclusion, unfortunately indecipherable, the incitement to privileged access is justified: the addressee is presented as a *místēs* who, as such, is exempt or freed of any penalty (*ápoinos*). The injunctive utterance of the Pherai *súmbola* thus ensures access to the sacred

---

[55] Text from Riedweg 1998:390 and commented, with bibliographic information, in Tsantsanoglou 1997:114–117, in Bernabé and Jiménez San Cristóbal 2001:201–208, and in Pugliese Carratelli 2001:123–124 (2003:127–128); *editio princeps*: Chrysostomou 1994:126–139 (on the archaeological site concerned). *Súmbola*: cf. B 11, 19 Riedweg = 475 F, 19 Bernabé, along with Bernabé 1999:58–59, who in this context proposed reading *phe[rsephonē* in the next line. See n44 above. Clarification on the right- or left-hand position of the spring to avoid in Pugliese Carratelli 1974:119–120.

[56] The symbolic practice of a bone shared between two guests is described by the scholiast to Euripides *Medea* 613 (II 175 Schwartz); on this, see commentary by Burkert 1999:68–69, as well as Tortorelli Ghidini 1991. Dionysus as a young adult: *Homeric Hymn* 7.3–4; on Brimo, see Apollonius Rhodius 3.861–863 and 1211, as well as Graf 1985:130–131.

[57] As Riedweg noted in 1998:362, the expressions *hieroì leimônes* and *íthi* are found, respectively, in the lamellae of Thourioi (A 4, 6 Zuntz = 487 F, 6 Bernabé) and of Rome (A 5, 4 Zuntz = 491 F, 4 Bernabé). On the location of meadows of love and meadows of the blessed, see references given in Calame 1996a:174–177.

meadow of the afterlife in a spatial-temporal itinerary which speaks of two ways of proceeding that we will have to return to: on the one hand, the voyage toward the world of the Blessed proposed by two Thourioi golden lamellae for the soul who has "expiated his penalty for unjust acts"; and on the other hand the destiny of the "unjust," paying "right here" in the Underworld the penalty (*poinán*) for their unjust acts in contrast with mortals allowed, for instance, by the Pindaric *Olympian Ode* already quoted to access the Isles of the Blessed.[58] Decidedly different from the concept of the *súnthēma* of Eleusis, where the initiand describes performatively and in the first person the ritual acts which he or she has just performed,[59] the *súmbola* procedure gives access to a new realm through repeating the invocation formulae. Its injunctive formulation in the second person recalls the long informative invitations from Hipponion, Petelia, or Pharsalus.

While it brings confirmation to the Dionysiac identity of the *mústai* and bacchants of Hipponion, this detour through Pherai also casts light on their role. It would be even more difficult to try to deprive the poetic Hipponion text of an interpretation in initiatory terms that the narrative is about ritual gestures. In the logic of ritual, the physical death and descent into Hades through inhumation could represent the phase of separation from the previous order as in the ternary structure of any rite of passage. In such a ritual logic, the thirst and sense of loss (*apóllumai*) expressed by the protagonist of the "initiation" could correspond to the symbolic death which is its center. And through drinking the waters of the Lake of Memory, the access to the realm of the "glorious" (with the complementary and community identity attached to that access) could in turn be interpreted as the final phase of aggregation for those whose identity, divided between Earth and Heaven, is known to the guardians of Hades.[60]

It is a widely held belief in classical Greece that privileged access to a realm of paradise close to that of the gods is reserved to those who, on earth, have undergone initiatory rites controlled by Dionysus. That means that

---

[58] A 2–3, 4 Zuntz = 489–490 F, 4 Bernabé: see below section 3.1; Pindar *Olympian* 2.57–58; on the debated meaning of this passage, see especially Lloyd-Jones 1985:252–256: see above n31 and n53.

[59] Clement of Alexandria *Protrepticus* 21.2, *pace* Burkert 1987:46 and 94, who lumps together *súmbola* and *súnthēma* (cf. n93 below); remember that Plutarch *De Consolatione* 611d, recalls concerning the survival of the soul the *mustikà súmbola tôn perì tòn Diónuson orgiasmôn*.

[60] B 1 Zuntz = 476 F, 7 Bernabé. For references on the history of concepts of the rite of passage and the initiation ritual, and for a critique on the overly systematic use of these categories, see my study of 1999:280–289, and chapter III, section 2.2 above.

the initiatory itinerary into the group of the blessed proposed by the golden lamella of the Hipponion implies a Dionysiac initiation during the life of the mortal. "Whoever reaches Hades without having known initiatory completion uninitiated and unsanctified (*amúētos kaì atélestos*) will be placed in the mire; he who arrives there purified and initiated (*kekatharménos te kaì telesménos*) will dwell with the gods," says the Socrates of the *Phaedo*, who is at the point of death, referring to an ancient belief. And he specifies that by initiation he means the Dionysiac rites, where "those who carry the thyrsos are many, but the bacchants (*bákkhoi*) are few."[61] The initiation which confers the state of purity required to belong to the small number of the elect who will share the life of the gods in Hades is thus inspired by Dionysus, even if for Socrates it represents a metaphor which finally refers to philosophic activity. And it has been noted that in the Hellenistic epigram of Poseidippos of Pella, perhaps the very same *mústēs* of that name on a lamella mentioned earlier, the speaker expresses his hope that thanks to the "mystic path," he will be near Rhadamanthys and dwell there after death.[62] In Hipponion, in Petelia, in Pharsalus, even in Entella, both the course through Hades promised only to *mústai*, and the privileged destiny which awaits them, imply a preceding Dionysiac type of initiation and rite of passage. As the knowledge of the epic Muse is about the past, present, and future, Mnemosyne guarantees the transition from the status of a mortal initiate to a divine status promised to the deceased. We find traces of such a double initiatory progression, completed by poetic memory, in other gold lamellae.

3. Modalities of funerary initiation

From an enunciative point of view, the discourse of the long poetic texts like the Hipponion lamella consists of a series of injunctive and performative indications, expressed in the second person and consequently addressed to the man or woman who carries the lamella. At the center of the text, the deceased

---

[61] Plato *Phaedo* 69c (with corresponding commentary by Olympiodoros, p. 48, 20 Norv.) = *Orphica* fr. 434 F III Bernabé (= fr. 5 and 235 Kern); see also *Gorgias* 493a–b = *Orphica* fr. 434 F II Bernabé, *Republic* 614b–d (with the two paths, one on the right leading toward the heavens, the other on the left leading down below the earth, that souls take after their judgment in the "myth" of Er), as well as Aristophanes *Frogs* 145–158, for the distinction between the mire where the unjust languish and the paradise reserved for the *memuēménoi*! See Edmonds 2004:87–88, 111–158, and 205–207.

[62] Poseidippos *Epigram* 705.21–25 Lloyd-Jones-Parsons; cf. n44 above for the Pella lamella, along with commentaries by Dickie 1995:83–84, and by Rossi 1996:61–62.

appears in the first person in a declaration of identity which approximately corresponds to the utterance in the short texts. That means that these "I" statements are supposed to be spoken directly to the wearer of the lamella; the "you" statements framing the "I" declaration offer in some way the context of enunciation of the statements assumed by the "I". One could imagine that the text was spoken by a male or female officiant during the funeral, or that on the enunciative level the statement is a password, supposed to be spoken at the moment in which the soul would find out its way through Hades.

The very same alternation between second person and first person is shown in texts revealed by the well-known lamellae found in two funerary tumuli in the Lucanian colony of Thourioi. With a few important variations, the three texts buried in the tomb called "the Timpone piccolo" and placed in the right hands of the three bodies (whose sex could not be determined), are in the first person, thus from the perspective of a speaker who corresponds to the deceased. On the other hand, the text of the lamella placed beside the head of a cremated body in the "Timpone grande" contains second-person forms referring to an officiant who seems to speak to the deceased.[63]

3.1. Thourioi: Purity and divine felicity

Without going into the details of texts which would require as thorough a commentary as the one presented here, we shall address only the spatial and temporal aspects of the itinerary traced out in the longest putting-into-discourse among those found in the "Timpone piccolo." Enunciated in the first person and dating from about the middle of the fourth century, this text sketches a route organized into three phrases.

> Pure, I come from among the pure, o sovereign of the
> Underworld,
> Eukles and Eubouleus and all of you, immortal gods;
> for I declare that I belong to your blessed race.
> But the Moira overwhelms me, and other immortal gods
> [...] and lightning from the stars.
> From the grievous circle, hard to endure, I have flown
> And on my swift feet I have dashed toward the desired
> crown,

---

[63] Texts enunciated in the first person: A 1 Zuntz = 488 F Bernabé (here) and A 2–3 Zuntz = 489–490 F Bernabé; in the second person: A 4 Zuntz = 487 F Bernabé. Description in Zuntz 1971:287–293 and 310–315, and in Pugliese Carratelli 2001a:98–111 (= 2003:98–115).

into the lap of the sovereign, of the queen of the
    Underworld, I have sunk.
"O fortunate one, o blessed one, rather than dead, you shall
    be a god."
A kid, I have fallen into milk.

> English version from the French translation
> by L. Brisson, slightly modified by C. Calame

Enunciated at the beginning of the discourse, the central phase of the
proposed spatial-temporal itinerary corresponds to the present of the
enunciation. Arriving in Hades (*érkhomai*, line 1) in a state of exceptional
purity, the *I*-speaker resorts to a feminine form (probably referring not to the
dead person but to the soul) to present himself to the gods of the Underworld:
the queen of the chthonian world, easily identified as Persephone, Eukles
(an avatar of Hades), and finally Eubouleus, identified by different parallels
sometimes with Dionysus, and sometimes with Pluto.[64] Invoked in the vocative
in the two shorter but similar texts also found in the "Timpone piccolo," these
three deities are combined with "other immortal gods." Before this divine
constellation, the speaker-soul declares himself in a well-marked speech act
(*eúkhomai*, line 3) which refers both to the utterance which he is making and to
the extra-discursive. He solemnly declares that he belongs to the same blessed
race (*ólbion génos*, line 3) as the deities invoked. The soul thus seems to have
direct access to the privileged domain reserved in Hades for those who can
claim divine ancestry.

    Described in aorist forms, the preceding initial moment is the moment
of death: the *I*-speaker says that he was vanquished by the fulfillment of that
part of destiny which falls to each mortal, in accordance with the idea of *moîra*
which makes up the destiny of heroes in the Homeric poems. In a perspective familiar to us from the epic world, where the power of Zeus contributes to
fulfill the destiny assigned to each individual, but in a syntactic anacoluthon
the meaning of which evades us, the fulfillment of the *moîra* is accompanied by
the lightning bolt of his celestial brilliance (*asteroblêta keraunón*, line 4); not that
the dead was really struck down by lightning, as one might think, but because
the intervention of Zeus' fire thus marks a death whose moment is determined
in advance. This divine fire seems to be part of the very ancestry claimed by the
various addressees of the long texts already read, as well as by the speakers of

---

[64] On these identifications, quite apart from any systematic association with Dionysus (but cf.
Plutarch *Symposiacs* 7.714c [*Moralia*]), cf. Zuntz 1971:310–312, and in an Orphic context, Morand
2001:165–168.

the brief texts also mentioned: they are all sons of celestial Ouranos (*asteróeis*), and, as previously mentioned, one of them is named Asterios.[65]

Still in the aorist, and thus in the past, the course after death is imagined first as a flight from the "circle of grievous and difficult sufferings," then as access to a crown of desire which some have characterized as mystic, but which could well be symposiac, and last as a refuge in the lap of Persephone, the "chthonian queen." Far from referring to any cycle of reincarnation or any concept of metempsychosis (maybe inspired by Pythagorism) the circle of afflictions no doubt refers much more simply to the "cycle of human affairs" spoken of by Herodotus; this sinusoidal concept of human time—already mentioned in Hesiod as seen in Chapter II—makes the lives of mortals an alternating sequence of happiness and misfortune.[66] And sinking into the lap of the queen of the Underworld recalls the legendary nursing of Demophoon in the *Homeric Hymn to Demeter*, as well as the nurse-like qualities attributed both to Demeter herself and to Persephone in Sophocles' *Oedipus at Colonus*.[67]

The ring-structured evocation of the queen of the dead leads the utterance back to the present. This present-tense wording is also found in the two other lamellae which came from the "Timpone piccolo": through this self-referential means, the speaker describes his arrival as a suppliant (*nûn d' hikétēs hékō*) of respectable Persephone.[68] In the longer text I quoted, this performative indication is replaced by a direct intervention in the second person, and it is undoubtedly spoken by the voice of Persephone herself. In the promise made in her speech act, the goddess opens the text to the future; she alludes thus to the third spatial-temporal stage in the course set out here, "O fortunate one, o blessed one, rather than dead, you shall be a god." Simultaneously happy as men may be (*ólbioi*) and blessed like the gods (*makáriste*), the deceased (or his soul) will pass from being a mortal to the status of a god (*theòs ésēi antì brótoio*).

---

[65] Cf. section 2.1.3 above, with n24. In the shortest texts A 2, 3 Zuntz = 489 F, 3 Bernabé and A 3, 3 Zuntz = 490 F, 3 Bernabé, death from being stamped out by the *moîra*, or by the flash of lightning (image of the will of Zeus) is presented as alternative. On the etymology proposed for *elúsion*, cf. Sourvinou-Inwood 1995:49–52; *contra*: Griffith 1997:229–230!

[66] Cf. Herodotus 1.5.4; 1.207.2, and 9.27.4, as well as Sophocles *Electra* 916–919 and, later, Aristotle *Problemata* 986a 22–29 (see above, Chapter II, section 5); but see also the "circle of heavy sorrows" cited by a late funerary stele from Panticapaeum near Olbia (= *Orphica* 467 V Bernabé) and interpreted as the cycle of rebirths especially by Casadio 1991:136–137. Pythagorean interpretation of this *kúklos* has been propsed by Zuntz 1971: 336–337, see also Edmonds 2004: 96–99.

[67] *Homeric Hymn to Demeter* 224–274; Sophocles *Oedipus at Colonus* 1050; see references I assembled on this in a study from 1998c:352–353 (with n40).

[68] A 2, 6 Zuntz = 489 F, 6 Bernabé; A 3, 6 Zuntz = 490 F, 6 Bernabé.

Such, then, is the course set out, again like a rite of passage, organized into three spatial-temporal stages: death and departure from the hazards of mortal life (past)—descent to the bosom of Persephone and the gods who surround her (present)—metamorphosis of the deceased into a deity (near future). It is as if the key to this text were given at its end, in a formula that rhythmically signs this poetic text, the rest of which is composed in dactylic meter.[69] In a final first-person utterance, the *I*-speaker indicates that this ternary movement is possible only because "A kid, I have fallen into milk." We will soon come back to the meaning of this strange declaration.

From the spatial-temporal point of view, the course proposed by the text from the "Timpone grande" and enunciated in the second person is based on a similar ternary structure. At the moment of enunciation of the partially dactylic text, the soul of the deceased is in an intermediate situation. Through the triple invocatory repetition of *khaîre* typical of the hymnic tradition, the deceased is called upon to rejoice. On the one hand, he has left behind the light of the sun "after undergoing (*pathṓn*) an ordeal (*páthēma*) he had never before suffered (*epepóntheis*)."[70] On the other hand he is invited to take the "right-hand path" which must lead him to the holy meadows and sacred woods of Persephone!

Composed in simple rhythmic prose much like the conclusion of the "Timpone piccolo" text, the central part of the short text takes up the formula "A kid, you have fallen into milk" in the second person, relating this enigmatic plunge either to the moment of death itself, or more likely to the ordeal (*páthēma*) which has just been mentioned: the moment when "from a man, you have become a god." No matter which prior moment is meant in the ritual reference (to which we shall return very soon), the spatial-temporal itinerary proposed to the deceased at the moment when his soul leaves the light of sun seems, by its rejoicing in the present, to follow also the ternary sequence "separation—marginal period—aggregation" of the rite of passage; this ritual progression corresponds to the access to a new status, that of immortal, anticipated by the first ritual gesture.

---

[69] Using categories which come more from semio-narrative analysis than from the anthropology of ritual, Riedweg 1998:319–383, also sees in the itinerary described by the speaker of text A 1 progress of an initiatory sort (on this, see also Calame 1996d:20–22). There can be found in this latter study additional elements of commentary referring to various earlier works, as well as the hypothesis that the last utterance of the text is composed in rhythmic prose, as befits its ritual function.

[70] A 4 Zuntz = 487 F Bernabé; on the relationships of this text with the lamellae exhumed at the "Timpone piccolo," as well as with the much later text A 5 Zuntz = 491 F Bernabé (enunciated in the third person), see most recently Riedweg 1998:368–375. The rhythmic structure of the central portion of text, interpreted in terms of *súmbola*, is analyzed by Watkins 1995:282–283.

3.2. Pelinna: Falling into milk and metaphor

The enigmatic utterance about falling into milk has lost at least some of its mystery since the 1987 publication of the two lamellae from Pelinna. Placed on the chest of a woman buried in that small city in Thessaly, the two gold lamellae were found with a coin slipped into the mouth of the body and intended to ensure the passage of its *psukhḗ* into the afterlife. These two fine lamellae shaped like ivy leaves present symmetric texts, in some ways giving "conditions of enunciation" much like those of the funerary passports mentioned earlier.[71]

In an earlier study I tried to follow the spatial-temporal course proposed in these homologous texts dating from the end of the fourth century, through the phenomena of their *mise en discours*. Here is the translation of the more complete text:

> Now, you are dead, now you are born, thrice blessed, on this day.
> > Say to Persephone that it is Bakkhios himself who delivered
> > > you.
> A bull, you have fallen into milk;
> immediately in the milk you sprang out:
> a ram, you have fallen into milk.
> Wine is your privilege, o blessed one,
> and below the earth the initiatory rites of the other blessed await
> > you.

In an anonymous address to the lamella's bearer, the double text from Pelinna contains utterances composed in the second person and in dactylic meter. Immediately related to the past moment of death and to the "becoming" linked to it (in forms of the aorist), the text insists heavily on the present of its enunciation, "now" (*nûn*, line 1), "on this day" (*hámati tôide*, line 1). The present moment is linked not just to the possession of wine, but especially to an introduction to Persephone. Brought about by a liberating movement linked to intervention by Bakkhios, whom we can identify with Dionysus, the invitation to speak to Persephone is enunciated in the injunctive infinitive (*eipeîn*, line 2), just as in Petelia and in Pharsalus. The text of the direct address itself takes up the formula which closes the longer text from Thourioi and repeats it two or three times in rhythmic prose. In this incantatory movement of repetition with variations, the ram is substituted for the kid: "a ram, you have fallen into

---

[71] P 1–2 Riedweg = 485 F and 486 F Bernabé; edition with commentary by Tsantsanoglou and Parassoglou 1987.

milk." This ritual utterance is preceded by "bull, you have sprung into milk"; doubled on one of the two lamellae, its wording evokes not only incantatory procedure, but also a springing forth which is found in other initiatory texts.[72]

Presented in the past (*éthores*, line 3 and 4; *épeses*, line 5), the immersion in milk corresponds both temporally and causally (*hóti ... éluse*, line 2) with liberation by a Bakkhios evoking Dionysus Lysius.[73] So the temporal outline of the lamella alludes to a ritual preceding death. Just as in the text from the "Timpone grande," the moment of earthly death coincides practically with the present moment, this correspondence brings about a sort of temporal oxymoron in the introductory expression: "now you died" (*nûn éthanes*, line 1). The present moment of enunciation of the gold text also coincides with the address directed to the deceased as "thrice blessed" (*trisólbie*, line 1). While evoking the double *makarismos* found, for example, at the end of the *Homeric Hymn to Demeter*, this description already announces the future reserved for the *you*-interlocutor of the text: initiatory rites (*télea*, line 7) will ensure him "below earth" the same destiny enjoyed by the other "blessed" (*ólbioi*, line 7), as in the Thourioi lamellae.[74] Its ring structure gives textual confirmation to the temporal relationship woven in this way between the introduction to Persephone and the near future reserved for the deceased. At the very center of the discursive circle are references to a past initiation through Bacchic immersion in milk. Composed and pronounced in rhythmic prose, this reference takes on the role of a *súnthēma*, like the password proffered by those initiated into the mysteries of Eleusis.

Even though the double text from Pelinna is unfortunately sparing with precise spatial indications, the funeral course sketched out by it presupposes a previous initiatory passage, as in the Thourioi texts. This rite of passage takes place during the life of the man or woman who has now passed into the other world; in the case of the Pelinna lamellae, it is explicitly attached to religious

---

[72] On the obvious affinities Dionysus shares with the bull, and less clearly with the ram, see Calame 1996d:17–19; on contacts with the kid (*ériphos*), cf. Casadio 1994:92–94, and Camassa 1994:176–178. On the meaning of *éthores* (relating to leaping), see references given in Calame 1996d:19n12.

[73] Independently of any Orphic allusion, the figure of Dionysus Lysius and his role as liberator are well described by Graf 1991:88–92 (see also 1993:243–247), where he proposes seeing in the wine mentioned in line 6 the *timé* attributed to the deceased, perhaps considered in the present moment an Elysian cupbearer! See also Bernabé and Jiménez San Cristóbal 2001:94–107. On the cult of Dionysus Lysius in Sikyon, in Corinth, and perhaps in Thebes, see most recently Casadio 1999:123–141, and Lavecchia 2000:116–121.

[74] *Homeric Hymn to Demeter* 480–482 and 486–489; for other versions of this *makarismos* formula and several bibliographic entries on this, cf. n96 below.

practices controlled by Dionysus the bacchant. Through association of the deceased with the other blessed who have also been liberated by Bakkhios, probably by drinking wine, the end of the initiation route traced by the poetic and declarative text from Pelinna evokes for us, through a previous rite of passage, the group of *mústai* and bacchants into which the deceased from Hipponion is integrated, after she has quenched her funerary thirst with the waters of Mnemosyne's lake. In the Petelia text, too, Bacchic initiation prior to death is required for a ritual and the initiatory access to the privileged realm of the "glorious" and its corresponding status.

4. From Bacchus to Orpheus: Comparisons and contrasts

So what about Orpheus? And Orphic death? If neither the figure of Orpheus nor Orphic practices have been mentioned thus far, it is purely intentional. Certainly, from the moment of their publication in 1879, then in 1880, the texts revealed by the funerary lamellae from Thourioi have enjoyed quasi-automatic inclusion within the Orphic circle. The mention in two of the texts from the "Timpone piccolo" of a "penalty" to be paid because of injustices committed, along with the description in the text from the "Timpone grande" of a "passion" to undergo induced the first interpreter of these lamellae to read in them an allusion to the famous narrative of Orphic anthropogony: humans born from the ashes of Titans, struck down by Zeus after they dismembered and ate the raw flesh of the young Dionysus.[75] Similarly, the gold text from Petelia, first mentioned in 1836, was subject to a similar interpretation from the end of the 19th century; some claimed that in the one who declares himself a son of the Earth and the starry Heaven they could recognize the double Titanesque and Dionysiac nature of the first men, born in the sixth and final phase of Orphic cosmo-theogony!

[75] Proposed by Comparetti 1882: (see earlier notes published by D. Comparetti in F. S. Cavallari, "Notizie degli scavi," in *Memorie dei Lincei. Scienze morali* 4, 1879:156, and 5, 1880:403–410; cf. Pugliese Carratelli 2001:113 and 99 = 2003:115 and 99). Specifically in reference to a similar reading of fr. 133 Maehler of Pindar (cf. n32 above), this Orphic interpretation of certain of the gold lamellae by reference to the "myth" of anthropogony attributed to Orpheus, through the intermediary of Eudemos' theogony, has been repeated ad nauseam recently: see notably Lloyd-Jones 1985:274–277, Graf 1991:90–91, Camassa 1994:178–182, Betz 1998:413–416, Riedweg 1998:380–382 (with the additional references given in n101), and Burkert 1999:60–68; see also now Graf and Johnston 2007:66–93. Tasteful skepticism in Musti 1984:62–64; see also Cole 1993:292–295: "there is no theme of rebirth in the Dionysian sepulchral texts," and Schlesier 2001:166–168. For a critical view on "Dionysos *patiens*," see now Edmonds 2004:102–109, who shows the ambiguities in the designation as "Orphic" of the texts of the funerary gold lamellae.

4.1. Original sin and Christian expiation

Not even taking into account the methodological abuse involved in seeing a ritual practice as the simple reflection of a "mythic" narrative, the narrative of Orphic anthropogony has itself often been interpreted in the Christian meaning of original sin. In its "Orphic" version, man's sin would be inscribed in the twofold nature of men, born from the badly digested remains of a god and the ashes of mortals guilty of a first transgression. With its truly dogmatic effect and its wide diffusion, this Christianizing hermeneutic attitude is able to skip over the controversial question of the date of an anthropogony which is supposed to serve as a conclusive phase of Orphic cosmo-theogony, but which is not attested before the neo-Platonic philosophers.[76] Consequently, the deceased from Thourioi who admit sins which must be ritually expiated seem capable of accepting responsibility for the original sin, committed on the child Dionysus by the Titans in the late Orphic "myth."

Through the works of the great historians of Greek religion in the twentieth century, and those of champions of the Hellenic concepts of the soul's destiny, divided among Christian and Puritan asceticism, oriental mysticisms, and platonically-inspired philosophical eschatologies, a *dóxa* was quickly established. In this perspective, any new document written on gold which saw the light of day could only be placed within the Orphic sphere of influence. The Hipponion lamella itself was first offered to learned readers as the gift of a new "Orphic text." As a result, among the roughly forty studies devoted to this document since its publication in 1974, the titles of more than a third contain the term *Orphic*, rarely placed between quotation marks, as the most basic interpretive caution would seem to demand.[77] Needless to say, the single appearance of the letters *orphik[* with what seems to be a mention of Dionysus (*dio[*) on a bone lamella found at Olbia fed new speculations from the very moment of its publication in 1978. The inscription of these few letters provided the Orphic *dóxa* with what was considered irrefutable proof.[78] But in

---

[76] See especially the precise historical study on this by Edmonds 1999:66–70, who again shows that the "Orphic" narrative of anthopogony is not attested before Olympiodoros! Complete bibliography and reply to this in Bernabé 2002:404–425.

[77] See bibliography given by Pugliese Carratelli 2001a:41–44 (= 2003:35–38, cf. n6 above).

[78] *SEG* XXVIII (1979), 659–661; the circumstances of discovery of these bone lamellae and an interpretation of the graffiti on them are given by West 1983:17–20 (with bibliographic references to the *editio princeps* given in n43); see also Zhmud' 1992:159–162, and Baumgarten 1998:89–92, who stresses the non-funerary use of these graffiti; Burkert 1999:61 and 70–72, specifically, finds confirmation of the Orphic nature of the gold lamellae in these documents with no explicit funerary purpose.

using these few crudely engraved words as "parallels" to the connected poetic texts of the gold lamellae, we forget that these bone lamellae, found in a sanctuary north of the Olbia Agora, have nothing funerary about them; indeed, we know nothing of the use of these graffiti, and consequently nothing of the nature of their pragmatic dimension.

4.2. Iconographic representations of the Underworld

If we limit it just to the terms used in the lamellae-passports which come from cities of Magna Graecia and from the continent, it is definitely the figure of Bacchus which can best provide a common denominator among all these ritually-related texts, and among the spatial-temporal itineraries they propose to the deceased.

The comparative method, applied in different ways in the three preceding chapters, could as an additional attestation lead us not toward cultural manifestations distant in time and space, not to texts belonging to some far-off historical paradigm, but rather to a different sort of semiotic manifestation— Apulian iconography. Not only do the Apulian vases offer a large number of representations of the Underworld, but these iconographic configurations also offer interesting temporal and spatial coincidences with the lamellae from Hipponion, Petelia, and Entella. Indeed, in the inventory of forty-one representations of the Underworld on Apulian vases dated from the beginning to the end of the fourth century, a dozen offer an image of Orpheus.[79]

In most of these representations, the young Orpheus appears with the traits and in the posture of an Apollo with a lyre; he is usually to the left of the *aedicule* which forms the center of the image and which shelters Persephone and Hades. That is the case, for example, in the image on one of the two faces of a volute crater in Naples which lists the proper names of most of the actors and actresses of the scene represented (Figure 6a).[80] At the center of the image, the young Persephone offers a phiale to a mature Pluto. To the left of the *naḯskos*, on three superimposed frames, Megara faces two Heraclids portrayed as adolescents; then, in the middle position, are two Erinyes designated as *Poinaí* (Punishments), called that because they are goddesses of vengeance and expiation; finally on the lower register Sisyphus is easily recognized, rolling his rock under the eye of a Fury, recognizable from the branch and the

---

[79] See the excellent and carefully prepared catalogue of these representations of the Underworld given in Moret 1993:349–351.
[80] Napoli H 3222 (inv. 81666) (*RVAp* I, 16/82); cf. Pensa 1977:24 (with plates I–IV) and Aellen 1994:61–66 and 202 (with plates 2–3).

whip she carries, and a young Hermes whose gaze connects him to the scene painted "below" the *naïskos*. To the right of the little aedicule, whose roof is supported by two Ionic columns and two caryatids, and symmetric to the left part, the young Pelops faces the charioteer Myrtilos, leaning against one of the wheels of his broken chariot, while a girl (perhaps Hippodameia) tries to attract his attention; below, in the middle level, one can identify Aeacus and Rhadamanthys, both duly named; finally the right part of the lower register is once again taken up by three figures, this time all female, of water bearers generally identified with the Danaids. Once again in the lower register, but in a central position and below the aedicule, Herakles is shown; framed on the one side by the triad with Sisyphus in its center and on the other side by the group of three hydrophoroi, the hero is fighting a three-headed Cerberus and a girl riding a hippocamp. Finally, in the middle level, the relationship among the various scenes with the divine couple sheltered by the *naïskos* is ensured both by an Orpheus in oriental dress playing the kithara (Figure 6b) and by a Triptolemos with a scepter, whose seat faces the aedicule while his gaze is turned toward Rhadamanthys, who carries a scepter topped by a bird.

Without necessarily being as rich in the number of heroic figures offered to the eye, several other Apulian representations of the afterlife present the same sort of composition in scenes connected around the *naïskos* which shelters Persephone and Hades, masters of the Underworld. That is the case for the volute crater in Karlsruhe, contemporary to the Naples crater.[81] With the exception of Theseus and Pirithous who are substituted for Pelops and Mirtylos, and without the triad formed by Triptolemos, Aeacus, and Rhadamanthys (replaced by a young man crowned with laurel and two anonymous girls), the same groups of characters are present. Once again dressed in rich oriental clothing and wearing a tiara, the kithara player easily identified as Orpheus, alone, faces the aedicule; he is illuminated by a torch carried by Hecate, who in this case relates the outside of the Underworld and the *naïskos* itself. A fragment from Ruvo, now lost, shows Orpheus marching to the sound of his kithara toward the same aedicule where he is received by the same Hecate: both are clearly identified by name (Figure 7).[82]

[81] Apulian volute crater from 350–340, Karlsruhe B4 (*RVAp* I, 16/81): cf. Pensa 1977:24 (along with plate V and figure 1) and Aellen 1994:58–65 and 205 (and plates 34–35).

[82] Ruvo, ex collection Fenicia: cf. Pensa 1977:25 (with figure 8) and Aellen 1994: 202–203 (with plate 6); see also, as an example of the same compositional scheme, the beautiful frescoes of the Apulian volute crater in Munich 3297 (J 849) (*RVAp* II, 18/282) dating from 330–310 (Pensa 1977:23, with figure 5; Aellen 1994:208, with plates 64–65) or, in a simpler manner, the volute crater Napoli SA 11 (inv. 80854) (*RVAp* I, 16/54) dating from 350–340 (Pensa 1977:25, with plate VII; Aellen 1994:205, with plates 32–33): Orpheus as Apollo.

Figure 6a. Apulian red-figure volute crater; side A: underworld scene with Hades and Persephone seated in their palace. Circle of the Lycurgus Painter, ca. 350–340 BC.

In forty-one of the representations of the Underworld indexed today, Orpheus appears (with more or less certainty) about fifteen times, sometimes with more Apollo-like traits and usually alone. In only one of these images, Orpheus, moved by a young winged Eros, holds Eurydice by the hand, but in a gesture where the hero seems to be leading his spouse toward Persephone and Hades rather than taking her away![83] Among those who interpret these different representations, consensus on the role to attribute to the hero with the lyre is far from being reached.

Figure 6b. Side A: detail, Orpheus in the underworld.

In this, another large Apulian volute crater offers a particularly interesting example, in that for the young Orpheus with the lyre, and in the same position, it substitutes a seated girl, her right hand holding a hydria and her left hand holding a mirror; turned toward the mirror and toward the central *naïskos*, the girl's gaze does what Orpheus' gaze does in the images already mentioned, in relating the outside of the Underworld and the aedicule where Hades and Persephone are seated, along with a Hermes who is probably psychopomp.[84] Above the young hydrophoros are a young couple, a youth carrying a laurel crown and a maiden depicted with an animal skin; the adolescent traits of both lead us to identify them as Apollo and Artemis.

But the same scene can be completely transposed into the Dionysiac domain, as it is in the Apulian volute crater acquired by the Toledo Museum

---

[83] Apulian volute crater, Napoli SA 709 (*RVAp* II, 18/284) dating from 330–310 (Pensa 1977: 27, with plate X, see n84); Aellen, 1994: 211, with plates 92–93); on this, see commentary by Moret 1993:318–327 (along with the catalogue of representations of Orpheus given at 321n185).

[84] Apulian volute crater Leningrad 1717 (St. 424) (*RVAp* II, 28/177) = painter of the Louvre K 67, dating from 325–310: cf. Pensa 1977:26, with plate VIII, as well as Aellen 1994:209, with plate 62.

of Art (Figure 8a–b).[85] Figures familiar from Apulian scenes of the Underworld, such as Herakles, Sisyphus, the Erinyes, hydrophoroi identified with the Danaids or the judges of the Underworld, all surrounding the *naískos* which shelters Hades and Persephone with their usual attributes, are replaced by characters who belong to the circle of Dionysus. The couple on the left in the upper register, formed by the son of Dionysus Oinops and a maiden carrying a torch and identified as Persis, matches the couple on the right, Actaeon and Pentheus, both heroes victims of their own disrespect for the god of the *manía*. In the middle frame, a Maenad identified as Acheta symmetrically reflects Agave, whose gaze is directed toward the central *aedicululum*, just as is the gaze of the young woman with the tambourine and thyrsos. It is no longer Herakles in the lower register, but rather a little Pan playing with the usual three-headed Cerberus. Instead of Orpheus, it is Dionysus on the left approaching the *naískos* and looking toward Hades while on the right is the young Hermes, whose gaze directed toward Persephone completes the careful symmetrical composition of the image.

4.3. Orpheus and Dionysus as musicians

All of the scenes cited so far represent either permanent guests or occasional visitors to the Underworld: residents of Hades' realm, not of the Elysian Fields or of the Isles of the Blessed! To see in these iconographic representations a confirmation of the spatial itinerary suggested in the texts of the gold lamellae would be to give in to the constant abuse of the comparative method, retaining only similarities and ignoring their differences and uniqueness. When Orpheus is represented, he is acting in precisely that domain that the deceased souls of Hipponion, Petelia, and Pharsalus seek to avoid. In addition, both by his place within the composition and by his appearance, Orpheus is found in a situation strongly related to Hades and Persephone, the couple under the *naískos*, either directly or as in the Karlsruhe crater and especially in the Ruvo fragment, mediated through Hecate, who lights the step (danced?) of the singer playing his kithara as he moves toward the aedicule: Orpheus accompanies no hypothetical *mústai* or disciples, but he does make the most of his qualities as a poet of divine origin and as the hero who founded the basic forms of song attributed to him in that classical tradition which sometimes makes him the son of Calliope. Orpheus communicates with Persephone

---

[85] Formerly New York, now Toledo 1994. 19 (*RVAp* Suppl. II, 18/41a 1, post-script p. 508): cf. Moret 1993:293–300, with plate 1a–d, and description given by Johnston and McNiven 1996:25–30; cf. Schlesier 2001:172n62.

Figure 7. Apulian red-figure vase fragment: Orpheus in the underworld. Unattributed, ca. 350 BC.

and her spouse, sometimes with Hades alone, through the art of the Muses, as on an Apulian amphora in the Hermitage Museum in what was formerly Leningrad (Figure 9).[86] Without the actors and actresses of the scene being named, and without any edifice which might evoke an Underworld dwelling, Orpheus wearing a tiara and once again dressed in a rich oriental mantle sings and accompanies himself on the kithara, facing Hades seated on a throne and with a scepter in his hand, while two women witness the scene, one holding a fan and the other holding a parasol and a phiale.

And when the scene becomes more specifically Dionysiac, when the god of wine and *manía* takes the place of Orpheus confronting the master and

---

[86] Leningrad 1701 (St. 498) (*RVAp* 23/46): cf. Pensa 1977:28, with plate XII; other examples of Orpheus facing Hades directly in Schmidt 1991:39–47. Orpheus as the poet who founded the art of the Muses (and the mysteries): Pindar *Pythian* 4.176–177, Aristophanes *Frogs* 1032–1036, and Timotheus fr. 791.221–236 Page; cf. Calame 2002c:392–397.

Figure 8a. Apulian red-figure volute crater; side A: underworld scene, Hades and Persephone in their palace, with Dionysus at left. The Darius Painter, ca. 340–330 BC.

Figure 8b. Side B: youth in *naïskos*, surrounded by youths and women.

mistress of the Underworld, it is as if a handshake, sometimes interpreted as marking the arrival of the hero or god in Hades and sometimes his departure, substitutes for the art of the Muses as a means of communicating with Hades and Persephone.[87] In comparison, both the way Orpheus' step is portrayed and the direction of his musical gesture indicate the moment when he addresses the god of the Underworld, who in other scenes confirms his welcome with a legitimizing gesture of recognition. As we have seen, the introduction and welcoming into Hades is often characterized by the presence of Hermes: he plays the role of guide for an Orpheus or a Dionysus who are simply protagonists passing through. Significantly, this god of transitions (not necessarily initiatory ones) is completely absent from the itineraries described in those passports for the afterlife which have been too quickly labeled as Orphic.

Whether they show Orpheus or Dionysus confronting Hades and Persephone, the Underworld scenes from Apulian ceramics are related to the epic narrative; they paint characters who belong to heroic legend. Whatever the role that either Orpheus or Dionysus assumes in them, they are foreign to any description of a ritual addressed to mortals. They offer a "mythological" representation of the Underworld which does not correspond in any way with the image governing the initiatory itinerary suggested by the gold funerary lamellae.

4.4. Dionysus, excluding Orpheus

And so from iconography we must return to the texts. In so doing, we return from "mythological" and narrative scenes involving gods and heroes to the performative description ritual practices involving mortals.

From this point of view, there is one document (despite its lacunae) which allows us to glimpse two things: the wording of a Dionysiac initiation prior to entering the privileged realm reserved for heroicized mortals and controlled by Persephone, and the Orphic over-interpretation to which this text is constantly subjected, just as is iconography. Dating from the end of the third century BC and included from the very beginning among collections of *Orphica*, the *Papyrus Gurôb*, like the gold lamellae, offers a liturgical sort of text.[88] Formulated in the third-person imperative and then in the first person, the instructions given concern the completion of an initiatory rite (*teletê*). Despite the very large lacunae in the text, we can see that it is about gathering

---

[87] Cf. Moret 1993:304–305 (waving goodbye), and Johnston and McNiven 1996:27–30 (gesture of recognition).

[88] *P. Gurôb* 1 = *Orphica* fr. 31 Kern = 578 F Bernabé; see most recently Hordern 2000:132–135.

Figure 9. Apulian red-figure amphora; side A: underworld scene; detail, Orpheus before Hades. Attributed to the Patera Painter, ca. 330 BC.

raw meat, eating the remains of sacrifice (probably a ram), consecrating an unknown object (probably by hiding it from view), affirming the uniqueness and divinity of Dionysus probably through signs of recognition which constitute *súmbola*, while an *I* affirms that he has drunk wine as a donkey and as a cowherd; after having pronounced a password (*súnthēma*), this speaker seems to consume food, then finally throws into a basket (*kálathos*) a top, a bullroarer, some knucklebones, and a mirror.

This sequence of ritual acts, whose reconstruction and interpretation should at the very least be taken with caution, is interrupted several times by the text of two prayers (*eukhḗ*). The first is a request for individual and collective salvation addressed to Brimo, Demeter, Rhea, and the armed Curetai, in exchange for ritual offerings; among the offerings are the sacrifice of a ram and a billy goat cited in the liturgical text itself. The second, also characterized enunciatively by its collective *we*, is a ritual and incantatory call to Eubouleus; the god is asked to intervene "for us" (after a time of parching and thirst?) alongside Demeter and Pallas, once again to ensure the salvation of the man or woman who prays. The name *Eubouleús* is apparently linked to the epiclesis *Ērikepaîos*, "of Springtime"—which sometimes describes the god in the *Orphic Hymns*; this name must refer to Dionysus just as it does on different lamellae from the "Timpone piccolo" in Thourioi, where it appears alongside Eukles-Hades.[89] The sacrifice of both the ram and the billy goat of course calls to mind the password mentioning immersion in milk, followed by possession of wine, in the Pelinna lamella.[90]

The objects placed in the ritual basket have of course been associated with the legend of the toys the Titans offered little Dionysus, who was amused as well by the choral dances of the armed Curetai, just before the sons of Ouranos tore the child apart. A top, a bull-roarer, dolls, and apples from the "soft-voiced" Hesperides are mentioned in the two dactylic hexameters attributed by Clement of Alexandria to Orpheus of Thrace, the poet of initiation; for this Father of the Church, these objects (to which he adds knuckle-

---

[89] A 1, 2 Zuntz = 488 F, 2 Bernabé and A 2–3, 2 Zuntz = 489–490 F, 2 Bernabé: cf. also A 5, 2 Zuntz = 491 F, 2 Bernabé, and section 3.2 above with n70. On the figure of Eubouleus, cf. n64 above, and on Erikepaios, cf. Morand 2001:189–194. On the identification with a donkey of the initiate called upon to pronounce the ritual text of *P. Gurôb*, we must recall that in allusions made at Aristophanes *Frogs* 158–160, to initiates (*memuēménoi*) of Eleusis, Xanthias compares himself to a donkey who celebrates the mysteries (*ónos ágō mustéria*). As for the term *teletḗ*, it generally concerns a mystery cult: cf. Burkert 1987:8–10.

[90] P 1–2, 5 = 485–486 F, 5 Bernabé; cf. section 3.2 above, with n71. On the Pherai lamella, cf. n55 above (on Brimo, n56 above).

bones and a mirror) are the *súmbola* of the Orphic initiation ritual.[91] So it is only very late that the narrative (itself quite late) of the Titans dismembering young Dionysus-Zagreus and his reassembly by Apollo is placed in relationship with the apparently ritual and initiatory objects whose enumeration is attributed to the founding poet Orpheus. While it brings together Demeter and Dionysus in a collaboration which, through the intervention of Eubouleus himself, recalls the collaboration of Persephone and Hades in certain ritual texts given by the funerary lamellae, the text of the papyrus of Gurôb sets forth religious prescriptions where Orpheus, at least in the current state of the document, plays no role at all! On the other hand, we must remember the presence in the text of *Gurôb* of Rhea, the mother of Demeter and Zeus' ambassador to the goddess in the corresponding *Homeric Hymn*, or the role attributed to Eubouleus, a native and inhabitant of Eleusis who, according to the inscriptions, receives offerings along with Demeter, as well as the use of a password (*súnthēma*), and the use of a ritual basket (*kálathos*) in a ritual context where sight and vision seem to play a central role; these four ritual instructions call to mind the sparse information we have on how the Mysteries devoted to Demeter and Persephone were conducted on the borders of Attica.[92]

In contrast to the recognized consensus on this, neither the Underworld scene from the Apulian crater in Toledo nor the text of the Gurôb papyrus ever refers to the founding hero, nor to the protagonists, nor to the time and space of an initiatory ritual reserved for followers of Orpheus.[93] Quite the opposite: both documents, one from the point of view of "mythological" scenography, the other in the functionality of ritual gestures, and both with the semiotic means appropriate to their specific "discourse," carry indications of the role Dionysus plays in initiatory practices which could ease mortals' access either to Hades, or to the realm governed by Persephone beyond Hades.[94] If integration into a specific temporality and territory proposed in the gold lamellae

---

[91] Clement of Alexandria *Protrepticus* 2.17.2 = *Orphica* fr. 34 Kern = 306 F and 588 T Bernabé; on this see Edmonds 1999:38–57 (*contra*: Bernabé 2002:404–420.)

[92] On these divine actors and ritual objects attested in Athenian celebrations of the Mysteries of Eleusis, I refer the reader to the texts mentioned in the careful commentary by Richardson 1974:295–296 (on the normative role of Rhea in the *Homeric Hymn to Demeter* 441–469, identified somewhat later with her daughter), 81–85 (concerning the Eleusinian figure of Eubouleus), 22–23 (on *súnthēma* and *kálathos*: cf. also n59 above), 26–29 and 310–311 (*epopteía*).

[93] In contrast to the confusion on this maintained by Johnston and McNiven 1996:32–34, according to the normative consensus among the authors they quote, n30; see also Burkert 1999:68–76.

[94] On the salvation role of certain initiatory practices devoted to Dionysus and mentioned in a funerary context, see especially Cole 1993:288–295, and Schlesier 2001:163–166.

does indeed presuppose a previous initiation, probably under the aegis of Dionysus-Bacchus, there is every reason to suppose that this initiatory preparation corresponded to the practice of an official mystery cult along the lines of Eleusis, as attested in several cities, especially in Magna Graecia.[95]

In this, the well-known double makarismos formula which concludes the *Homeric Hymn to Demeter* is highly meaningful. To the man or woman who has had the vision of the *órgia* instituted by Demeter herself, this call promises not only prosperity for his or her household in this life, but also a more favorable share in the afterlife than that reserved for common mortals in the world down below. A similar formula, taken up both by Pindar and by Sophocles and explicitly related to Eleusis, also offers a new life in Hades limited just to initiates.[96] In the Sophocles fragment, they are thrice blessed (*trisólbioi*) who "go into Hades after having seen the mysteries (*telé*)," just as in the Pelinna lamella she is *trisólbios* who, liberated by Bakkhios and received by Persephone, can expect down below the *télea* enjoyed by the other blessed.[97] These lexical correspondences are striking, to say the least, in very similar representations of ritualized time and space.

5. Passwords for a collective funerary identity

Through the orientation of their spatial-temporal configuration, the texts of most of the gold lamellae ensure ritual passage to a final condition and status. The axial point of this regime of temporality is found in a glorious future which will take place in eternity, concomitantly with the space constituted by the Elysian Fields. And so, no transmigration of souls, and no "Orphic" reincarnation! But rather a very prosaic eschatological course, promised through the rhythm of a rite of passage to male and female citizens, the

---

[95] Eleusinian-type mystery cults apart from Eleusis are examined by Graf 1985:273–277. We should remember that first West 1975:234–236, then Musti 1984:65–68, brought together the way followed by *mústai* and bacchants in the Hipponion text (n31 above) with the sacred way leading Athenian initiates to Eleusis. On the image of the path in the context of Dionysian *órgia*, see for instance, Feyerabend 1984:1–10.

[96] *Homeric Hymn to Demeter* 480–489; cf. Pindar fr. 137 Maehler and Sophocles fr. 837 Radt, to compare with P 1–2, 1 and 7 = 485–486 F, 1 and 7 Bernabé (cf. section 3.2 above); on this, see Richardson 1974:310–321, and, for comparison, Calame 1996d:19–23; cf. also Empedokles fr. 31 B 132, 1 Diels-Kranz (see Scarpi 1987:207–210). Notice that the text of lamella A 1, 8 Zuntz = 488 F, 8 Bernabé also shows a form of makarismos: cf. n63 . On the absence of any idea of reincarnation in the *Orphic Hymns*, cf. Morand 2001:212–230.

[97] P 1–2, 1 Riedweg = 485 F, 1 and 486 F, 1 Bernabé ; cf. section 3.2 above; for a preliminary Dionysiac initiation, see also Graf and Johnston 2007:158–164

bourgeois of small cities, and that at the conclusion of an initiatory itinerary, as prerequisite probably within a mystery cult.

The aspiration here is essentially heroic, nourished by the *post mortem* destinies of protagonists in the great epic poems still sung in Panhellenic religious celebrations. Beginning perhaps with Herakles, whose death, according to the *Catalogue of Women* attributed to Hesiod, means transfer into the realm of Hades. But at the moment of the poem's enunciation (*nûn!*), the hero has become a god (*theós*); having escaped all the ills of mortal life and set apart from any cyclical concept, he enjoys the same Olympian dwelling as other deities; immortal and eternally young, he lives alongside his wife, Hebe, who incarnates this youth, and Hera's hatred for him is now finally transformed into love (*pephíleke*, in the perfect)![98]

But a bit closer to the eschatological hopes that the average citizen might nourish, the "song of Harmodios," mentioned by Aristophanes himself, was also sung in the symposiac meetings of fifth-century Athens. Like Achilles and probably Diomedes as well, the young hero of the struggle against the tyrants sons of Peisistratos did not really die; but rather at the end of a process of heroization like that experienced by the most courageous heroes of the Trojan War, he lives in the Isles of the Blessed, in the company of heroes of the Trojan war, the heroes whom Pindar also places in this golden age realm, in his second *Olympian Ode*.[99] Initiation before death into a mystery cult apparently could indeed nourish such hopes of heroization, since Plutarch, in the dialogue he devotes to love, can promise disciples and *mústai* of Eros (*orgiastaîs kaì mústais*) the same happy destiny (*beltíona moîran*) in Hades as those who have participated in the Eleusis initiation.[100]

In ending this trip through concepts and spatio-temporal configurations related to a "pleasant" eschatology, we must stress the central ritual role played by these texts which present practical instructions in a poetic form, placed under the sign of Memory, these poetic speeches, ensure a status of practical regime of truth to the spatial-temporal regime thus configured. In the Hipponion gold lamella, for example, not only is the bearer's declaration of identity situated in the present, where enunciated time, time of narration, and time of enunciation (which coincides with the moment of physical death) coincide, but this present also corresponds to the intermediate stage

---

[98] Hesiod fr. 25, 24–33 Merkelbach-West; Nagy 1979:165–169.

[99] *Carmina conviviala* 894 Page, mentioned at Aristophanes *Acharnians* 979, and quoted by the scholia *ad loc.* (I B, p. 124 Wilson); Pindar *Olympian* 2.71–80: cf. n31 and n51 above.

[100] Plutarch *Dialogue on Love* 761f–762a.

of the course proposed, itself divided into three spatial and temporal phases. This means that in the constant tension between past and near future already discussed concerning other practical Greek spatial-temporal regimes, the chanted recitation of the inscribed words, because of its "performative" nature, is capable of accomplishing the ritual transformation. With its rhapsodic rhythm, poetic composition can thus realize the eschatological expectations of citizens who are initiates and who carry the lamellae, quite separate from any Orphic mysticism which our contemporary paradigm of mystical recomposition proposes to the modern interpreter of these texts.

A hermeneutic response based on such aspirations is all the more ill-suited and even less pertinent in that the new identity proposed by the recitation of the gold lamellae texts is a collective identity. In Calabria and in Thessaly, in Sicily and in Crete, at least from the end of the fifth century to the third century, the deceased who are to recite the gold texts exhumed with them all claim the same ancestry: through their declaration of identity which works as a password, they all declare themselves descendants of Earth and Heaven. And those who will have the privilege of drinking from the cool spring of Memory will be taken into a group of glorious and blessed heroes in a specific Adamic space. Borrowing from the philosopher Ricoeur his distinction between "*mêmeté*" and "*ipséité*," the regime of temporality (and of spatiality) configured in Hipponion-type poetic texts can be seen as a means discursive and ritual for a mortal to allow his *ipse*-identity to accede to an *idem*-identity, but a communal one.[101] With their rhythm which is both narrative and initiatory, these configurations of time and space help to insert through the action of a ritual and poetic memory new and collective individual destinies into a collective status.

But this enunciative transformation from an individual *ipse* to a collective *idem* and this access to a new common status through the powers of poetic discourse can come about only through a prior initiatory temporal path. Inserted into the calendar time of a Dionysiac mystery cult, the initiatory course is intended to confer on the time of the individual life and on its unstable *ipséité* a collective dimension capable of establishing it in a community *mêmeté*, with a spatial-temporal dimension brought about by the eschatological promise. A collective *idem*-identity, since male and female initiates will be admitted to the same group of heroes, the glorious, and the blessed, through words of identity pronounced at the moment of death under the sign

---

[101] On the dialectic of individual "*ipséité*" and "*mêmeté*," see Ricoeur 1990:11–35; on this cf. chapter I, section V.

of Memory; and this is permanent, a form of immortalization realized in a specific time and space, separated from any idea of metempsychosis, reincarnation, or resurrection, and thus separated from any return to the world of mortals ... The mystical perspective opened up by pronouncing the texts of the gold lamellae leads to a spatial-temporal configuration whose axial point and geographic anchor is no longer in the past, but in a practical future, set in immortalizing eternity of a poetic memory.

This testing of Greek funerary texts thus leads us to reformulate Ricoeur's investigation of the hermeneutic composition of the "I" and of the self; it invites us to reorient this study toward the spatial and temporal configuration of an *idem* shared by several individuals. No doubt this need for community can be attributed to the aspirations and nostalgia found within this study, which still leans heavily on the paradigm of social thought from the 1960s, and on the implementation, most often chaotic and repressive, of a Maoism which was socially generous in its priniciples.

The hermeneutic and enunciative complexion conferred on scholarly discourse through paradigms and preoccupations of the moment, and also through the scholar's own sensitivities, is perhaps best illustrated by the image which Benjamin Constant gave us at the beginning of the nineteenth century, of a Greek Underworld divided into two distinct spaces and two distinct temporalities.[102]

> On one of the Fortunate Isles, gently cooled by Ocean's winds and ornamented with beautiful flowers, under eternal sunshine and free from trials and worries, live the thrice-blessed who rejected the temptations of crime and injustice in this life. Their days, free from tears, are spent in the company of those favored by the immortals. Their occupations are songs, hymns, races, concerts, games, or else they sit in a shade perfumed by offerings made to the gods by those on earth, and retrace their memories of the past in their conversations with one another. Saturn governs them, helped by Rhadamanthys and perhaps by Aeacus, who once ruled on the disputes of the gods themselves. In Erebos, on the other hand, where perpetual night reigns, criminals condemned to eternal oblivion are prey to the torments of worry which will never cease. Ancient Greece, in its eschatological hopes is apparently not the land of the eternal return ...

---

[102] Constant 1824 (1999):477.

Who could mistake the progression of ideas here? In Homer, the entire realm of shadows is a place of suffering. Pleasures and pains are purely physical. There are no judges for the actions of this life. Aeacus is not named, Rhadamanthys dwells in Elysium, not in the realm of the dead, and Minos' jurisdiction is only accidental arbitration over those passing through. Pluto punishes murders when he is told of them, but his purpose is not to punish crime: he merely gives in to the invocations of those who implore him, and gives them what they ask, not dealing out justice but rather granting this prayer as he would any other. He does not simply await humans in the Underworld, but rather sends the Furies against the living on earth, just as Jupiter and Juno send Iris and Mercury down to pursue their enemies.

In Pindar, the Underworld is different, a place of deserved punishment and reward; punishments and pleasures are intellectual and moral. There is a tribunal presided by Saturn, the same Saturn whom Homer shows us deposed by Jupiter and covered in chains.

Ancient Greece, with its eidiatological hopes, is apparently not the land of the "eternal return." If Mnemosyne is the figure of a poetic memory evoking an heroic past through divine revelation, Memory also gives to the mortal man, submitted to the vicissitudes of life on earth, the guarantee that he will get, in a stable future and in a particular space, a form of divine permanence. The condition of access to that specific regime of spatio-temporality are the initiatory practices, during life, as reformulated in the *Phaedo* by the Socrates depicted by Plato.

BY WAY OF CONCLUSION
Returns to the Present

Truth loves to prevail,
and all-conquering time
always fosters the deed that is well done

> Bacchylides 13.204–207 (trans. Campbell 1992:201)

I NSERTED INTO A POEM BY BACCHYLIDES which celebrates the victory of an
athlete of Aegina in the Nemean games, this aphorism on truth (*alḗtheia*)
which always triumphs with time (*khrónos*) might well serve as the very
foundation for the representation of time we might attribute to any good
classical Greek. Variations on the theme can be found throughout Hellenic
culture, not only in the poems of the poet of Keos, but in those of his Theban
colleague Pindar, who also sang of victory in the Panhellenic games. Praises
for one young winner in the Games of Olympia include this variation:

> And at that founding ceremony (of Zeus' shrine at Olympia)
> the Fates stood near at hand
> as did the sole assayer
> of genuine truth, Time ...[1]

> Pindar *Olympian* 10.51–55 (trans. Lattimore 1947/1976:35)

From the Homeric poems on, this truth guaranteed by time fits into a tensive
continuity among past, present, and future. In the first book of the *Iliad*, the
seer Calchas is introduced as one who, through the divinatory arts granted
by Apollo, "knows what is, what will be, and what was." In the long and
poetically-inspired scene which opens Hesiod's *Theogony*, the Muses confer on
the poet the power to glorify the past, and future, and the eternal present of
the gods; the Hesiodic Muses in unison sing "what is, what will be, and what

---

[1] Bacchylides 13.204–207; Pindar *Olympian* 10.51–55, see also *Olympian* 1.30–34 or fr. 159 Maehler
("Time is par excellence the savior of just men.").

was."[2] In each case, the place where this truth is set forth in its temporality is far from indifferent: the assembly of the Achaeans in the *Iliad*, the sacred mountain of Helicon in the prelude to the *Theogony*. There is one basic difference, since in the *Iliad*, among the assembled heroes, reorientation of the future as it relates to the past comes about through human action: they must appease the wrath of Apollo by making up for the affront to the god committed in the abduction of the daughter of Apollo's priest Chryses. In the song to the Muses which opens the *Theogony*, on the other hand, the temporal dimension of the truth revealed by the Muses to the young shepherd and poet is annulled in an eternal present; the past genealogy of the blessed gods leads to a stable present it includes past and future in a divine eternity, in contrast to the hazards of the ephemeral destiny set aside for mortals.

But in both cases, truth as related to divinity is revealed by an inspired voice, the voice of the seer who speaks for Apollo in the *Iliad*, or the voice of the poet inspired by the Muses of Helicon in the *Theogony*. The same is true of the (less narrative than ritual) compositions of Bacchylides and Pindar: aphorisms about time as the guarantor of truth must be placed within their intended contexts. In the epinician composed by the poet from Keos, the work of time, which makes great deeds triumph and ensures their truth, fits into the dialectic of praise and reproach which is at the basis of all classical Greek poetics. If critical words by badly intentioned people lose their force, it is thanks to works of justice by the wise man (*sophós*), who finally corresponds to the speaker of the poem, singer of hymns inspired by the Muse Clio. And Pindar attributes the revelation of Herakles' founding of the Olympic Games to the very tradition claimed by those who perform his poem.

Logics of temporality and thus logics of truth; spatial-temporal regimes whose dissemination and permanence depend on the powers of the poet's word, generally inspired by the gods; configurations of the time and of the space perceived to transform them in a collective and ritualized memory. That is also what the *melopoiós* sings in the famous epigram composed to praise those who died at the Battle of Thermopylae. Neither mold nor time "which vanquishes all" (*pandamátōr*) can erode the eternal radiant beauty of Leonidas' valor; poetic praise transforms the tomb of the Spartan king and his soldiers into a shrine with its altar, just as for Bacchylides the art of the Muses, daughters of Memory, together with time, contributes to ensuring after death the truth of beautiful deeds. The site of memory is the poem itself, in orchestrating the relationship

---

[2] Homer *Iliad* 1.68–72; Hesiod *Theogony* 24–40; on the affinities between the seer's words or truth and the inspired words of the poet, see especially Nagy 1991:57–62.

between past and future in a ritualized present, inscribed in the time of the calendar.[3] There is no need to stress the role given throughout the Hellenic tradition to the poetic word, overcoming through a divinely-inspired form of eternity the vicissitudes and finality of the temporality assigned to mortals. For Simonides, as well, the time of happiness experienced by mortal men is subject to changes as unpredictable and as rapid as the flight of a fly.[4]

The four examples of spatial-temporal poetics and practice studied in the preceding chapters must all be placed within this conceptual frame, this ensemble of representations. In each of these configurations, the present voice of the *historiopoietes* ensures the effectiveness of a representation of the past in a precise geographic and historical situation, to ensure its orientation in the immediate future: the voice of the didactic poet (Hesiod) who hopes to resolve the conflicts of political justice by narrating the succession of different kinds of mortal men accounting for a present situation, the choral voice orchestrated by a melic poet (Bacchylides) who makes of the Athenian national hero and his companions the ambiguous heroic model for the choral group performing in worship which under Apollo's aegis celebrates and consecrates the city's control over a maritime domain; the voice of the people inscribed on a stele (at Cyrene) and consecrated to the same god in order to re-found a colonial city whose origins are oracular; the voices (on the funerary gold lamellae) of officiants allowing the previously initiated deceased to escape from the hazards of mortality and to attain beyond Hades, through ritual memory, an eternity close to that of the gods.

"Modern time has only been conceived as such since expectations have moved away from all previous experiences."[5] It was in these words that Koselleck, thirty years ago, defined the feeling of accelerating time which characterizes modernity, in a work he devoted to defining the historian's "horizon of expectation" as it relates to history's "space of experience." With Lamartine

---

[3] Simonides fr. 531 Page; cf. also fr. 645 Page (at Olympia, Simonides praised time, presenting it as the wisest of all; see also Thales fr. 11 A 1, 35 Diels-Kranz) with a moral meaning, see also Theognis 963–970; see now Bakker 2002.

[4] Simonides fr. 521 Page, cf. also fr. 527 Page; on the hazards of the temporality of human mortality, see above chapter V, section 2.3.1. Often commented on, the form of immortalizing memory conferred by the poetic word is well described by Bouvier 1993:1134–1140, with references to the numerous works on the subject.

[5] Koselleck 1990:323, in a study programmatically entitled in its original version "Erfahrungsraum und Erwartungshorizont—zwei historische Kategorien," in U. Engelhardt, V. Sellin, H. Stuke (eds.), *Soziale Bewegung und politische Verfassung. Beiträge zur Geschichte der modernen Welt*, Stuttgart (Klett) 1975:13–33. (English translation of quotation from Reinhart Koselleck, *The Practice of Conceptual History: Timing History, Spacing Concepts*, trans. Todd Samuel Presner et al., Stanford University Press, 2002:128); see also Hartog 2003:19–28.

especially ("The speed of time compensates for distance"), the hopes placed in progress during the Enlightenment, after disconnecting the future from the past, have contributed to erasing the substance of a present regularly projected into the future. In classical Greece, on the other hand, it is through recalling a past in a space shared with the gods and through different modes of the poetic word in its present ritual force that one attempts to orient both the development of the community and the future of individuals subject to the hazards of mortality; it is in this way that one may attempt to reduce and overcome the distance placed between mortal men and immortal gods by the fragility and mobility of space-time situations. In the elegiac poetry composed for groups of citizens often meeting together in symposia, for example, Solon at the beginning of the sixth century takes up a Homeric formula on the oracular revelation of past, present, and future deeds and applies it to the social and civic reality of contemporary Athens. But in attributing awareness of these acts to Justice, who records them silently, the Athenian legislator reorients the epic formulary expression, setting aside a future whose revelation and realization he seems to reserve for the poet's voice. Though it is through time that *Díkē* makes citizens pay for their misdeeds, we learn at the end of the poem that the reestablishment of justice and order among men, through the straightening of "twisted" speeches, belongs to Eunomia: this beautiful civic order is attributed to the teachings of the one who sings the elegiac poem.[6]

"Presentism" as characteristic of post/hypermodernity was defined by way of prelude to the definition of several practical regimes of Hellenic spatio-temporality, but the feeling of being out of breath from full immersion in the immediate really dates only from the transition between the twentieth and twenty-first centuries. Drawing in particular on the thought of Charles Péguy, Jean Chesneaux recently called on the community of historians to become part of the Copernican revolution proposed by Walter Benjamin, reversing the traditional relationship between the past and the present. "The Copernican revolution in history's vision is this: the Past was considered the fixed point and the present moved gropingly to try to bring knowledge closer to this fixed element. From now on, the relationship must be reversed and the Past must become dialectic reversal and irruption of awakened consciousness. Politics now takes precedence over history."[7] The proposed reversal of perspective

---

[6] Solon fr. 3.14–17 and 30–39 Gentili-Prato; cf. also fr. 1.25–32 on the idea of the vengeance of Zeus which takes place over time and finally touches each man. On this see commentary by Noussia 2001:247–249 and 255–257.

[7] Benjamin 1989 (1982:405–406), in a quotation taken from *K1*; see Chesneaux 1996:135–150 as well as 173–184 (quote on 183).

makes the present, not the past, the point of reference. A revolution all the more necessary in that it allows us to break with the ideology of continuity and with the evolutionary (even teleological) progress of history; a revolution which is all the more engaged in that by postulating "compenetration" of privileged moments of the past and the present, it allows the present to be shaken up by the past, to make action on the future a revolutionary act. Chesneaux himself concludes, "For Benjamin as for Péguy, the relationship with the past has no meaning except to the extent that it challenges the present and opens up a different future."

We have seen that calendar time, conceived of as one of those third times which allows us to articulate world time with lived phenomenological time, seems (as Benveniste suggested) to be situated in relationship to an axial point at the beginning of its linear and measurable development. But we added that this time, when only barely grasped in its discursive representation, is automatically situated in relationship to a second pole, that of the moment and the place of its putting-into-discourse. Which is to say that if there is a "third time," it must be sought in the present putting-into-discourse of our spatial-temporal configurations; they are based on the work of the individual and collective memory, along with the processes of archiving and preparing documents in order to produce a historio-poetic memory. Even more, it means that we must add to this Copernican revolution brought about by a view of the past centered on the *hic et nunc* of its production yet another reversal, in reaction to the aporia of a phenomenology of time, far too marked by Heideggerian metaphysics: and thus a reversal between this invented time and space which make up the spatio-temporality of the lived, and the physical space-time of the world; quite apart from any transcendence (even phenomenological), it is in this spatial-temporal frame that the present moment and the present place belong, in the perception we have of them, in the experience we make of them, in the ways we have of configuring them and of inserting them in a memory of the past they come from.

And so the space-time of the physicists replaces the atemporal eternity and the ubiquity of the Greek gods; space-time with its curvature which includes us is subject to this "unpredictable determinacy" which in turn substitutes for the immortal will of Zeus to bring to its conclusion the *moîra*; this is the inevitable destiny which falls to the lot of every mortal man, realized in all its vicissitudes and in an ephemeral time. As Chesneaux himself recognizes, the present cannot be assimilated to a simple fixed point. Not only does the present illuminate the past by reflection, then to be subjected in turn to the past's reflection; not only can this optic metaphor be extended forward, since this movement of "reflexion" continues toward the future. But in the Copernican revolution in history proposed by Benjamin, the fixed point into which the present seems to be transformed proves to be a mobile point.[8] The present, our individual and collective present, is inevitably both situated in and drawn along by what the layman might understand as the arrow of physical and cosmic space-time. Seemingly subject to the second law of thermodynamics which states the irreversible degradation of energy through entropy, space-time encompasses and integrates these cyclical manifestations within its curve.[9] Within the tiny room for maneuver left to him in an unpredictable causal determinism, there remains to man the possibility of imprinting on a largely unpredictable future some slight reorientations in light of the past; a past undoubtedly based on lived and individual memory, but maintained and configured by the work in an efficient and shared of those historians most engaged in a present which is fundamentally unpredictable and elusive; and that in spite of the predominant power exercised by the agents of neo-imperialist economic development, naturalized as determinism of the market.

In this spatial-temporal system as clarified by physicists, man occupies an ambiguous position, that of a being who is within the system and who perceives it. Carried along as it is by inevitable movement, human perception of the world changes as it tries to grasp the world and to act within it, just as the world on which we act also changes concomitantly. An incomplete animal in his very makeup, man thus tries in a constantly moving *hic et nunc* to make up for the situation of *aporia* in which he is plunged by a determinism without predictability, inherent in his organic and physical spatial-temporal framework. These attempts (which generally take the symbolic form of cultural manifestations) are among the community practices by which men try, in a constant process of collective "anthropopoiesis," to compensate for a basic incompleteness. In the context of the human being's crafting and symbolic construction of himself and his transformation into civilized man, spatial-temporal configurations which are the result of work by historians on individual and collective memory can take on a purpose of both practical regulation and active reflection.[10] In a constantly moving present, they may help to establish a few relationships of reflexive continuity between a fading past and a future subject to the hazards of a space-time which dominates us.

---

[8] Chesneaux 1996:141–142.

[9] See Paty 1993:172–186.

[10] The innumerable processes through which man makes himself in a constant effort to compensate for his innate incompleteness have been the object of research conducted collectively by Affergan, Borutti, Calame, Fabietti, Kilani, and Remotti 2003; see also Remotti 1999:20–30.

The human sciences, of which the methods of history are but one part, are themselves subject to the same movements of temporal development and spatial diffusion,[11] due to the historicity and spatiality of "anthropopoietic" practices; history and geography place them within logics of spatial-temporality and thus within regimes of truth subject to constant change. And to the extent that these configurations of time and space constructed by historians have recourse to verbal language and are thus dependent on the different modes of putting-into-discourse, they create a regime of spatial-temporality which, while distinct, is not autonomous, since that would deprive it of reference; the enunciative aspect of any discursive work must reckon with this regime, verbally and discursively constructed in relationship to the spatial-temporal parameters of the *hic et nunc* of *la mise en discours* itself; it also depends on the different situations when historiographic and historiopoietic creation is received.

What we have tried to illustrate here is precisely that inevitable intermingling, within the flux of both the world's spatial-temporality and of university teaching, between the spatial-temporal logics of several "anthropopoietic" processes of ancient Greece and the hermeneutic paradigms dependent on regimes of truth which are themselves subject to fluctuating (academic) historicity and geography. The spatial-temporal impact of Hesiod's didactic poetry which substitutes for the word of Zeus in reestablishing justice to recover a civic time rooted in the golden age permitted us to test the structural paradigm of academic France in the 1970s. In the sexual and poetic ambiguities of a national hero, the protagonist of an episode intended through religious celebration of Apollo to justify the present and the immediate future of a policy of territorial and economic expansion, it was the perspective of sex relationships widely adopted by the American academic world in the 1980s which was illustrated. In the founding act of a colony established by the will of Apollo and his Delphic oracle, the practical spatial-temporal regime offered by a decree of colonial citizenship appeared as a political and religious act of civic memory which escapes the philosophical and idealistic concepts of cyclical time which European scholars throughout the twentieth century attempted to attribute to the Greeks. Finally, the gold funerary lamellae, in their pragmatic function as passport, proposing a spatial-temporal itinerary with initiatory meaning and permitting the deceased to pass from the ephemeral and unstable regime

---

[11] Recently Revel 2001:59–64, reminded us of the consequences of the double historicity of the situation of knowledge which is that of the social sciences generally: historicity of the object and historicity of the observer.

of temporality of the mortal's life to a form of immortality near that of the gods, allowed us to confront the mysticizing hermeneutics which for the past half century has marked the history of Greek religion throughout its expansion in the west.

Together with the four comparative approaches proposed here, this confrontation should lead us to attempt to establish in the human sciences generally a position of relativist modesty; such an attitude finally takes into account our own insertions and spatial-temporal orientations, as producers of new configurations which model time and space, intended to integrate and to clarify actively the "anthropopoietic" actions of men.

It is not far from New York and the Island of Manhattan, in nearby New Jersey, a city on the banks of the Passaic River, crossed on one of those extraordinary railroad lift bridges which only North American industrialists could have imagined. New Work/Newark, which carries within its name the mark of its recent creation, offers a strange map to the visitor who is not afraid of being directly confronted with the social problems brought about by the democracy of economic liberalism. Leaving Penn Station, the visitor feels a difficulty in orienting himself which is not normal in American cities. This is because in Newark the usual orthogonal plan of the colonial city is combined with a diagonal orientation: Central Street does not intersect Broad Street at a right angle, and Broad Street itself, like Broadway in New York, runs obliquely from a "green" which is triangular rather than rectangular. References in archives show that the usual paradigm of European and colonial urbanism in Newark was influenced by the Indian trail which led from Hackensack, the site of the Lenni Lenape Indians, to the little port on the Passaic.[12]

History is inscribed in space, in the very country of presentism, within an organic spatial-temporal configuration which puts greatest emphasis on the most soaring and transparent contemporary architecture. At the intersection of Broad Street and Washington Street is a modest obelisk which commemorates the construction of the first bridge over the Passaic. Leaning against it on one side is an Indian, wearing a loincloth, his long hair held back by a headband, and on the other side a Puritan, wearing long straight trousers, lavallière, and high hat. Their gazes are high, and both are looking along the axis of the street, but their backs are to one another: one looking toward the past

---

[12] Here I follow a study completed several years ago (1988) by the architectural historian of architecture Jacques Gubler, a sensitive critic of American city planning.

and the other toward the future? Even in the simplification of sculpture, the process of configuring an anthropopoietic history can only be symbolic, and holds multiple meanings.

In no way does this prevent that symbolic process from becoming a way to appropriate human time and space in order to try to orient them both from a practical and an experiential standpoint.

ἀλλ᾽ ἐκδιδάσκει πάνθ᾽ ὁ γηράσκων χρόνος

But, aging, time teaches everything.[13]

---

[13] Aeschylus *Prometheus* 981, in a statement addressed by the hero Prometheus to Hermes. See on this topic the semantic study proposed by Fränkel 1960:9–22, who concludes: "Von der 'Zeit' wird immer nur im Sinne der Zukunft gesprochen, oder der sich weiter vorwärts erstreckenden Dauer, oder der späteren Zeit—also der relativen Zukunft." (10–11)

BIBLIOGRAPHY

Adam, J.-M. 1991. *Le récit.* 3rd ed. Paris.

Adam, J. -M., and Heidmann, U., eds. 2005. *Sciences du texte et analyse de discours: Enjeux d'une interdisciplinerité.* Geneva.

Adam, J.-M., Lugrin, G., and Revaz, F. 1998. "Pour en finir avec le couple récit/ discours." *Pratiques* 100:81–97.

Aellen, Ch. 1994. *A la recherche de l'ordre cosmique: Forme et fonction des personnifications dans la céramique italiote.* Zurich.

Affergan, F. 1987. *Exotisme et altérité: Essai sur les fondements d'une critique de l'anthropologie.* Paris.

Affergan, F., Borutti, S., Calame, C., Fabietti, U., Kilani, M., and Remotti, F. 2003. *Figures de l'humain: Les représentations de l'anthropologie.* Paris.

Aristophane, les femmes et la cité. 1979. Cahiers de Fontenay 17. Paris.

Assmann, J. 1992. *Das kulturelle Gedächtnis: Schrift, Erinnerung und politische Identität in frühen Hochkulturen.* Munich.

Atlan, H. 1999. "Possibilités biologiques, impossibilités sociales." In Atlan et al. 1999, 17–41.

Atlan, H., et al., eds. 1999. *Le clonage humain.* Paris.

Auger, D. 1979. "Le théâtre d'Aristophane: Le mythe, l'utopie et les femmes." In *Aristophane, les femmes et la cité,* 71–101.

Azara, P., Mar, R., and Subías, E., eds. 2001. *Mites de fundació de ciutats al món antic: Mesopotàmis, Grècia i Roma; Actes del col·loqui.* Barcelona.

Bagordo, A., and Zimmermann, B., eds. 2000. *Bakchylides: 100 Jahre nach seiner Wiederentdeckung.* Munich.

Bakker, E. J. 2002. "The Making of History: Herodotus' *Histories Apodexis.*" In Bakker, de Jong, and van Wees 2002, 3–32.

Bakker, E. J., de Jong, I. J. F., van Wees, H. eds. 2002. *Brill's Companion to Herodotus.* Leiden.

Ballabriga, A. 1998. "L'invention du mythe des races en Grèce archaïque." *Revue de l'histoire des religions* 215:307–339.

Baumgarten, R. 1998. *Heiliges Wort und heilige Schrift bei de Griechen: Hieroi Logoi und verwandte Erscheinunges.* Tübingen.

Benjamin, W. 1989. *Paris: Capitale du XIXe siècle; Le Livre des Passages*. Trans. J. Lacoste. Paris. Orig. pub. as of *Das Passagen-Werk* (Frankfurt am Main, 1982 [texts from 1927 to 1940]).

Benveniste, E. 1974. *Problèmes de linguistique générale*. Vol. 2. Paris.

Bernabé, A. 1991. "El poema órfico de Hiponion." In López Férez 1991, 219–235.

———. 1999. "La laminetta orfica di Entella." *Annali della Scuola Normale Superiore di Pisa* IV.1:54–63.

———. 2002. "La toile de Pénélope: A-t-il existé un mythe orphique sur Dionysos et les Titans?" *Revue de l'histoire des religions* 219:401–433.

Bernabé A., and Jiménez San Cristóbal, A. I. 2001. *Instrucciones para el más allá*. Madrid.

Bernal, M. 1996. *Black Athena: Les racines afro-asiatiques de la civilisation classique*. Vol. 1: *L'invention de la Grèce antique: 1785-1985*. Paris. Orig. pub. as *Black Athena: The Afroasiatic Roots of Classical Civilization*. Vol 1: *The Fabrication of Ancient Greece 1785-1985* (New Brunswick, NJ, 1987).

Berthelot, J.-M., ed. 2001. *Épistémologie des sciences sociales*. Paris.

Bettini, M. 1992. *Il ritratto dell'amante*. Turin.

Betz, H. D. 1998. "'Der Erde Kind bin ich und des gestirnten Himmels.' Zur Lehre vom Menschen in den orphischen Goldblättchen." In Graf 1998, 399–419.

Bichler, R., and Rollinger, R. 2000. *Herodot*. Hildesheim, Zurich, and New York.

Blaise, F., Judet de La Combe, P., and Rousseau, Ph., eds. 1996. *Le métier du mythe: Lectures d'Hésiode*. Lille.

Bloch, M. 1964. *Apologie pour l'histoire ou Métier d'historien*. Paris.

Bonnechere, P. 1998. "La scène d'initiation des *Nuées* d'Aristophane et Trophonios: Nouvelles lumières sur le culte lébadéen." *Revue des Études Grecques* 111:436–480.

Borgeaud, Ph., ed. 1991. *Orphisme et Orphée: En l'honneur de Jean Rudhardt*. Geneva.

Borutti, S. 1996. "Verità dell'evento e ruolo del soggetto nella coscienza storica." In Fagiuoli and Fortunato 1996, 235–256.

———. 1999. *Filosofia delle scienze umane: Le categorie dell'Antropologia e della Sociologia*. Milan.

———. 2003. "Fiction et construction du l'objet en anthropologie." In Affergan et al. 2003, 75–99.

Borutti, S., and Fabietti, U., eds. 1999. *Fra antropologia e storia*. Milan.

Boschetti, P. 2004. *Les Suisses et les nazis: Le rapport Bergier pour tous*. Geneva.

Bourdieu, P. 1982. *Ce que parler veut dire: L'économie de l'échange linguistique*. Paris.

Bouvier, D. 1993. "'Mneme': Le peripezie della memoria greca." In Settis 1993, 1131–1146.

———. 2000. "Temps chronique et temps météorologique chez les premiers historiens grecs." In Darbo-Peschanski 2000, 115–141.

Bremmer, J., ed. 1987. *Interpretations of Greek Mythology*. London and Sydney.

———. 2001. "Myth and History in the Foundation of Cyrene." In Azara, Mar, and Subías 2001, 155–163.

Brown, A. S. 1998. "From the Golden Age to the Isles of the Blessed." *Mnemosyne* IV.51:385–410.

Bühler, K. 1934. *Sprachtheorie: Die Darstellungsfunktion der Sprache*. Jena.

Burkert, W. 1987. *Ancient Mystery Cults*. Cambridge, MA and London.

———. 1999. *Da Omero ai Magi: La tradizione orientale nella cultura greca*. Venice.

Burnett, A. P. 1985. *The Art of Bacchylides*. Cambridge, MA and London.

Calame, C. 1996a. *Mythe et histoire dans l'Antiquité grecque: La création symbolique d'une colonie*. Lausanne. Trans. by D. W. Berman as *Myth and History in Ancient Greece: The Symbolic Creation of a Colony* (Princeton and Oxford, 2003).

———. 1996b. *Thésée et l'imaginaire athénien: Légende et culte en Grèce antique*. 2nd ed. Lausanne.

———. 1996c. "Le proème des *Travaux* d'Hésiode, prélude à une poésie d'action." In Blaise, Judet de La Combe, and Rousseau 1996, 169–189.

———. 1996d. "Invocations et commentaires 'orphiques': Transpositions funéraires de discours religieux." In Mactoux and Geny 1996, 11–30.

———. 1998a. "Éros revisité: La subjectivité discursive dans quelques poèmes grecs." *Uranie* 8:95–107.

———. 1998b. "Mémoire collective et temporalités en contact: Somare et Hérodote." *Revue de l'histoire des religions* 215:341–367.

———. 1998c. "Mort héroïque et culte à mystère dans *l'Œdipe à Colone* de Sophocle." In Graf 1998, 326–356.

———. 1999. "Indigenous and Modern Perspectives on Tribal Initiation Rites: Education according to Plato." In Padilla 1999, 278–312.

———. 2000a. *Le Récit en Grèce ancienne: Énonciations et représentations de poètes*. 2nd ed. Paris. Trans. by J. Orion as *The Craft of Poetic Speech in Ancient Greece* (Ithaca, NY and London, 1995).

———. 2000b. *Poétique des mythes dans la Grèce antique*. Paris. Trans. by J. Lloyd as *Greek Mythology: Poetics, Pragmatics, and Fiction* (Cambridge, 2009).

———. 2000c. "Temps du récit et temps du rituel dans la poétique grecque: Bacchylide entre mythe, histoire et culte." In Darbo-Peschanski 2000, 395–412.

———. 2002a. *L'Éros dans la Grèce antique*. 2nd ed. Paris. Trans. by J. Lloyd as *The Poetics of Eros in Ancient Greece* (Princeton, 1999).

———. 2002b. "Interprétation et traduction des cultures: Les catégories de la pensée et du discours anthropologiques." *L'Homme* 163:51–78.

———. 2002c. "La poésie attribuée à Orphée: Qu'est-ce qui est orphique dans les *Orphica?*" *Revue de l'histoire des religions* 219:385–400.

———. 2005a. *Marques d'autorité: Fiction et pragmatique dans la poétique grecque antique*. Paris. Trans. by P. Burk as *Masks of Authority: Fiction and Pragmatics in Ancient Greek Poetics* (Ithaca, NY and London, 2005).

———. 2005b. "Pragmatique de la fiction: Quelques procédures de deixis narrative et énonciative en comparaison (poétique grecque)." In Adam and Heidmann 2005, 119–143.

Calame, C., and Kilani, M., eds. 1999. *La fabrication de l'humain dans le cultures et en anthropologie*. Lausanne.

Camassa, G. 1994. "Passione e rigenerazione: Dioniso e Persefone nelle lamine 'orfiche.'" In Cassio and Poccetti 1994, 71–182.

Carlier, P. 2003. "Regalità omeriche e regalità greche dell'alto arcaismo." In Luppino Manes 2003, 13–29.

Carrard, Ph. 1998. *Poétique de la Nouvelle Histoire: Le discours historique en France de Braudel à Chartier*. Lausanne.

Carpenter, Th. H., and Faraone, Ch. A., eds. 1993. *Masks of Dionysus*. Ithaca, NY and London.

Carrière, J.-C. 1986. "Les démons, les héros et les rois dans la cité de fer: Les ambiguïtés de la justice dans le mythe hésiodique des races et la naissance de la cité." In *Lire les polythéïsmes I: Les grands figures religieuses*, 193–261. Besançon and Paris.

———. 1991. "Mystique et politique dans *Les Travaux et les Jours* d'Hésiode: L'authenticité et les enjeux du vers 108." In *Mélanges Etienne Bernand*, 61–119. Besançon and Paris.

———. 1996. "Le mythe prométhéen, le mythe des races et l'émergence de la Cité-État." In Blaise, Judet de La Combe, and Rousseau 1996, 431–463.

Casadio, G. 1991. "La metempsicosi tra Orfeo e Pitagora." In Borgeaud 1991, 119–155.

———. 1994. "Dioniso Italiota. Un dio greco in Italia meridionale." In Cassio and Poccetti 1994, 79–107.

———. 1999. *Il vino dell'anima: Storia del culto di Dioniso a Corinto, Sicione, Trezene*. Rome.

Casevitz, M. 1985. *Le vocabulaire de la colonisation en grec ancien: Etude lexicographique des familles de ktizo et de oikeo-oikizo*. Paris.

Cassio, A. C. 1994. "*Pienai* e il modello ionico della laminetta di Hipponion." In Cassio and Poccetti 1994, 183–205.

Cassio, A. C., and Poccetti, P., eds. 1994. *Forme di religiosità e tradizioni sapienzali in Magna Grecia*. Pisa and Rome.

Célis, R., and Sierro, M., eds. 1996. *Autour de la poétique de Paul Ricœur*. Lausanne.

Cerri, G. 1998. "L'ideologia dei quattro elementi da Omero ai Presocratici." *Annali dell'Istituto Universitario Orientale di Napoli* 20:5–58.

Certeau, M. de. 1975. *L'écriture de l'histoire*. Paris.

Chamoux, F. 1952. *Cyrène sous la monarchie des Battiades*. Paris.

Chaniotis, A. 2000. "Das Jenseits: Eine Gegenwelt." In Hölscher 2000, 159–181.

Chantraine, P. 1968. *Dictionnaire étymologique de la langue grecque: Histoire des mots*. Paris.

Chartier, R. 1998. *Au bord de la falaise: L'histoire entre certitudes et inquiétude*. Paris.

Chesneaux, J. 1996. *Habiter le temps: Passé, présent, futur: esquisse d'un dialogue politique*. Paris.

Clarke, M. 1999. *Flesh and Spirit in the Songs of Homer: A Study of Words and Myths*. Oxford.

Clay, J. S. 2003. *Hesiod's Cosmos*. Cambridge.

Cole, S. G. 1993. "Voices from beyond the Grave: Dionysus and the Dead." In Carpenter and Faraone 1993, 276–295.

Comparetti, D. 1882. "The Petelia Gold Tablet." *Journal of Hellenic Studies* 3:111–118.

Constant, B. 1824–1831. *De la religion considérée dans ses formes et ses développements*. Repr., Arles, 1999.

Couloubaritsis, L. 1996. "Genèse et structure dans le mythe hésiodique des races." In Blaise, Judet de La Combe, and Rousseau 1996, 497–518.

Crosby, A. W. 1997. *The Measure of Reality: Quantification and Western Society, 1250–1600*. Cambridge.

Crubellier, M. 1996. "Le mythe comme discours. Le récit des cinq races humaines dans *Les Travaux et les Jours*." In Blaise, Judet de La Combe, and Rousseau 1996, 431–463.

Culioli, A. 1999. *Pour une linguistique de l'énonciation*. Vol. 2: *Formalisation et opérations de repérage*. Paris.

Darbo-Peschanski, C. 1995. "Fabriquer du continu. L'historiographie grecque face au temps." *Storia della storiografia* 28:17–34.

———. 1998. "L'historien grec ou le passé jugé." In Loraux and Miralles 1998, 143–189.

———, ed. 2000. *Constructions du temps dans le monde grec ancien*. Paris.

Depew, M. 1997. "Reading Greek Prayers." *Classical Antiquity* 16:229–258.

Detienne, M. 1988. "L'espace de la publicité: Ses opérateurs intellectuels dans la cité." In Detienne 1988, 29–81.

———. ed. 1988. *Les savoirs de l'écriture: En Grèce ancienne*. Lille.

———. ed. 1994. *Transcrire les mythologies: Tradition, écriture, historicité*. Paris.

———. 1998. *Apollon le couteau à la main: Une approche expérimentale du polythéisme grec*. Paris.

———. 2000. *Comparer l'incomparable*. Paris.

Dickie, M. W. 1995. "The Dionysiac Mysteries in Pella." *Zeitschrift für Papyrologie und Epigraphik* 109:81–86.

Dobias-Lalou, C. 1994. "*SEG* IX, 3: Un document composite ou inclassable?" *Verbum* 3/4:243–56.

Duku, A., and Dodille, N., eds. 1993. *L'Etat des lieux en sciences sociales*. Paris.

Dumézil, G. 1968. *Mythe et Épopée*. Vol. 1: *L'idéologie des trois fonctions dans les épopées des peuples indo-européens*. Paris.

Dušanić, S. 1978. "The ὅρκιον τῶν οἰκιστήρων and Fourth-Century Cyrene." *Chiron* 8:55–76.

Edmonds, R. G. III. 1999. "Tearing Apart the Zagreus Myth: A Few Disparaging Remarks on Orphism and Original Sin." *Classical Antiquity* 18:35–73.

———. 2004. *Myths of the Underworld Journey: Plato, Aristophanes, and the "Orphic" Gold Tablets*. Cambridge.

Edmunds, L., ed. 1990. *Approaches to Greek Myth*. Baltimore and London.

———. 2001. *Intertextuality and the Reading of Roman Poetry*. Baltimore and London.

Else, G. 1967. *Aristotle's Poetics: The Argument*. Cambridge, MA.

Engelhardt, U., Sellin, V., and Stuke, H., eds. 1976. *Soziale Bewegung und politische Verfassung: Beiträge zur Geschichte der modernen Welt*. Stuttgart.

Fabian, J. 1983. *Time and the Other: How Anthropology Makes its Object*. New York.

Fabietti, U., ed. 1998. *Etnografia e culture: Antropologi, informatori e politiche dell'identità*. Rome.

———. 1998. *L'identità etnica*. 2nd ed. Rome.

———. 1999. *Antropologia culturale: L'esperienza e l'interpretazione*. Rome and Bari.

Fagiuoli, E., and Fortunato, M., eds. 1996. *Soggetto e verità: La questione dell'uomo nella filosofia contemporanea*. Milan.

Fearn, D. 2007. *Bacchylides: Politics, Performance, Poetic Tradition*. Oxford.

Felson, N. 1999. "Vicarious Transport: Fictive Deixis in Pindar's *Pythian* Four." *Harvard Studies in Classical Philology* 99:1–31.

Feyerabend, B. 1984. "Zur Wegmetaphorik beim Goldblättchen aus Hipponion und dem Proömium des Parmenides." *Rheinisches Museum* 127:1–22.

Ferri, S. 1925. "Alcune iscrizioni di Cirene." *Abhandlungen der Preussischen Akademie der Wissenschaften. Philologisch-historische Klasse* 5:1–40.

Fornara, C. W. 1977. *Translated Documents of Greece and Rome.* Vol. 1: *Archaic Times to the end of the Peloponnesian War.* Baltimore and London.

Foti, G. 1974. "Il sepolcro di Hipponion e un nuovo testo orfico." *La Parola del Passato* 29:91–107.

Foucault, M. 1969. *L'archéologie du savoir.* Paris.

Fränkel, H. 1960. *Wege und Formen des frühgriechischen Denkens: Literarische und philosophiegeschichtliche Studien.* 2nd ed. Munich.

Gawantka, W. 1975. *Isopolitie: Ein Beitrag zur Geschichte der zwischenstaatlichen Beziehungen in der griechischen Antike.* Munich.

Gallavotti, C. 1975. *Empedocle: Poema fisico e lustrale.* Milan.

Genette, G. 1973. *Figures.* Vol. 3. Paris.

Gentili, B. 1954. "Il ditirambo XVII Sn. di Bacchilide e il cratere Tricase da Ruvo (*CVA*, Robinson II, tav. 31–2)." *Archeologia Classica* 6:121–125.

———. 1995. *Poesia e pubblico nella Grecia antica: Da Omero al V secolo.* 3rd ed. Rome and Bari.

Gentili, B., et al. 1995. *Pindaro: Le Pitiche.* Milan.

Gilbert, M. 1996. "Pour une contribution narrative à la problématique du temps." In Célis and Sierro 1996, 37–54.

Ginzburg, C. 1989. *Mythes, emblèmes, traces: Morphologie et histoire.* Trans. M. Aymard. Paris. Orig. pub. as *Miti, Emblemi, Spie* (Turin, 1986).

Goldschmidt, V. 1950. "Theologia." *Revue des Études Grecques* 63:20–42. Repr. in Goldschmidt 1970, 141–159, with an Addendum (159–172).

———. 1970. *Questions platoniciennes.* Paris.

Graf, F. 1985. *Nordionische Kulte: Religionsgeschichtliche und epigraphische Untersuchungen zu den Kulten von Chios, Erythrai, Klazomenai und Phokaia.* Rome.

———. 1991. "Textes orphiques et rituel bachique: A propos des lamelles de Pelinna." In Borgeaud 1991, 87–102.

———. 1993. "Dionysian and Orphic Eschatology: New Texts and Old Questions." In Carpenter and Faraone 1993, 239–258.

———, ed. 1998. *Ansichten griechischer Rituale: Geburtstags-Symposium für Walter Burkert.* Leipzig and Stuttgart.

Graf, F., and Johnson, S. I. 2007. *Ritual Texts for the Afterlife: Orpheus and Bacchic Gold Tablets.* London and New York.

Graham, A. J. 1960. "The Authenticity of the *horkion tôn oikisterôn* of Cyrene." *Journal of Hellenic Studies* 80:94–111. Repr. in Graham 2001, 83–112.

———. 2001. *Collected Papers on Greek Colonization.* Mnemosyne Supplement 214. Leiden, Boston, and Cologne.

Griffith, R. D. 1993. "In the Dark Backward: Time in Pindaric Narrative." *Poetics Today* 14:607–623.

———. 1997. "The Voice of the Dead in Homer's *Odyssey* and Egyptian Funerary Texts." *Studi Micenei ed Egeo-Anatolici* 39:219–240.

Grossberg, L., Nelson, C., and Treichler, P. A., eds. 1992. *Cultural Studies.* New York and London.

Guarducci, M. 1974. "Laminette auree orfiche: Alcuni problemi." *Epigraphica* 36:7–32.

———. 1985. "Nuove riflessioni sulla laminetta 'orfica' di Hipponion." *Rivista di Filologia e di Istruzione Classica* 113:385–397.

Gubler, J. 1988. "Notes on Newark's Urban History." *Architecture et comportement* 4:157–174.

Halbwachs, M. 1925. *Les cadres sociaux de la mémoire.* Paris.

Hamilton, R. 1989. *The Architecture of Hesiodic Poetry.* Baltimore and London.

Hartog, F. 2000. "Le témoin et l'historien." *Gradhiva* 27:1–14. Repr. in Hartog 2005, 191–214.

———. 2001. *Le miroir d'Hérodote: Essai sur la représentation de l'autre.* 3rd ed. Paris.

———. 2003. *Régimes d'historicité: Présentisme et expériences du temps.* Paris.

———. 2005. *Évidence de l'histoire: Ce que voient les historiens.* Paris.

Hartog, F., and Lenclud, G. 1993. "Régimes d'historicité." In Duku and Dodille 1993, 18–38.

Hauser-Schäublin, B. 1995. "Puberty Rites, Women's Naven, and Initiation: Women's Rituals of Transition in Abelam and Iatmul Culture." In Lutkehaus and Roscoe 1995, 33–53.

Heidegger, M. 1996. *Being and Time: A Translation of* Sein und Zeit. Trans. J. Stambaugh. Albany, NY. Orig. pub. as *Sein und Zeit* (Tübingen, 1927).

Heidmann, U., ed. 2003. *Pratiques comparées des mythes.* Lausanne.

Heitsch, E., ed. 1966. *Hesiod.* Darmstadt.

Henry, H. S. 1977. *The Prescripts of Athenian Decrees.* Mnemosyne Supplement 49. Leiden.

Herdt, G. 1994. *Guardians of the Flutes.* Vol 1: *Idioms of Maculinity.* 2nd ed. Chicago and London.

Hölscher, T., ed. 2000. *Gegenwelten zu den Kulturen Griechenlands und Roms in der Antike.* Munich and Leipzig.

Hoff, R. von den, and Schmidt, S. eds. 2001. *Konstruktionen von Wirklichkeit: Bilder im Griechenland des 5. und 4. Jahrhunderts v. Chr.* Stuttgart.

Hordern, J. 2000. "Notes on the Orphic Papyrus from Gurôb (P. Gurob 1: Pack² 2464)." *Zeitschrift für Papyrologie und Epigraphik* 129:131–140.

Hornblower, S. 1991. *A Commentary on Thucydides.* Vol. 1: *Books I–III.* Oxford.

Hose, M. 1995. "Bakchylides, *Carmen* 17: Dithyrambos oder Paian?" *Rheinisches Museum* 138:299–312.

Humbert, J. 1960. *Syntaxe grecque.* 3rd ed. Paris.

Hurst, A., ed. 1985. *Pindare.* Entretiens sur l'Antiquité classique XXXII. Vandœuvres and Geneva.

Ieranò, G. 1989. "Il ditirambo XVII di Bacchilide e le feste apollinee di Delo." *Quaderni di Storia* 30:157–183.

Izard, M., and Smith, P., eds. 1979. *La fonction symbolique: Essais d'anthropologie.* Paris.

Jaccottet, A.-F. 2003. *Choisir Dionysos: Les associations dionysiaques ou la face cachée du dionysisme.* Zurich.

Janko, R. 1984. "Forgetfulness in the Golden Tablets of Memory." *Classical Quarterly* 34:89–100.

Jeffery, L. H. 1961. "The Pact of the First Settlers at Cyrene." *Historia* 10:139–147.

Johnston, S. I. 1999. *Restless Dead: Encounters Between the Living and the Dead in Ancient Greece.* Berkeley and Los Angeles.

Johnston, S. I., and McNiven, T. J. 1996. "Dionysos and the Underworld in Toledo." *Museum Helveticum* 53:25–36.

Jones, N. F. 1999. *The Associations of Classical Athens.* New York and Oxford.

Jouanna, J. 1987. "Le souffle, la vie et le froid: Remarques sur la famille de *psúkhō* d'Homère à Hippocrate." *Revue des Études Grecques* 100:203–224.

Käppel, L. 1992. *Paian: Studien zur Geschichte einer Gattung.* Berlin and New York.

Kassel, R., and Austin, C., eds. 1983. *Poetae Comici Graeci.* Berlin and New York.

Kilani, M. 1992. *La construction de la mémoire: Le lignage et la sainteté dans l'oasis d'El Ksar.* Geneva.

———. 1994. *L'invention de l'autre: Essais sur le discours anthropologique.* Lausanne.

———. 1999. "L'archivio, il documento, la traccia: Antropologia e storia." In Borutti and Fabietti 1999, 24–39.

———. 2003. "L'art de l'oubli: Construction de la mémoire et narration historique." In Heidmann 2003, 213–242.

Kneppe, A., and Metzler, D., eds. 2003. *Die emotionale Dimension antiker Religiosität.* Munster.

Koselleck, R. 1976. "*Erfahrungsraum* und *Erwartungshorizont*—zwei historische Kategorien." In Engelhardt, Sellin, and Stuke 1976, 13–33.

———. 1990. *Le futur passé: Contribution à la sémantique des temps historiques.* Trans. J. Hoock and M.-C. Hoock. Paris. Orig. pub. as *Vergangene Zukunft: Zur Semantik geschichtlicher Zeiten* (Frankfurt, 1979).

———. 2002. *The Practice of Conceptual History: Timing History, Spacing Concepts.* Trans. T. S. Presner et al. Stanford.

Koselleck, R., and Stempel, W. D., eds. 1973. *Geschichte: Ereignis und Erzählung.* Munich.

Kowalzig, B. 2007. *Singing for the Gods: Performance of Myth and Ritual in Archaic and Classical Greece.* Oxford.

Kugel, J. L., ed. 1989. *Poetry and Prophecy: The Beginnings of a Literary Tradition.* Ithaca, NY and London.

Lacocque, A. 1983. *Daniel et son temps: Recherches sur le mouvement apocalyptique juif au IIe siècle avant Jésus-Christ.* Geneva.

Lanza, D. 2004. "Nés de la même mère? Quelques observations en marge d'une anthropogonie grecque." *Mythe et mythologie dans l'Antiquité gréco-romaine = Europe* 904/905:38–54.

Laks, A., and Most, G. W., eds. 1997. *Studies on the Derveni Papyrus.* Oxford.

Lavecchia, S. 2000. *Pindari dithyramborum fragmenta.* Rome and Pisa.

Lefkowitz, M. 1995. "The First Person in Pindar Reconsidered—Again." *Bulletin of the Institute of Classical Studies* 40:139–150.

Lenclud, G. 1994. "Qu'est-ce que la tradition?" In Detienne 1994, 24–44.

Létoublon, F. 1989. "Le Serment Fondateur." *Métis* 4:101–115.

Lincoln, B. 1991. *Death, War, and Sacrifice: Studies in Ideology and Practice.* Chicago.

———. 1997. "Competing Discourses: Rethinking the Prehistory of *Mythos* and *Logos*." *Arethusa* 30:341–367. Repr. in Lincoln 1999, 3–18.

———. 1999. *Theorizing Myth: Narrative, Ideology, and Scholarship.* Chicago and London.

Lire les polythéismes I: Les grandes figures religieuses. 1986. Besançon and Paris.

Livingstone, A. 1989. *Court Poetry and Literary Miscellanea.* Helsinki.

Lloyd, G. E. R. 1990. *Demystifying Mentalities.* Cambridge.

Lloyd-Jones, H. 1985. "Pindar and the After-Life." In Hurst 1985, 245–279. Repr. with an addendum in Lloyd-Jones 1990, 80–109.

———. 1990. *Greek Epic, Lyric, and Tragedy.* Oxford.

Long, A. A., ed. 1999. *The Cambridge Companion to Early Greek Philosophy.* Cambridge.

Lonis, R. 1980. "La valeur du serment dans les accords internationaux en Grèce classique." *Dialogues d'histoire ancienne* 6:267–286.

López Férez, J. A., ed. 1991. *Estudios actuales sobra textos griegos.* Madrid.

Loraux, N. 1980. "Thucydide n'est pas un collègue." *Quaderni di storia* 12:55–81.

———1996. *"Back to the Greeks?* Chronique d'une expédition lointaine en terre connue." In Revel and Wachtel 1996, 275–297.

Loraux, N., and Miralles, C., eds. 1998. *Figures de l'intellectuel en Grèce ancienne.* Paris.

Luppino Manes, E., ed. 2003. *Storiografia e regalità nel mondo greco.* Alessandria.

Luraghi, N. ed. 2001. *The Historian's Craft in the Age of Herodotus.* Oxford.

Lutkehaus, N., ed. 1990. *Sepik Heritage: Tradition and Change in Papua New Guinea.* Durham, NC.

Lutkehaus, N. C., and Roscoe, P. B., eds. 1995. *Gender Rituals: Female Initiation in Melanesia.* New York and London.

Mactoux, M. M., and Geny, E., eds. 1996. *Discours religieux dans l'Antiquité.* Besançon and Paris.

Maehler, H. 1997. *Die Lieder des Bakchylides* II: *Die Dithyramben und Fragmente.* Leiden, New York, and Cologne.

Maffi, I. 2004. *Pratiques du patrimoine et politiques de la mémoire en Jordanie: Entre histoire dynastique et récits communantaire.* Lausanne.

Malighetti, R. 1998. "Dal punto di vista dell'antropologo: L'etnografia del lavoro antropologico." In Fabietti 1998, 201–215.

Malkin, I. 1987. *Religion and Colonization in Ancient Greece.* Leiden and New York.

———. 1994. *Myth and Territory in the Spartan Mediterranean.* Cambridge.

Marchegay, S., Le Dinahet, M.-Th., and Salles, J.-F., eds. 1998. *Nécropoles et pouvoirs: Idéologies, pratiques et interprétations.* Paris.

Marcus, G. E., and Fischer, M. M. J. 1986. *Anthropology as Cultural Critique: An Experimental Moment in the Human Sciences.* Chicago and London.

Marincola, J. 1997. *Authority and Tradition in Ancient Historiography.* Cambridge.

Meiggs, R., and Lewis, D. 1969. *A Selection of Greek Historical Inscriptions.* Oxford.

Mélanges Etienne Bernand. 1991. Besançon and Paris.

Merkelbach, R. 1999. "Die goldenen Totenpässe: Ägyptisch, orphisch, bakchisch." *Zeitschrift für Papyrologie und Epigraphik* 129:1–13.

Meschonnic, H. 1990. *Le langage Heidegger.* Paris.

Miller, R., and Miller, H. 1996. *Myst: The Surrealistic Adventure That Will Become Your World.* 2nd ed. Novato, CA.

Mills, S. 1997. *Theseus, Tragedy, and the Athenian Empire.* Oxford.

Morand, A.-F. 2001. *Etudes sur les* Hymnes orphiques. Leiden, Boston, and Cologne.

Molet, L. 1990. "Histoire du comput et de quelques calendriers." In Poirier 1990, 189–268.

Momigliano, A. 1966. "Time in Ancient Historiography." *History and Theory* 6:1–23. Repr. in Italian in Momigliano 1982, 63–94.

———. 1982. *La storiografia greca*. Turin.

Moreau, A., ed. 1992. *L'initiation*. 2 vols. Montpellier.

Moret, J.-M. 1982. "L''Apollinisation' de l'imagerie légendaire à Athènes dans la seconde moitié du Ve siècle." *Revue archéologique* 1:109–136.

———. 1993. "Les départs des enfers dans l'imagerie apulienne." *Revue archéologique* 2:293–351.

Most, G. W. 1997. "Hesiod's Myth of the Five (or Three or Four) Races." *Proceedings of the Cambridge Philological Association* 43:104–127.

Most, G. W., and Laks, A., eds. 1997. *Studies on the Derveni Papyrus*. Oxford and New York.

Müller, G. 1968. *Morphologische Poetik: Gesammelte Aufsätze*. Tübingen.

Murari Pires, F. 2003. "Prologue historiographique et proème épique: Les principes de la narration en Grèce ancienne." *Quaderni di Storia* 58:73–94.

Musti, D. 1984. "Le laminette orfiche e la religiosità d'area locrese." *Quaderni Urbinati di Cultura Classica* 45:61–83.

Nagy, G. 1979. *The Best of the Achaeans: Concepts of the Hero in Archaic Greek Poetry*. Baltimore and London.

———. 1989. "Ancient Greek Poetry, Prophecy, and Concepts of Theory." In Kugel 1989, 56–64.

———. 1990a. *Greek Mythology and Poetics*. Ithaca, NY and London.

———. 1990b. *Pindar's Homer: The Lyric Possession of an Epic Past*. Baltimore and London.

Neschke, A. 1996. "*Dikè*: la philosophie poétique du droit dans le 'mythe des races' d'Hésiode." In Blaise, Judet de La Combe, and Rousseau 1996, 465–478.

Nicolai, R. 2001. "Thucydides' Archaeology: Between Epic and Oral Tradition." In Luraghi 2001, 263–285.

Nora, P. 1984. "Entre Mémoire et Histoire. La problématique des lieux." In Nora 1984, xvii-xlii.

Nora, P., ed. 1984. *Les lieux de mémoire I: La République*. Paris.

Noussia, M. 2001. *Solone. Frammenti dell'opera poetica*. Milan.

Olender, M. 1989. *Les langues du paradis: Aryens et Sémites; un couple providentiel*. Paris.

Oliver, J. H. 1966. "Herodotus 4, 153 and *SEG* IX 3." *Greek, Roman, and Byzantine Studies* 7:25–29.

Oliviero, G. 1928. "Iscrizioni di Cirene 2: La stele dei Patti." *Rivista di Filologia e di Istruzione Classica* 56:222–232.

Onians, R. B. 1951. *The Origins of European Thought about the Body, the Mind, the Soul, the World, Time, and Fate.* Cambridge.

Osborne, R. 1996. *Greece in the Making: 1200–479 BC.* London and New York.

Padilla, M. W., ed. 1999. *Rites of Passage in Ancient Greece: Literature, Religion, Society.* Lewisburg, London, and Toronto.

Palagia, O., ed. 1997. *Greek Offerings: Essays on Greek Art in Honour of John Boardman.* Oxford Monographs 89. Oxford.

Parker, R. 1983. *Miasma: Pollution and Purification in Early Greek Religion.* Oxford.

———. 1987. "Myths of Early Athens." In Bremmer 1987, 187–214.

Parmelin, H., Guillot, M., et al. 1972. *Psychologie comparative et art: Hommage à I. Meyerson.* Paris.

Paty, M. 1993. *Einstein philosophe: La physique comme pratique philosophique.* Paris.

Payen, P. 1997. *Les îles nomades: Conquérir et résister dans l'Enquête d'Hérodote.* Paris.

Pensa, M. 1977. *Rappresentazioni dell'oltretomba nella ceramica apula.* Rome.

Poirier, J., ed. 1990. *Histoire des mœurs.* Vol. I.1: *Les coordonnées de l'homme et la culture matérielle.* Paris.

Prost, A. 1996. *Douze leçons sur l'histoire.* Paris.

Pucci, P. 1998. "The Proem of the *Odyssey.*" In Pucci 1998, 11–29.

———. 1998. *The Song of the Sirens: Essays on Homer.* Lanham, MD.

Pugliese Carratelli, G. 1974. "Testi e monumenti." *La Parola del Passato* 29:108–126.

———. 1975. "Sulla lamina orfica di Hipponion." *La Parola del Passato* 30:226–231.

———. 1976. "Ancora sulla lamina orfica di Hipponion." *La Parola del Passato* 31:458–466.

———. 2001. *Le lamine d'oro orfiche: Istruzioni per il viaggio oltremondo degli iniziati greci.* Milan

———. 2003. *Les lamelles d'or orphiques: Instructions pour le voyage d'outre-tombe des initiés grecs.* Trans. A.-Ph. Segonds and C. Luna. Paris.

Rancière, J. 1992. *Les noms de l'histoire: Essai de poétique du savoir.* Paris.

Reitzenstein, R. 1924/5. "Altgriechische Theologie und ihre Quellen." *Vorträge der Bibliothek Warburg* 4:1–19. Repr. in Heitsch 1966, 523–544.

Remotti, F. 1990. *Noi primitivi: Lo specchio dell'antropologia.* Turin.

———. 1999. "Thèses pour une perspective anthropopoiétique." In Calame and Kilani 1999, 15–31.

Revel, J., and Wachtel, N., eds. 1996. *Une école pour les sciences sociales.* Paris.

———. 2001. "Les sciences historiques." In Berthelot 2001, 21–76.

Richardson, N. J. 1974. *The Homeric Hymn to Demeter*. Oxford.

Ricœur, P. 1983. *Temps et récit*. Vol. 1: *L'intrigue et le récit historique*. Paris.

———. 1984. *Temps et récit*. Vol. 2: *La configuration dans le récit de fiction*. Paris.

———. 1985. *Temps et récit*. Vol. 3: *Le temps raconté*. Paris.

———. 1990. *Soi-même comme un autre*. Paris.

———. 1998. "La marque du passé." *Revue de Métaphysique et de Morale* 1:7–31.

———. 2000. *La mémoire, l'histoire, l'oubli*. Paris.

Riedweg, C. 1998. "Initiation—Tod—Unterwelt: Beobachtungen zur Kommunikationssituation und narrativen Technik der orphisch-bakchischen Goldblättchen." In Graf 1998, 359–398.

———. 2002. "Poésie orphique et rituel initiatique: Eléments d'un 'Discours sacré' dans les lamelles d'or." *Revue de l'histoire des religions* 219:459–481.

Roscoe, P., and Scaglion, R. 1990. "Male Initiation and European Intrusion in the Sepik: A Preliminary Analysis." In Lutkehaus 1990, 414–423.

Rose, V., ed. 1967. *Aristotelis qui ferebantur librorum fragmenta*. Stuttgart.

Rossi, L. 1996. "Il testamento di Posidippo e le laminette auree di Pella." *Zeitschrift für Papyrologie und Epigraphik* 112:59–65.

Rudhardt, J. 1971. *Le thème de l'eau primordiale dans la mythologie grecque*. Berne.

Saïd, S. 1998. "Tombes épiques d'Homère à Apollonios." In Marchegay, Le Dinahet, and Salles 1998, 9–19.

Sahlins, M. 1979. "L'apothéose du capitaine Cook." In Izard and Smith 1979:307–339.

———. 1981. *Historical Metaphors and Mythical Realities: Structure in the Early History of the Sandwich Islands Kingdom*. Ann Arbor.

———. 1985. *Islands of History*. Chicago.

Scarpi, P. 1987. "Diventare dio: La deificazione del defunto nelle lamine auree nell'antica Thurii." *Museum Patavinum* 5:197–217.

Scheid, J., and Svenbro, J. 1994. *Le métier de Zeus: Mythe du tissage et du tissu dans le monde gréco-romain*. Paris.

Schlesier, R. 2001. "Dionysos in der Unterwelt: Zu den Jenseitskonstruktionen der bakchischen Mysterien." In Hoff and Schmidt 2001, 157–172.

———. 2003. "Die Leiden des Dionysos." In Kneppe and Metzler 2003, 1–20.

Schmid, J., and Schmid, Ch. K. 1992. *Söhne des Krokodils: Männerhausrituale und Initiation in Yensan, Zentral Yatmul, East Sepik Province, Papua New Guinea*. Basel.

Schmidt, J. U. 1986. *Adressat und Paraineseform: Zur Intention von Hesiods Werken und Tagen*. Göttingen.

Schmidt, M. 1991. "Bemerkungen zu Orpheus in Unterwelts- und Thraker darstellungen." In Borgeaud 1991, 31–50.

Schröder, S. 2000. "Das Lied des Backchylides von der Fahrt des Theseus nach Kreta (C. 17 M.) und das Problem seiner Gattung." *Rheinisches Museum* 143:128–159.

Scodel, R. 1984. "The Irony of Fate in Bacchylides 17." *Hermes* 112:137–143.

Scott, D. W. 1986. "Gender: A Useful Category of Historical Analysis." *American Historical Review* 91:1053–1075. Repr. in Weed 1989, 81–100.

Segal, C. 1979. "The Myth of Bacchylides 17: Heroic Quest and Heroic Identity." *Eranos* 77:23–77. Repr. in Segal 1998, 295–314.

———. 1998. *Aglaia: The Poetry of Alcman, Sappho, Pindar, Bacchylides, and Corinna.* Lanham.

Seibert, J. 1963. *Metropolis und Apoikie: Historische Beiträge zur Geschichte ihrer gegenseitigen Beziehungen.* Wurzburg.

Settis, S., ed. 1993. *I Greci: Storia Cultura Arte Società 2: Una storia greca II.* Turin.

Sourvinou-Inwood, C. 1990. "Myths in Images: Theseus and Medea as a case Study." In Edmunds 1990, 395–445.

———. 1995. *'Reading' Greek Death: To the End of the Classical Period.* Oxford.

———. 1997. "The Hesiodic Myth of the Five Races and the Tolerance of Plurality in Greek Mythology." In Palagia 1997:1–21.

Stanek, M. 1983. *Sozialordnung und Mythik in Palimbei: Bausteine zur ganzheitlichen Beschreibung einer Dorfgemeinschaft der Iatmul, East Sepik Province, Papua New Guinea.* Basel.

Stengel, P. 1920. *Die griechischen Kultusaltertümer.* 3rd ed. Munich.

Stockton, D. 1990. *The Classical Athenian Democracy.* Oxford and New York.

Stoddard, K. 2004. *The Narrative Voice in the* Theogony *of Hesiod.* Leiden and Boston.

Suárez de la Torre, E. 2000. "Bemerkungen zu den Mythen bei Bakchylides." In Bagordo and Zimmermann 2000, 69–85.

Tessier, A. 1987. "La struttura metrica della laminetta di Hipponion: Rassegna di interpretazioni." *Museum Patavinum* 5:232–241.

Tortorelli Ghidini, M. 1991. "Semantica e origine misterica dei 'simbola.'" *Filosofia e teologia* 5:391–395.

———. 2006. *Figli della Terra e del Cielo stellato: Testi orfici con traduzione e commento.* Naples.

Trépanier, S. 2004. *Empedocles: An Interpretation.* New York and London.

Tsantsanoglou, K. 1997. "The First Columns of the Derveni Papyrus and their Religious Significancy." In Most and Laks 1997, 93–128.

Tsantsanoglou, K., and Parassoglou, G. M. 1987. "Two Gold Lamellae from Thessaly." *Hellenica* 38:3–17.

Tuzin, D. 1997. *The Cassowary's Revenge: The Life and Death of Masculinity in a New Guinea Society*. Chicago and London.

Vamvouri-Ruffy, M. 2004. *La fabrique du divin: Les* Hymnes *de Callimaque à la lumière des* Hymnes *homériques et des hymnes de culte*. Kernos Supplement 14. Liège.

Vegetti, M. 1999. "Culpability, Responsibility, Cause: Philosophy, Historiography, and Medicine in the Fifth Century." In Long 1999, 271–289.

Vernant, J.-P. 1960. "Le mythe hésiodique des races: Essai d'analyse structurale." *Revue de l'histoire des religions* 157:21–54. Repr. in Vernant 1985, 19–47.

——— 1966. "Le mythe hésiodique des races: Sur un essai de mise au point." *Revue de Philologie* 40:247–276. Repr. in Vernant 1985, 48–85.

———. 1972. "Ébauches de la volonté dans la tragédie grecque." In Parmelin, Guillot, et al. 1972, 277–306. Repr. in Vernant and Vidal-Naquet 1972, 43–74.

———. 1985. *Mythe et pensée chez les Grecs: Études de psychologie historique*. 2nd ed. Paris.

Vernant, J.-P., and Vidal-Naquet, P. 1972. *Mythe et tragédie en Grèce ancienne*. Paris.

Veyne, P. 1971. *Comment on écrit l'histoire: Essai d'épistémologie*. Paris.

Vidal-Naquet, P. 1983. *Le chasseur noir: Formes de pensée et formes de société dans le monde grec*. 2nd ed. Paris.

———. 1991. *Les Juifs, la mémoire et le présent*. Vol 2. Paris.

———. 1995. *Les Juifs, la mémoire et le présent*. Vol. 3: *Réflexions sur le génocide*. Paris.

Vian, F. 1963. *Les origines de Thèbes: Cadmos et les Spartes*. Paris.

Villard, L. 1997. "Tyche." *Lexicon Iconographicum Mythologiae Classicae* VIII.1:115–125. Zurich.

Wakker, G. 1990. "Die Ankündigung des Weltaltersmythos (Hes. *Op.* 106–108)." *Glotta* 68:86–90.

Walker, H. J. 1995. *Theseus and Athens*. New York and Oxford.

Waltkins, C. 1995. *How to Kill a Dragon: Aspects of Indo-European Poetics*. New York and Oxford.

Weed, E., ed. 1989. *Coming to Terms: Feminism, Theory, Politics*. New York and London.

West, M. L. 1975. "Zum neuen Golgblättchen aus Hipponion." *Zeitschrift für Papyrologie und Epigraphik* 18:229–236.

———. 1966. *Hesiod. Theogony*. Oxford.

———. 1978. *Hesiod. Works and Days*. Oxford.

———. 1983. *The Orphic Poems.* Oxford.

———. 1997. *The East Face of Helicon: West Asiatic Elements in Greek Poetry and Myth.* Oxford.

Woodard, R. D. 2007. "Hesiod and Greek Myth." In *The Cambridge Companion to Greek Mythology,* ed. R. D. Woodard, 83–165. Cambridge.

Zhmud', L. 1992. "Orphism and Grafitti from Olbia." *Hermes* 120:159–168.

Zuntz, G. 1971. *Persephone: Three Essays on Religion and Thought in Magna Graecia.* Oxford.

IMAGE CREDITS

Figure 1. Metropolitan Museum of Art, purchase, Joseph Pulitzer Bequest, 1953; acc. no. 53.11.4. Photo, all rights reserved, The Metropolitan Museum of Art.

Figure 2. Musée du Louvre, acc. no. G 104. Photo, Réunion des Musées Nationaux / Art Resource, NY.

Figure 3. Copenhagen, Ny Carlsberg Glyptotek, acc. no. IN 2695. Photo, Ny Carlsberg Glyptotek.

Figure 4. Arthur M. Sackler Museum, Bequest of David M. Robinson; acc. no. 1960.339. Photo, Harvard University Art Museums, Photographic Services.

Figure 5. Plan after *Cirene*, ed. Nicola Bonacasa et al. (Milan: Electa, 2000), p. 63, by permission of Mondadori Electa SpA.

Figure 6. Naples, Museo Archeologico Nazionale, acc. no. H 3222 (inv. 81666). Photo, Erich Lessing / Art Resource, NY.

Figure 7. Drawing after Michele Jatta, "Vasi dipinti dell'Italia meridionale," *Monumenti Antichi* 16 (1906), tav. III.

Figure 8. Toledo Museum of Art, gift of Edward Drummond Libbey, Florence Scott Libbey, and the Egypt Exploration Society, by exchange; acc. no. 1994.19. Photo, Toledo Museum of Art.

Figure 9. St. Petersburg, Hermitage Museum, acc. no. 1701 (= St. 498). Photo, The State Hermitage Museum, St. Petersburg.

INDEX

CPSIA information can be obtained
at www.ICGtesting.com
Printed in the USA
LVHW101112310123
738081LV00001BA/3